No Place for Grief

THE ETHNOGRAPHY OF POLITICAL VIOLENCE

Tobias Kelly, Series Editor

A complete list of books in the series
is available from the publisher.

NO PLACE FOR GRIEF

Martyrs, Prisoners, and Mourning
in Contemporary Palestine

Lotte Buch Segal

PENN

UNIVERSITY OF PENNSYLVANIA PRESS

PHILADELPHIA

Published by
University of Pennsylvania Press
Philadelphia, Pennsylvania 19104-4112
www.upenn.edu/pennpress

Printed in the United States of America
on acid-free paper

1 3 5 7 9 10 8 6 4 2

A catalogue record for this book is available from the
Library of Congress.
ISBN 978-0-8122-4821-0

For Sune, David, and Elias

CONTENTS

PREFACE

My time in Palestine has left me with a sadness that flows from the experiences of the people I encountered there. The question of whether this influences my interpretation of words, human beings, and situations is at best rhetorical. Many times I did not know how to respond to the words, tears, or gestures of the human beings at the heart of this book. How could I reply? As a female researcher from one of the most affluent societies of the world. As a woman whose life is not imperiled by the systematic exhaustion of the Palestinian occupation. As someone who feels empathy with the people she meets without certainty that empathy is ever exhaustive or necessarily the pathway to knowledge.

A student in my Psychology in Anthropology course asked me after having read Chapter 2 of this book for class: "Do you understand these women?" To this question I replied with a qualified "Yes." It is a yes only if we mean knowledge in the sense of acknowledgment, which I offer here. I have done my best not to simplify these women's experiences, but I also know that I could not entirely avoid it.

I feel compelled to act upon what I know, but I am not sure of the consequences. I write. I tell. Who listens? Some do. Does it matter? I do not know. João Biehl once asked me what I thought was the most powerful part of my work. It took me an hour to dare to say that it may have been sitting down and listening to those women, so at least they knew that I had heard their stories. They knew, and I knew. Now you know.

NOTE ON TRANSLITERATION

In transliterating Arabic words to English I follow Hans Wehr, *A Dictionary of Modern Written Arabic: Arabic–English,* edited by J. Milton Cowan (London: MacDonald and Evans, 1980). For smoother reading, the names of people have been transliterated without diacritical markings.

Introduction

I merged a little with the void
sitting in a nocturnal room and was filled
with your silence
that trembled in the picture

—Ghada al-Shafi'i

Luma's husband was killed in an air raid near their house on the outskirts of a major Palestinian city. She heard the bombing and knew immediately that her husband was its most likely target.

Thirteen years have passed since his death. Luma has mourned him, and she could remarry without any social censure, as other widows have done. But she adamantly refuses. The first time we met she told me so, though not in so many words. She revealed her conviction in the slight upward tilt of the chin and click of the tongue that means "no, of course not," among Palestinians.

Whenever she spoke of her husband's death, her voice would rise to a higher pitch and her face and cheeks would color. The adrenaline coursing through her body was evident. Talking about his death in its minutest details, Luma recounted how she went through stages of fear, anticipation, and an uncanny sense of knowing that her husband was dead, even before official confirmation. When she was finally certain that her husband had been killed, she descended into a state of desolation.

Luma spoke about his death in a way that conveyed the sorrow of losing a husband in culturally appropriate terms and emphasized her feelings for him. As the wife of a politically active man, she had to put her life on hold when her husband was detained in Israeli prisons, after he had fled and hid preceding his incarceration. Up to his death in 2002, their twelve-year relationship had oscillated between moments of happiness, like their wedding and the birth of their children, and moments of anxiety and hardship during his imprisonment. Luma told me how his first imprisonment occasioned nearly as much grief as his death ten years later. We may even surmise that her husband's death allowed Luma to reconnect with a certain normalcy, because, in her words, it was not until a year after her husband's death that life again, or perhaps for the first time, became normal.

When Luma finished her story, she dried her tears, rushed to her kitchen, and proudly brought back two kinds of homemade cake for us to have with our coffee. She said it had done her good to cry.

However, not all kinds of conjugal loss lend themselves so easily to a story of mourning and desire. Luma's loss—the possibilities and the limitations of how she could express it—instigated my study of the consequences of being in a population, and a kind of marriage, that tend to be cast by Palestinians and academics alike in a language of heroism, perseverance, and national solidarity. I wanted to consider what happens when the emotional remains of being a bereaved wife appear to outweigh the sense of belonging to a collective, and when life in the shadow of heroism is unable to find expression.

One woman, Yara, appears to encapsulate precisely this dilemma. Her husband has been detained since 2001, and Yara herself has also been imprisoned. Yet with seven hundred thousand Palestinians incarcerated in Israel since 1967 (Btselem 2015), the confinement of Yara's husband is nothing out of the ordinary. Imprisonment is lived, felt, and endured by the vast majority of families in occupied Palestine.

Yara lived next door to a Palestinian friend of mine in an upscale neighborhood of Ramallah. It was a rainy November day in 2007 when we first met. Gently ushering my assistant Rawan and me inside her living room, Yara seemed somewhat uneasy at the prospect of talking about her husband's confinement, of presuming that her own words mattered as much as her husband's. I explained that part of my project was to invite women to describe the experience of confinement for those left behind.

To a woman like Yara, the history of the Palestinian resistance movement and its varying intensities are woven into her account of her emotions about her husband's imprisonment. As she recounted the early phases of resistance, she remembered how, at that time, political men were highly respected among Palestinian people and society.

However, Yara also explained how doubt had slowly but persistently crept into her conviction that she and her husband should devote their lives to politics: "I was thinking, 'Why are you leaving your house and your wife and your kids; who are you doing this for?' No one cares anymore."

Despite these doubts, Yara is still loyal to the cause for which her husband is in prison. This comes through powerfully when she is invited to speak in public. One such occasion illustrates the imbrication of politics and intimate lives to which this book is dedicated. In 2012 yet another international campaign for the release of Palestinian prisoners in Israel was being launched. A series of meetings on the problem of the Palestinian prisoners followed. Despite the organizer's expectations, very few people showed up for the meeting. Yara began her talk by emphasizing that she was speaking to raise awareness of the conditions for all Palestinian prisoners and not only for her own husband. She spoke about the large number of people held in detention and their common plight. Through illustrative examples of her husband's difficulties in prison she voiced her concern about the general issues at stake for the Palestinian prisoners in Israeli custody. During the talk she subtly reminded the audience that she had not seen her husband for the last six years, as he was being held in isolation. When the floor opened for questions, a woman from a human rights movement asked if Yara would say something about the conditions faced by the prisoners' family members. Yara recounted the humiliation many families endure when visiting their relatives in prison; how they employ human rights lawyers for years on end in the hope that yet another hearing might lead to their loved one's release.

When a woman asked a more personal question, "What about you?" Yara's voice suddenly fell. She was quiet for a while, took a deep breath, and then gestured toward me and said, "ask her, Lotte knows." Given that I was neither an activist member of the host organization nor a regular participant in these meetings, the woman looked at me with a somewhat puzzled expression and urged Yara to continue talking. Yara then began speaking again in a more pensive tone of voice. Whereas her talk about the prisoners, the Israeli penal system, and the conflict at large was coherent, persuasive, and well rehearsed, it seemed to me that the words she needed to talk about her own experience were not readily at hand. At least not in the context of a political meeting on the cause of the Palestinians and more specifically the release of the prisoners. She did not say anything personal about how it felt to be her. Instead, she subtly changed the subject to that of the effect of her and her husband's confinement on their children. She could not hold back her tears as she spoke about her daughter's psychological distress and the ensuing difficulties of finding her a suitable spouse. This part of Yara's story was not rehearsed. And in contrast to the evocative force of Yara's political speech, the more personal revelations did not elicit any reaction from the audience. Neither the activists in the solidarity movement nor the members of the audience responded to what Yara confessed. While I am speculating here, the audience seemed simply unable to take in the full extent of her experience—that even though she continued to be politically active, she was expressing doubt about the worth of the struggle. Judging from the lack of response in the meeting to Yara's more personal account in contrast to the clear acknowledgment of the political struggle, her experiences seemed relevant to the attendees only to the extent that she could represent the brave but suffering wife of the prisoner, and thus contribute to the political cause.

It is not that Yara's predicament is ignored by distant or intimate witnesses. For instance, the leader of the professional organization in which Yara's daughter works told me that they do what they can in the workplace to support her, not only as the child of a heroic detainee but also as a human being who is marked by the episodic imprisonment that both her father and mother have been through since her early childhood. During my conversation with Yara on that rainy November day in Ramallah, she seemed most distraught when speaking about the effect that her and her husband's detention may have had on their children.

Grieving in Private

What do Luma's and Yara's stories each tell us about absent spouses and the ways in which they can and cannot be mourned in both the private and public lives of Palestinians? These small glimpses of conjugal life, or lack thereof, help reveal how the death or indefinite absence of a spouse suffuses many Palestinian relationships. My interest here is not only in the sadness that the women express over such a loss but also in how this is braided with a disenchantment with politics and a feeling of unbearable loss for many activists wrought by their participation in the Palestinian cause. This is not to say that the language of suffering and loss is unimportant or irrelevant in the history of the Palestinian national movement. The notion of the martyr, for example, is central to Palestinian iconography and political discourse. The figure of the victim has also played a central role in Palestinian human rights practices.

However, the dominant ways in which loss and suffering have been framed have, I argue, effectively excluded the experience of many Palestinians.

For Yara, the losses she has had to endure are not easily expressed or publicly received within the repertoire of stories that women tell about loss in Palestine. Her loss does not lend itself well to the process of mourning, and to the relief that mourning can potentially bring. Her sorrow simply has to be borne in private anguish. To the martyr's widow Luma, in contrast, the language of mourning, such as her lamentations, allows her both to inhabit and admit to feelings of love and desire in a way that is socially accepted, insofar as these feelings are directed toward her deceased husband. In Yara's case, however, there is no available language by which to express the grief that invades her being. Her grief includes not only the continual loss of her husband but also her doubt about the roles she has filled and continues to fill in the Palestinian political community, as a committed activist, a female ex-detainee, and the proud wife of a hero.

A core argument of this book is that the language of a hopeful future for the Palestinian project almost *requires* blocking out the full extent of what it feels like to be in Yara's position. A result of this is therefore a loss of language regarding marital separation that is not caused by death, among other inarticulable losses.

The predominant line of scholarship on Palestinian adversity would propose one of two things. Either that women like Yara may indeed suffer in their predicament but, at the same time, they occupy a space of agency and can feel consoled by the shared language of *sumūd*, the local idiom of perseverance and steadfastness often used to connote the power of simply enduring rather than engaging in violent means of resistance (Meari 2014). Or that Yara's experience is just an example of the chilling statistics about psychiatric disorders in Palestine. Psychiatry, too, is a common language to describe and understand life as a Palestinian in the occupied West Bank. In this language, 24.3 percent of Palestinian women display major lifetime depression, despite the fact that men are more directly exposed to traumatic events than women (Madianos, Lufti Sarhan, and Koukia 2012; Punamäki et al. 2005). But for Yara, neither the language of widowhood deployed by women like Luma nor the language of psychiatry sufficiently encapsulates her feelings and experiences.

Over the course of my engagement with affliction among Palestinians, I have come to think of the mutually absorbing languages of sumūd and trauma as a standing language of acknowledgment of suffering in con-temporary Palestine. I am drawing here on Ludwig Wittgenstein's argument in *Philosophical Investigations* against the existence of a private language, that is, a language that belongs only to an individual, and his related idea that words represent sensation (1953 [2009]: §244–§271; see Chapter 1 in this book for elaboration). What intrigues me is how language then works in terms of another of Wittgenstein's concepts, namely, "forms of life."[1] Philosopher Stanley Cavell sums up the idea of forms of life this way:

> We learn and teach words in certain contexts, and then we are
> expected, and expect others, to be able to project them into further
> contexts. Nothing ensures that this projection will take place (in
> particular, not the grasping of universals nor the grasping of books
> of rules), just as nothing ensures that we will make, and understand,
> the same projections. That on the whole we do is a matter of sharing
> routes of interest and feeling, modes of response, sense of humor
> and significance and of fulfillment, of what is outrageous, of what is
> similar to what else, what a rebuke, what forgiveness, of when an
> utterance is an assertion, when an appeal, when an explanation—all
> the whirl of organism Wittgenstein calls "forms of life." Human
> speech and activity, sanity and community, rests on nothing more,
> but nothing less than this. (1976: 52)

On this premise, a "standing language" refers to agreement in criteria as to what "forms of life" are human. My concern, however, is not whether particular experiences pertain to being human. Rather, I am pondering how, in complex ways, the standing language shapes what kinds of suffering can be put into words, and acknowledged, before the limits of agreement about what it means to be human in contemporary Palestine are reached. With this as my analytical point of departure I hope to offer details on what it means to be a prisoner's wife in occupied Palestine, and to help conceptualize the entanglement of everyday endurance, intimacy, and the ordinary in the face of an occupation that has become part and parcel of Palestinian social life.

Beginning with the ways in which so-called heroic women's endurance and suffering are understood, the book casts the ethnography of prisoners' wives in the light of three mutually interacting contexts of understanding that these women are often seen within: first, the idea of trauma as capturing the derivative suffering of the women related to either martyrs or prisoners;

second, a Palestinian moral discourse that entwines resistance, sumūd, and suffering; and, third, the temporality of endurance, and how this waxes and wanes with the temporality of both trauma and resistance.

Trauma with No Aftermath

Given the long history of the conflict between Israel and the Palestinians[2] and, significantly, the outside world's involvement in it, "trauma" is a most powerful language for talking about the affliction of the Palestinians. The language of trauma is where the twin experiences of enduring and suffering seem to have a home for both Palestinian health professionals and international observers (Fassin 2008; Fassin and Rechtman 2009). This is because the psychosocial organizations that offer the women their services work through languages of traumatization as a way to acknowledge the emotional effects of the occupation, be it imprisonment, loss, or violence. I am interested here in the gap between the language of trauma and the women's experiences, and the political implications and nature of that gap.

During a stretch of fieldwork in 2008 I had an informal meeting on mental health, gender, and trauma in Palestine with an esteemed lecturer and now research colleague from the Institute of Community and Public Health at Birzeit University, which was then located in the West Bank town of Ramallah. When I asked her how she understood the notion of trauma in Palestine, she said with a smile that "Raija-Lena brought trauma to Palestine." Since the early 1990s, the Finnish professor of psychology Raija-Lena Punamäki has had a highly acclaimed and locally respected collaboration with researchers at the Gaza Community Mental Health Program and, later, at Birzeit University on the occupation's impact on the mental health of Palestinian adults and children (Punamäki et al. 1997; 2005). Punamäki was not alone, however, in bringing the idea of trauma to Palestinians. One figure in particular is mentioned whenever anthropologists contemplate the notion of trauma in occupied Palestine: the late Dr. Eyad al-Sarraj, an internationally renowned British-trained psychiatrist who established the Gaza Community Mental Health Program in 1993 (Fischer 2007; Fassin and Rechtman 2009). Under his direction, the psychological impact of war and occupation became what we might think of as household models of distress among Palestinians, not least in Gaza. Naturally, this is not because every single Gazan has been enrolled in individual therapy. Rather, "the program" (or al-barnamij Gaza as-saher nafsiyah, as it is called in the local vernacular) grew into four smaller centers across the strip, each of which functioned as a center for vocational training, awareness raising on the impact of violence on families, and individual and group counseling. Throughout its existence, the program has had the support of prominent Western and Israeli psychiatrists, who have coauthored what has become important and often-cited quantitative and qualitative documentation of the psychological effects of the occupation on Palestinians (Punamäki et al. 1990, 2005; Afana et al. 2010). Sarraj passed away in 2013, but the program continues to operate and has been frequently cited on the matter of women and children's traumatization, most recently in the wake of the war on Gaza in the summer of 2014.

The Gaza Community Mental Health Program may be among the best-known Palestinian organizations of its kind internationally, but there are at least three other Palestinian institutions that play a crucial role in defining and offering treatment to victims of occupation-related violence.

The first organization with a psychosocial mandate in the West Bank was the Palestinian Counseling Center, which had ties to the left-wing movement in Palestine, prominent figures of Palestinian civil society, and key mobilizers of the first Intifada, or uprising, from 1987 to 1993. The center has branches across the West Bank for Palestinians. The second institution is the YMCA in Beit Sahour, a Christian organization that spearheaded the treatment of people with physical disabilities caused by the armed clashes between Palestinians and the Israeli military during the first Intifada. Among therapists in the occupied[3] territory the counselors trained at the YMCA generally enjoy a good reputation for being among the most professional and up-to-date therapists. The last institution, which works differently, through a primarily medical rather than community-anchored approach, is the Treatment and Rehabilitation Center for Torture Victims. This center, too, was founded by a psychiatrist, Dr. Mahmoud Sehwail, in 1997. In contrast to centers that offer treatment for the effects of the occupation more universally, this organization's original mandate was to focus on helping victims of torture. But since its inception, the Treatment and Rehabilitation Center has broadened its services to include the families of torture victims along with prisoners' and martyrs' families more generally. The state of Israel changed its interrogation practices after the second Intifada, and physical torture is allegedly less prevalent among detainees in Israel today (B'Tselem 2010) compared to two decades ago. Israeli nongovernmental organizations (NGOs) nonetheless continue to testify about ongoing incidents of torture and ill treatment of Palestinians in Israeli confinement (PCATI 2009, 2011). Lori Allen's work further reveals that torture in Palestinian Authority prisons and detention centers across the occupied territory is a continuing practice that is common knowledge among Palestinians (2012: 2; see also PHRG 2014) Some of the families in my study have family members who have suffered torture or ill treatment both at the hands of Israel and the Palestinian Authority.

The omnipresence of violence, actual and potential, in its different guises indeed conveys how the idea of the Palestinians as a traumatized population is a powerful vehicle by which to make their suffering legible to a global audience (see also Fassin and Rechtman 2009). But the characterization of a traumatized victim has a downside. As Ruth Leys (2007) has shown in her genealogy of trauma and derivative concepts, the diagnosis of posttraumatic stress disorder has been a battleground for different understandings of the human psyche. According to Leys, the removal of survivor's guilt from the *Diagnostic and Statistical Manual of Mental Disorders* third edition laid the groundwork for the theory of a victim who was traumatized by a specific external event rather than through identification with his or her aggressor, as Sigmund Freud had earlier theorized. One may speculate as to whether the idea of a victim farther removed from the initial act of violence is what allowed the notion of a traumatized war victim to be recognized globally—especially since it was precisely in the 1990s that we saw an increase in the proliferation of psychosocial programs to war-affected populations across the globe, Palestine being no exception (Pupavac 2001; Summerfield 1999; Giacaman et al. 2011). Though there is a vast body of literature that testifies to the permeability of victim and perpetrator categories in situations of violence, the notion of a victim as someone to whom something has happened is still a powerful vehicle for designing interventions for so-called target groups (Jensen and Rønsbo 2014).

As Giacaman et al. (2011) have noted, trauma-based interventions in populations that suffer from war-induced distress go only part of the way in offering solace for their suffering. The three internationally funded NGOs and three smaller initiatives are most certainly the drivers behind the "psychosocialization" of the response to the occupation, but the Palestinian Ministry of Health struggled for years to agree on the Psychosocial Bill, in which such services could also be part of an already inferior and underfunded health system. The negotiation of the bill was difficult due to the conflicting

perspectives on mental health as either a medical or a political issue. As Giacaman et al. point out, the Palestinian health system is modeled on a colonial
understanding of psychiatry. Accordingly, the mentally ill who were taken
care of in their family homes before the British colonialization are now hos-
pitalized in the Mental Health Hospital of Bethlehem in the West Bank. In
the local vernacular, this is also known as the hospital for the mad (Giacaman et al. 2011). Patients with a congenital mental disorder thus belong
to this system, whereas psychiatric patients whose illness is due to violence pose complexity and difficulty, given the heroic politics associated
with participation in the struggle. That this participation is to a great many
participants psychologically painful has been documented time and again,
yet the stigmatization of poor mental health is hugely prevalent as well.
During fieldwork in Gaza as well as the West Bank, I witnessed psychiatrists
and counselors in NGOs go to great lengths before handing over their clients, both men and women, to the conventional psychiatric care system.

Whereas psychologists, psychiatrists, and physicians have indeed documented the consequences of the occupation for mental and physical health,
I aim to offer in anthropological terms what it means to live with violence at
your front door as a permanent feature of life rather than as an occasional,
discrete occurrence. Allan Young (1995) wrote in his study of the diagnosis
of posttraumatic stress disorder that events dominate the discipline of psychology, with its reliance on notions of trauma and traumatic memory ce-
mented in Western thought with Freud's writings in the early twentieth
century (1928 [1969]). Yet anthropologists align themselves with psychologists
in how they write and theorize violence related to suffering as, respectively,
event and aftermath (see Herman 1992 and for comparison Leys 2000). In
anthropology, a focus on violent events and a linear temporality of suffering
may be an apt way to conceptualize affliction, but such a framework fails to
account for suffering of an ongoing, chronic, and enduring character (see Das
2015 for an elaborate discussion of this point). I intend to shed light precisely on
these entangled languages of trauma and heroism, and their residual effects on
those who do not occupy the center stage: namely, Palestinian prisoners' wives.

An Anthropological Grammar of Suffering

If we set aside for now the concept of trauma as a way to understand suffering
in occupied Palestine, how then do we describe the emotions that arise in

the wake of a spouse's absence? Wittgenstein's notion of "forms of life" may help us think about loss that is not caused by death. Veena Das calls our attention to how the duality in the notion of forms of life is often missed in anthropology (Das 1998, 2013): only *forms,* understood as different cultures, seem to grasp our attention as anthropologists. In contrast, Cavell emphasizes form *and* life, both the social and the natural. There is therefore an ethnological or horizontal form of life and a vertical or biological form of life. "It is the vertical sense of the form of life that he suggests marks the limit of what is considered human in a society," Das remarks, "and provides the conditions of the use of criteria as applied to others" (1998: 180).

These thoughts are pertinent to an ethnography of endurance in the occupied territory because the pressure of military occupation exerted on the Palestinians slowly but steadily suffocates social lives and intimate relations. How can an ethnography on Palestinian women's contradictory emotions about the death or imprisonment of their husbands further advance our thinking about loss, mourning, and grief, as well as forms of life? There is an elaborate repertoire of narrative styles, laments, folk songs, poetry, and performance of bodily gestures through which mourning (including the mourning that is tied to a political cause) can be articulated in occupied Palestine. Why are these collective forms of expression inadequate in the cases of detainees' wives?

A salient aspect of loss is the fact that human life goes on, even in the face of harrowing bereavement. Interpreting Ralph Waldo Emerson's text (1844) on the death of his young son Waldo, Das writes, "When Emerson says that grief has nothing to teach me he is overcoming an illusion that any publicly available institutions such as religion could offer consolation. 'Nothing is left now but death'—the issue is not that the father-philosopher does not know how to go on *but to make sense of the fact that he does go on*" (2011: 948). This analysis of the subtleties of finding a place in language for grief marks the beginning of my dual focus on different registers of loss in Palestinian marriages, and what it means to endure in such a context. I emphasize what intimate, if never truly private, experience means in regard to grief in a context where loss, especially loss caused by death, is often framed in religious terms (e.g., their travails are a test from God) or as a political sacrifice. In public speech as well as in everyday talks with acquaintances, women will often use these two languages. During my time in Palestine I found that not only was it easier for the widows of martyrs to present their suffering in these terms than it was for the wives of prisoners, but also that this vocabulary of mourning did not convey the full extent of their grief, even for the widows of martyrs.

Anthropologists use an array of analytical approaches to understand how life and social arrangements are restructured for women who are bereaved (see Brison and Levitt 1995). It seems to me, however, that anthropology has not, to the same extent as other disciplines, honed a language to talk about experiences when such social arrangements fail to do their work. One possible approach to this issue would be to follow Wittgenstein's claim that language can never be truly private. It is a part of sociality. Grief and loss of belief in the political project are removed from the narratives that circulate in the public realm, even narratives that at the outset appear to include the entire scale of affliction brought upon the Palestinians by the military occupation.

There is, however, another way that detainees' wives have a different relation to the standing languages of mourning: Those languages do not account for the painful feeling of betrayal that remains once the personal cost of engagement in the struggle becomes heavier than the value accorded to heroically supporting the Palestinian collective (Kelly 2010). A feeling of betrayal, writes Vincent Crapanzano (2011), is the more or less intentional loss of belief in the "we" as a vantage point. And since Palestinians understand that the objective of the military occupation is to splinter the Palestinian population and prevent it from becoming a national "we," doubting the value and worth of the struggle amounts to an admission that the occupation has won. This doubt is part and parcel of the grief felt by prisoners' wives, as is the loneliness that necessarily follows it, even if it is suppressed in order for the struggle to endure. To acknowledge the doubt and grief of prisoners' wives would be to acknowledge doubt in the Palestinian project.

Sumūd, Suffering, and Nationalism

Another register of loss that currently suffuses social life in the occupied territory is something that I tentatively term the "loss of politics" (Buch Segal 2015). I am not suggesting that Palestinians have renounced any engagement with politics. Yet while violent death still causes people to mobilize and express anger at the political situation, less grievous forms of loss increasingly fail to register, as they are absorbed into everyday life—not quite normalized, but not worthy of public acknowledgment, either (see also Allen

2012 and Kelly 2009 for an ethnographic elaboration of this point). Media attention to "release parties," which are broadcast live across the Middle East, to celebrate the return of Palestinian prisoners like those who were exchanged for the Israeli soldier Gilad Shalit in 2011 might seem to contradict the "loss of politics." Nonetheless, I suggest that even words for political resistance appear to have lost their force, by dint of repetition. They are still uttered, but they ring hollow. Loss of politics is a loss of hope for a future for a Palestinian form of life (Buch 2010; Buch Segal in press; Das 1998: 174).

How is the idea of a loss of politics plausible among a population that is best known as *the* quintessentially resistant people? Were we to judge on the basis of much of the academic literature Palestinian nationalism is an idea that still, at least to some extent, mobilizes people (Allan 2013; Sayigh 2008; Peteet 2005; Khalili 2007; Hammami 2004; Tamari and Hammami 2001). As Laleh Khalili (2007) writes, there seem to be collective ways of wording solace for the price exacted by adamant resistance, whether that price is detention, martyrdom, or everyday suffering. A gatekeeping concept in Palestinian studies is therefore also sumūd, which has appeared in scholarship on the occupied territory and refugee camps across the Levant since the 1980s (see Sayigh 1993; Perdigon 2011; Meari 2014). Sumūd expresses an ethos of standing tall, of persevering no matter what is inflicted on you and your people. It implies that women like Yara and Luma endure by keeping the family together in the face of any negative effects that accompany the heroic deeds of their husbands, sons, and fathers.

Yet if we look at the most recent studies, based empirically on the time during or after the second Intifada, it is clear that the call for resistance is at best ambiguous in contemporary Palestine. Lori Allen argues that the rallying cry of human rights in the Palestinian nationalist discourse is permeated by a collective feeling of participation in a farce, or even a charade (2012: 2), and hence characterized by cynicism. Allen conducted the bulk of her fieldwork during and after the second Intifada. Similar research by Tobias Kelly (2009), undertaken at the same time, considers why some young men don't take up weapons, but, rather, hope for jobs in accounting; he concludes that the violent struggle for statehood, characterized by inefficiency and hopelessness, is not the only future imaginable. Beyond doubt, there is indeed still intact a strong national rhetoric that reflects belief in and rallies citizens to work for a Palestinian state. But doubt in the worth of the struggle, framed as a desire for an ordinary life, is similarly detectable.

This double register of doubt and hope in the national project was re-formulated for me during a conversation with a Palestinian acquaintance, a significant figure in Palestinian left-wing activism and in the health sector. Over a lemonade he said, "Look, Lotte, if you ask your question in terms of the prisoners themselves it is easy. During the first Intifada there was a packed suitcase under our bed all the time. Ready to go to prison. If you ask me about what it meant for women and children, that is an entirely different story." Even he admitted that in private conversations, Palestinians will tac-itly agree now that the golden era of Palestinian resistance is but a faint memory. The language of resistance nonetheless still represents collective hope for Palestinian freedom from occupation. People in Palestine have no option but to act as if they still believe in a collective future, even though the words with which collective hopes are narrated are emptied of life. The need to keep reiterating the Palestinian national narrative, even though its affect is in fact further dissolved by the hour, makes it hard to acknowledge what has happened to the wives of detainees. But whereas the audience that heard Yara's revelations about her daughter's psychological disorder was not able to acknowledge the extent to which the resistance struggle causes human hearts and minds to break, the people who live through these experiences on a day-to-day basis understand these costs only too well.

Once at a small gathering in my flat in Ramallah with three friends, all of whom have husbands serving lengthy prison sentences, one woman, Amina, told us about how nervous her husband was on the occasion of her last visit. In this atmosphere of casual women's talk she ended her account say-ing, "kulhum majaniin, bnhibhum"—meaning they (the prisoners, or our husbands) are all mad, we love them. Her words illustrate the ambivalent self that is eclipsed by the grandiose political speeches made in national and international forums. Amina, Yara, and other women in the same situation perhaps inhabit the most delicate space of all. They experience the wound at the heart of the conjugal relation, but must go on loving and sup-porting their husbands in small everyday gestures, such as visiting prison, writing letters, sending photos, and engaging in other acts of caring. Am-ina's words crystallize the tragic recognition that while the occupation is said to foster endurance in those who suffer its consequences, what it causes is sometimes madness. Despite Amina's lighthearted tone, all the women in my living room that day knew the pain that would come from the confession that living through a fourteen-year stretch as a wife of a de-tainee tends to deaden the heroic impulse. Her words were but one instance of the murmured conversations within families and among friends, in which it is said that the long detentions of so many may turn out to have been simply a debilitating loss of time and sanity for the prisoner himself and his relatives.

The Exhaustion of Endurance

I have asked myself how to read these private conversations about frayed relations vis-à-vis the idea of resistance in contemporary Palestine. Thus hesitancy runs adjacent to my attempt to voice that which cannot be voiced—namely, the effects of more than sixty years of military occupation on the social institution called upon to embody ṣumūd: the Palestinian family. My work on the vulnerability of relationships in the occupied territory continually forces me to consider the responsibility of the anthropologist. Who am I to voice that which by Palestinian standards is best kept silent? Who decides what Palestinian standards are, and who is supposed to embody them? My verbalization of the experiences of those who supposedly epitomize how the occupation's penetrating force comes to a halt at the doorstep of *ad-dar*, the Palestinian household, arguably could be read as a violation of the laborious work done by Palestinians to counter the occupation with dignity. It is, however, precisely the minutiae of this work that holds the key to understanding and acknowledging the exhaustion of endurance. Describing these women's practices of endurance allows for the recognition of Palestinian voices that are heard but seldom listened to, as Yara's example illustrates.

One figure in particular has inspired social analysis of voice, violence, and gender: the Greek heroine Antigone, who seems to epitomize a woman who balances loyalty to the state with loyalty to close kin (Das 2007; Saint Cassia 2005; Butler 2000; Willner 1982). In an act intended to secure the heroic burial of her brother, she defeats her uncle Creon and, as a consequence, is walled up in a tomb, where she commits suicide. By insisting on burying her brother, Antigone chooses kinship over the state, at the cost of her own life. To Judith Butler, Antigone's choice is a conflict between the law of the state and the law of the family (2000: 6). In Chapter 6 below, Antigone appears as a thought-provoking figure who may help us understand the knife's edge balanced by prisoners' wives in their experiences of frayed relations with Palestinian resistance.

In the contemporary atmosphere of skepticism, women who are married to long-term detainees occupy a subject position that crystallizes just how profoundly Palestinians lack secure knowledge of their future, and world, in the hands of the occupation. But to recognize this would constitute betrayal. Admission that these women live through a slow, persistent erosion of their sense of self and their intimate lives equals the poisonous admission that the Israeli occupation has permeated the family. This admission ultimately testifies to how the language of *sumūd* may indeed still circulate, but has long been emptied of consolation, and has given way to what I think of as profound skepticism.

The Temporality of Endurance and the Ordinary

The infrastructure of the military occupation of the Palestinian territory is of such magnitude that it has seeped through the permeable boundaries of interiority so profoundly that we need to ask what occupation does even to Palestinian subjectivity and ways of intimacy. Kelly (2013) asserts that the crucial task in such a context is to tease out how the particular markers of suffering affect people's acts of care and kindness to each other, and where the limits of kindness are drawn. The emphasis here, then, is to show how far endurance is stretched, to gauge its elasticity as well as its limits.[4] Because there are, in fact, limits to endurance, and the important thing here is for anthropology to elucidate that which is eclipsed by the rallying of Palestinian resistance. This provokes one of this book's main questions: what becomes of endurance when that which is to be endured is without end? Ultimately this book testifies to the slow grind of violence that is not spectacularly catastrophic, not generally categorized by immediate and large-scale death. What is most violent about the situation in occupied Palestine is that it continues without end.

Even though the call to endure, to stand tall and to show sumūd in the face of occupation, is still heard, responses to this call are saturated with doubt. In an attempt to detail and give form to this slow, steady erosion of the means of resilience in Palestine, I use ethnography to describe human beings in terms of the particular lifeworlds they inhabit (Jackson 2014). There is also a moral impulse in this description: the maintenance of narratives of agency and steadfastness in spite of the occupation constitutes at best a partial and fractured picture of how Palestinians at this time see the situation and themselves within it (see Peteet 2005: x). In this sense this book focuses on lives for which the regular narratives appear to be dissolving, a focus so clearly exemplified in the work of Sarah Pinto (2014) on women and mental disorder in North India. Thinking about the dissolving narratives of Palestinian resistance and the dissolving ascription of meaning in loss and adversity in the wake of such dissolution poses a conceptual challenge to an anthropology in which the work of narrative is seen to have a great impact (see the works of Mattingly, Lutkehaus and Throop 2008; Mattingly 1998; and Jackson 2002, 2014). Enduring distress, be it due to chronic mental illness or detention, begs conceptualization that can accommodate not only the efficacy of but also the failure of narrative.

Endurance as Duration

How then do we think about the temporality of endurance in occupied Palestine? The absence that these wives experience does not follow the linear time line of a traumatic event, an emotional reaction, and an attendant aftermath. Such traumatic events are often marked by spectacular characteristics that separate them from everyday routine. They are a radical "other" that has suddenly upended the lifeworlds of those who engage with violence, as either victims or perpetrators, or both. In other words, the traumatic is an event that occurs at a particular moment, and lasts for a definite duration. Through a foregrounding of temporality, I hope to further anthropological understanding of how human relationships are configured in an ordinary life that is imbued with the presence of violence, but is, at the same time, generally uneventful (Povinelli 2012). This perspective unsettles precisely the notion of an aftermath—that is, the time after a violent event in which the pieces of normal life are presumably gathered and reassembled. In Palestine, by contrast, the everyday is where violence, betrayal, and fear are actualized.

Thinking about the temporality of endurance, then, requires that we think about the everyday as repetitious, or in the words of Das and colleagues (2014), habitual. For example, Adam Reed's writing on inmates in Papua New Guinea underscores the temporality of the prison as being intrinsically linked to a "tiresome, weighty now" (2003: 100). Reed's finding reverberates with Chapter 3's conclusion that life as a relative of a Palestinian detainee seems to be structured by repetition.

The idea of "duration," introduced by the French Philosopher Henri Bergson, here mainly through Deleuze's (1988) reading of him in *Bergsonism*, helps us understand enduring violence and its intensities. Over the last decade, Bergson has inspired anthropologists—in particular, it seems, those who are concerned with the intricacies of violence and temporality (Das 2007; Pedersen and Holbraad 2013; Khan 2012; Caton 2014). Here, the notion of duration aptly describes the time of incarceration, an aspect of life that is potentially permanent or that constantly lacks the certainty of a final date of release. Moreover, the idea of duration has enabled me to think more closely about the relation between the enduring violence and the temporality of relatedness in occupied Palestine.

Endurance as the Ordinary

The Arabic word *'ādi* means "nothing unusual or spectacular, plain, ordinary." Among Palestinians, *'ādi* is a frequent response in everyday conversations to questions like "kīfik" (How are you?), "šu akbārik" (What's your news?), and "kīf aḥsāsik" (How do you feel?). It was also the word I encountered during my fieldwork as a response to my question of if and how life had changed after a husband had gone into prison. Yet knowing the wives of long-term detainees and the way in which their lives changed, during their husbands' detentions, I wondered how they could they answer "'ādi" to describe a life that, to me, seemed uncanny. In contrast, Ghada al-Shafi'i's poem "Maps of Absence," quoted in the epigraph to this Introduction, expresses a sense of self that merges with the void left by a disappeared other. Resonating with this book's attention to the lack of a language available to Yara to voice the emotional effects of her husband's detention, the poetry of al-Shafi'i investigates the subject of female voices on the Palestinian art scene (Khankan 2009). The poem conveys the embeddedness of absence, of someone who has left—but is not lost. It gestures at the uncanniness of an enduring, infinite void in the intimacy of relations around the absent husband.

In line with al-Shafi'i's faceless "I," the void left by the women's imprisoned husbands becomes over time an integral part of the women's lives to the extent that it is *'ādi*, ordinary. At the same time, the women are obliged to project sumūd; they must not show any signs that other feelings exist parallel to pride in the honor generated by their husbands' acts of resistance. Even in the current atmosphere of fatigue with ever more losses, detentions, and general adversity, unconditional support for the national struggle is perceived as ʿādi.

A pivotal question then concerns the meaning of ʿādi, the ordinary, under circumstances of absence and military occupation. Terming these circumstances "ordinary," when confinement in fact molds the entire existence of the detainees' wives, can be conceived as a denial of the suffering that accompanies the absence. Continuing a line of inquiry that finds expression most clearly in the work of Das (2007, 2010) and in regard to contemporary Palestine Kelly (2009), Allen (2012) and Feldman (2015), I work toward an understanding of how far individual notions of what is allegedly ordinary can be stretched, in order to turn inside out a key notion in contemporary n anthropology: "the ordinary" or its ethnographic twin, "the everyday." I take maintaining the everyday as an achievement that is created through habitual actions. For my interlocutors, this means acting with the aim of sustaining their split families (Das 2010: 376).

This does not mean that every aspect of these women's quotidian lives is enacted dramatically as suffering. It does mean, however, that the everyday is the place in which the braiding of the ordinary and the extraordinary occurs. The picture of endurance that emerges here shows us women's labor of making an everyday life for themselves and their intimate relations while their husbands are imprisoned, and how the characteristics of such a life are simultaneously allowed and denied a place in the standing language.

Any work of endurance is intrinsically and necessarily in dialogue with Elizabeth Povinelli's and João Biehl's work on life marked by abandonment (Povinelli 2012; Biehl 2005 [2013]). Biehl's writing introduces us to lives at the intersection of abandonment by kin, psychopharmaceuticals, and a state that has seemingly given up on caring for its citizens (2005; Biehl and Moran-Tomas 2009). Povinelli's concern on the other hand is with the conceptualization of the effort to endure (2012: 471).

I think of endurance from a different angle. In contrast to Biehl's description of his main protagonist Catarina's abandonment by her relatives, none of my interlocutors have been abandoned by their kin. In fact, it is quite the contrary, as families offer support in the absence of husbands. Women have been integrated even more tightly into kin intimacy due to their husbands' absences, whether those husbands are dead or in prison. Nor are the women necessarily deprived of material sustenance; some are even financially independent of these kin networks. Yet it is within the scene of care and support and even dramatic performances of kin solidarity that I could detect a feeling of suffocation, in the sense that these women were bound to represent what others wanted them to be, as an act of solidarity to their lost husbands and to the Palestinian cause.

While I share Povinelli's wish to investigate the potential for a life lived Otherwise in the permeable boundary between endurance and exhaustion, her emphasis on the possibility of a different life would here translate into documentation of Palestinian inventiveness and vitality born out of exhaustion. My emphasis, however, is on the kind of endurance that cannot be separated from its limitations. Ethnographically, this is about the minutiae of the emotional labor that endurance requires, such as Luma's effort to offer her guests refreshments the second her tears dried, or Yara's participation in political campaigning whose efficacy she herself doubts. Consequentially, I put aside the idea of the Otherwise for a time. I am simply trying to work out what endurance means, and its dimensions, when it is considered as an aspect of the ordinary for the women figuring in this book.

Becoming an Intimate Stranger

This direction of my work came to me through a realization during three months of fieldwork in Gaza in 2005, where I was part of a research project under the auspice of RCT—The Danish Rehabilitation and Research Centre for Torture Victims right after Israel's withdrawal of its settlements from the strip. At the beginning of the holy month of Ramadan, I found myself in a research office in Gaza overlooking the Mediterranean Sea. In front of me was a list with twenty names, a response to a request from the research team of which I was a part. We had asked our partners in a psychosocial organization to provide a randomized list of torture survivors, half of them men and half women. I was puzzled by the absence of any female names on the list. When I asked why there were only men, our Palestinian research leader answered with a shrug, "Women are not torture victims, they are the wives of the victims."

The fact that women rarely are torture survivors or detainees in Israeli prisons is hardly a mystery, bearing in mind the gendered distribution of labor in the resistance against Israel (see Peteet 1991; Jean-Klein 2003; Sabbagh 1998; Gren 2009). However, the language in which the research leader noted that these women were wives rather than victims appeared to refer to notions of proper adversity, of who deserved services. My attempt to understand the rationales behind such assumptions grew into my examination of the acknowledgment, or lack thereof, of lives and forms of suffering, as well as the criteria used to evaluate affliction among those related to the heroes and victims of the Palestinian resistance. My field comprised a variety of venues and activities: the baking hours on Fridays in the village, the Prisoners' Support Center's appointments with donors, meetings in Europe or in the occupied territory of donors about allocations of funds to different interventions and conferences in Europe, the Middle East, and Canada, where the most recent knowledge on trauma, interventions, and conflict was being discussed by those most knowledgeable in their field.

My fieldwork began through the Prisoners' Support Center in Ramallah, where I asked to meet clients who were secondary victims. I spent the first two months of my fieldwork accompanying therapists on outreach sessions and meetings with donors and other nongovernmental, psychosocial organizations in the West Bank and Jerusalem. Given that the Prisoners' Support Center initiated a group therapeutic project for wives of detainees a couple of months into my fieldwork I soon came to spend most of my time with the five women of that therapeutic group. I compounded my research efforts around another group of women in the similar, though still different, situation of being the widows of martyrs in another town in the West Bank.

The two sites are here termed Dar Nūra and Bāb aš-šams, respectively. These are not the proper names of the villages because their disclosure, in combination with the personal details conveyed in this book, could betray the anonymity and confidentiality of my interlocutors. Recognizing that belonging to a village, a region, or a town in the occupied territory is as significant as being a Palestinian (Swedenburg 1990; Muhawi and Kanaana 1989), I have omitted detailed descriptions of these two sites, for the sake of protection. In the cases of particular interlocutors and their lives and stories, I have included as much local detail as confidentiality allows. I have done this while keeping the ethnographic problems involved in making such representative choices firmly in mind.

The bulk of data was created within, among, and about intimate relationships in the families of detainees, and secondarily in the families of martyrs. Intimate relationships in families were therefore a primary site of study rather than, say, a village, a town, or any other geographically bounded site.

Intimate relations for the women appearing in this book unfold primarily in the domesticities around the women's homes. Notably, however, the domestic is not necessarily private, nor is intimacy always connoted as positive. Following Das, Ellen, and Leonard, I understand the domestic as "somehow always implicated in the non-domestic—be that the domain of the politico-jural, the idea of the non-domesticated wilderness, or as suffused by affects that circulate in the wider politico-jural domain" (2008: 351). The domestic, then, is the site where betrayals of relations and of oneself can take place in the wake of a violence that trespasses the porous boundary between the domestic and the outside (Das 2007: 11; Kelly and Thiranagama 2010).

Amina, her sisters Layla and Aisha, and the kin network around them are the women among the detainees' families with whom I had and still have the closest relationships. Among my interlocutors, it is their company that I seek upon returning to the occupied territory and with whom I stay in touch through the occasional e-mail or text message.

I consider these relationships to be based on mutuality, differences at every imaginable level aside. Amina, the woman with the least education of the group, welcomed me wholeheartedly into her home after we first spoke. On this occasion she commented on the character of our conversation, which covered topics she discussed with many people, but, she said, in a different way. Voicing our conversations as "different" tells me that even if only sometimes and with some people I did in fact succeed in listening "differently" to my interlocutors, a method of anthropological inquiry that in Lisa Stevenson's thoughtful words make room for hesitancy, the uncertain, and the unsettled (2014:2). Indeed, my hope is that this work overall will convey precisely knowledge in a way that allows us to think about voice, heroism, and gender in an alternative light.

Listening differently may in fact have been the most important aspect of how I conducted my fieldwork and why I was not only accepted but welcomed with a sincerity that I had not envisioned, in Amina's home or elsewhere. I thus accepted Amina's welcome and used her house as a base during the days and nights I spent in Dar Nūra. This was the place to which I returned and where her unmarried sister Layla, their mother, and their brother, as well as Amina's four children, welcomed me. They never made anything special out of my presence, yet we enjoyed each other's company, whether we were baking together under the watch of Amina's and Layla's strict eyes, sharing a meal, watching old Indian action movies before bedtime, or walking through the village in the cool evenings.

Aisha, a highly educated, politically active, professional woman, I got to know slowly through conversations and joint activities. During our first encounters she spoke entirely in the language of nationalist rhetoric. It was only over time and after I had shared hours in her home, at her workplace, and in her car with her two children that she expressed the paradoxes intrinsic to her situation. For shorter periods I was part of the rhythm of Aisha's daily routine by coming to her office for a couple of hours, reading or talking with her and other staff members there. We then drove home, cooked lunch for the children, and visited friends, family, and in-laws, before she either dropped me off at Amina's house or drove me to Birzeit, from where I took a minibus to Ramallah or Jerusalem. Eventually, both Amina and Aisha spoke confidentially with me, using words that they did not share with either their kin or children. Since being with the women often also meant being with their families, it was only on particular, orchestrated occasions that they could speak differently with me about their lives as detainees' wives.

When I first met most of my interlocutors, they were accompanied by their therapists from either the Prisoners' Support Center's headquarters in Ramallah or the branch office in Bāb aš-šams. Such an introduction meant that the therapist acted as both a female confidante and a fellow Palestinian who guaranteed my trustworthiness. This proved invaluable, especially with regard to the families of detainees: betrayal, treason, and rumors are real and experienced elements of their everyday life and part of the cause of their husbands' detainments (Kelly 2010). This form of introduction thus dramatically facilitated my access. In addition, choosing a therapeutic organization rather than a detainees' club as a point of access confirmed to the women that I was interested in their own experiences, rather than those of their men. It expressed to them that they were not a gateway to knowledge about events or the suffering or political lives of their husbands: I was concerned with the women and their lives with and without their absent husbands.

I have had conversations with forty-two women who were either married to detainees, the widows of martyrs, or the mothers of either detainees or martyrs. Among them, twelve women stand out. Seven were married to detainees, and five were the widows of martyrs. The ethnography of these women forms the backbone of the book, which is based on our recurrent meetings. I met all of them at least three times individually and once each in the company of their mother, mother-in-law, sisters, or sisters-in-law, respectively, or at times collectively. Seven of the twelve are women whom I visited regularly with or without the intention of conducting a formal interview. This is why I refer to the main part of my data as conversations. As one aspect of my dialogue with the seven women, I gave them diaries in which to record their thoughts, feelings, or anything that sprang to their minds. I asked them to fill the diaries in for a week, after which I would read them, too. However, I also made clear to the women that if they did not feel like writing or showing me their writings, that was fine. Four of the women returned their diaries to me, and their content is discussed mainly in Chapter 6.

As for the thirty women who constitute only a peripheral part of my ethnographic material, conversations with them have provided me with knowledge about nationalist rhetoric in the nexus of the personal and the collective.

With five of the seven women, I had the most intimate conversations and relationships that developed over time: Amina, Aisha, Fatemeh, Nadia, and Luma. Amina, Aisha, and Fatemeh formed part of the support group for detainees' wives and all live in Dar Nūra. Nadia and Luma are from the outskirts of Bāb aš-šams. Nadia is the widow of a martyr and currently married to a detainee. Luma is the widow of a martyr. My relationships with Nadia, Luma, and less so Fatemeh centered on our conversations, and however close we came through words, I did not at any point form part of their everyday life. I joined Fatemeh on a visit to her husband in prison, yet I did not spend an extended period of time in her home. In the case of all seven women, I accompanied them on visits to their female relatives and also received guests together with them in their homes.

I am cautious about how close a stranger can possibly become to another human being, to say nothing of a stranger who does not master Arabic fully and has had utterly different life circumstances. Yet insofar as we assume that the words through which we express ourselves are the result of our relations to one other, the fact that I was a stranger, Western, and then unmarried meant I could not judge the women morally by the criteria they were normally assessed by. Therefore I was allowed to ask particularly probing questions, and they frequently answered. Of course, they had to trust that I would not betray them, not only to the Israelis but also to their families, their families-in-law, and the community of the village. This is why I have concealed not only their true names but also the names of their villages and the circumstances under which their husbands came to be detained in Israel.

On the morning after I arrived at the wonderful house in East Jerusalem that was to become my base during fieldwork, Rose, my caring landlady, said over a cup of coffee: "So, do you want to get started *habibti*?" She ushered me into her green Citroën in which we drove to Ramallah in order for me to meet a friend of hers who, as it turned out, was one of the most esteemed psychological counselors in Palestine. Our meeting was the beginning of my friendship with a sharp-witted and generous woman who at one point formulated my research as "looking into the effects on women of our crutches of heroism" in occupied Palestine. For a number of reasons, those words would and could never be mine. Yet they frame with almost stunning accuracy the question of why at times particular experiences of distress among those who are "only the wives" of the heroes cannot be acknowledged without impairing the collective hope for the Palestinian project. In essence, this is the fundamental question that I examine in this book. I do so through by pondering questions such as what it means to endure when that which is endured is without end and how to grieve when that which is grieved does not lend itself to a language of loss and mourning. In *No Place for Grief* I give no easy answers, nor do I claim to offer irrefutable facts or knowledge. What I do offer is the kind of knowledge, which is more akin to acknowledgment that such questions persist and pose particular kinds of pressure on its subjects.

CHAPTER 1

══════

The Grammar of Suffering
in Occupied Palestine

From the late autumn of 2007 through the end of winter the following year, five women married to long-term political detainees met every Wednesday at 11 A.M. in a chilly meeting room at the town hall in a sleepy West Bank village. The group was facilitated by a female therapist, Muna, and her assistant, both from the Prisoners' Support Center.[1] The five women participating in the two-hour sessions appear throughout this book, less however as therapeutic subjects than as wives, mothers, and daughters who are living through the absence of their husbands.

Even before they participated in the group therapy, the women knew each other. They all live in Dar Nūra, a village of around five thousand inhabitants, and are related to each other through either consanguine or affinal kinship, or, in most cases, both, as patrilateral parallel cousin marriage is the preferred form of marriage in the village.[2] They are thus folded into each other's lives, and know of each other either through firsthand accounts or, more often, rumors and reputation. The knowledge shared in the therapeutic group was therefore anything but confidential. None of the women ever risked her reputation as the proud, dutiful wife of a heroic detainee.

On the first two occasions, the group met downstairs in the library of the town hall. With children browsing through books and playing, and secretaries working with open doors, the library was not an appropriate therapeutic space, the therapists found. Since one of the participants, Aisha, enjoyed considerable social esteem in the village, the group was thereafter allowed to meet in a more private room. Moving two floors up and under the auspices of the town council, we were served tea and coffee by the council's cook at every meeting. When the women who formed part of the group met and asked each other whether they would attend the next session, they would say "bt-rohiila al-baladiyyeh?" (Are you going to the town hall?), rather than referring to it as either a women's or a therapeutic group.

In this way the women distanced themselves from the fact that they were involved in a process that problematized their relationship to the detainees. Local assumptions hold that being a relative of a detainee inspires a sense of honor and feelings of pride for those who are active against the Israeli occupation. Among Palestinians, being the wife of a detainee is therefore not considered a genuine reason for distress proper, save for the affliction that the wife may feel vicariously on behalf of her detained husband. That life as a detainee's wife is not in fact lived exclusively in the glow of derivative honor is no surprise to fellow Palestinians or international observers of Palestine. Nonetheless, there are difficulties in acknowledging that "form of life" for the very same Palestinians and foreigners alike, difficulties that are the theme of this chapter.

Muna, who was facilitating the Dar Nūra town hall group, hoped to create a social space in which these women's lives and suffering were recognized. During the span of the therapeutic group project, the Prisoners' Support Center hosted a training course in group therapy on its Ramallah premises for twenty Palestinian counselors. Two Spanish psychotherapists led the course. A vital element of the course concerned how to enable clients to establish what is termed "a safe place," in therapeutic vernacular. A safe place refers to both a state of mind and a physical space or a material object that evokes a feeling of comfort and safety in the client. Ideally this personal space is established for the group members before they express their traumatic experiences. During the training course, Muna raised her hand to voice a concern. She was already halfway through the group therapeutic process for the detainees' wives. Muna asked, "What if the clients do not have and cannot create a safe place?" The teacher replied, "We have to help them establish a safe place." Muna continued, "I have a problem with a member of this group, Amina. She feels more victimized than all the others. How can I deal with that?" The teacher answered, "The feeling of victimhood is a feeling that 'no one can understand me.' You could try asking her how she would feel if someone actually understood her. Because she thinks that she is not allowed to be okay. She reacts like she expects her husband to prefer that she is not

okay. Ask her to look toward the future. Because she's not staying the same:
life changes."

Later in the day's packed training schedule, the participating therapists
were asked to enact a situation from their therapy using the therapeutic intervention of psychodrama. This form of therapy is based on the work of the
Brazilian psychotherapist Jacob Moreno (1946). His central idea is the powerful potential of reenacting a psychic conflict in front of an audience. Ideally,
this performance will transform a traumatic experience into something that
can be shared and thereby externalized from the inner, allegedly ineffable
register of the traumatized person.

As a therapeutic method, psychodrama enjoys widespread popularity
across Gaza and the West Bank. It is an intervention believed to be well
suited to clients, such as women and children, who are not quite comfortable
in providing coherent narratives of past and difficult experiences (Burmeister and Maciel 2007; Moreno 1946). That psychodrama also figured in the
training program for group therapy is no surprise, since psychodrama and
group therapy both emphasize collective sharing as a way to heal painful
experience.

During such an exercise in psychodrama, Muna enacted the role of
Amina, whom she represented as feeling too much like a victim. Still shaken,
Muna told me afterward, "When I played the role of Amina and told the
audience why I felt like a victim, I started crying and I could not stop; I just
cried and cried. I felt for that moment that I was Amina. Esmail [Muna's
husband] is also political, he could just as well be in prison."

Why did the enactment of Amina cause Muna to cry? The training
session for the Palestinian therapists appears to convey at least two modes
of understanding distress. One is a Palestinian moral discourse on suffering
captured by Muna as the concerned wife of a politically active and potentially heroic husband at risk of both violent death and detention in Israel. The
local idiom of perseverance, sumūd, summarizes this discourse. By this
understanding, women like Amina are praised as the patient, supportive,
and proud wives of heroic husbands, suffering as spouses, albeit differently
according to the gendered division of labor in the Palestinian project (see
Peteet 2005; Jean-Klein 2003). The second, underlying concept of suffering
is the one offered by the Spanish trainers, an idea of victimhood as an emotional experience that one can recover from with time. This framework
grounds affliction on the psychological terrain of trauma (Fassin and Recht-

man 2009; Argenti-Pillen 2000; Leys 2000). The two modes of understanding anguish, both demonstrated in the vignette, together constitute how suffering is addressed and understood in the occupied territory.

This compound framing of affliction resembles what Didier Fassin has termed the hero-victim subjectivity, but there are important differences between his and my engagement with trauma among Palestinians. Fassin's work (2008) is primarily based on professional immersion as well as fieldwork among medical and management staff in the organization Medecins sans Frontiers in Paris and its programs for Palestinians. In contrast my analysis privileges the view from rather than on subjectivities, in the sense that the bulk of empirical data is based on fieldwork in occupied Palestine among people who are labeled as traumatized and their therapists. This ethnographic premise allows me to ponder how the experiences of wives of Palestinian detainees are not adequately contained in the framing of their suffering as either trauma or heroic sacrifice.

By asking why Muna was crying as an initial question, this chapter offers both an ethnographic analysis and a conceptualization of the problem of experiences that evade what Sally Engle Merry and Susan Bibler Coutin (2014) term "commensurability." This term refers to the globally circulating indicators used to register, for instance, suffering in the shape of violence, sexual assault, or poverty and the lives that can get lost in this registration. This chapter brings to light how the forms of affliction for detainees' wives are incommensurate with, and elude, the languages of these indicators.

What Counts as Suffering in Palestine

Muna's difficulty with Amina's case suggests precisely the degree of incommensurability between the therapeutic premise of change and the uneventful life it is supposed to heal. This premise emerges in the Spanish teacher's presentation of Amina's inability to engage in life as related to the onset of an event—her husband's imprisonment—to which Amina responded with an immediate show of overwhelming emotion. Following an emotional response, Amina was supposed to recover. By this understanding, suffering is caused, and defined, by an extraordinary human experience that befalls an individual. The problem with women like Amina, however, is that while they are included in therapy because they are wives of potentially traumatized men, and witnesses of potentially disturbing events of detention, these women's experiences are arguably not "events" set apart from the ordinary, nor do they unfold in a temporally linear fashion with an onset, an emotional response, and an aftermath in which recovery can occur. Muna speaks about her client Amina by using the vocabulary of therapeutic progress, while identifying with Amina's situation of being the wife of a man who is politically active. Muna thereby employs a language of affect that merges psychological jargon with Palestinian modes of knowing affliction. The complex resonances[3] between these two modes of knowing suffering together form what I think of as a "grammar of suffering." This grammar merges a global psychological understanding of suffering as trauma and a Palestinian moral discourse on suffering expressed in terms of events, heroism, and endurance in the face of hardship.

The Palestinian moral discourse of suffering is polyvocal. Khalili's triad of heroic, tragic, and sumūd narratives captures the three main genres in which Palestinians tend to recount their experiences, depending on whether they are recounting a heroic past or current stories of tragedy and suffering (2007: 224). Heroic narratives, Khalili argues, are those that privilege the courageous aspects of a person or an experience, leaving, for instance, the cost of such courage unspoken. More often than not, heroic narratives are set in the past tense. Tragic narratives on the other hand increasingly have become part of the Palestinian narrative repertoire, as instances of loss and consistent discrimination against Palestinians in Lebanon, Palestine, and Israel are extremely common. Lastly, what Khalili calls sumūd narratives tend to describe a range of experiences not easily accounted for. At first glance, sumūd narratives would seem to sum up and include the experiences of, say, detainees' wives. As this chapter proceeds, however, it will become clear that I am hesitant to agree with Khalili's point that the value and efficacy of the sumūd narratives is that they allow their narrators a breathing space. Drawing my inspiration from Deleuze's thoughts on convergence,[4] I suggest instead that breathing space is precisely what is missing for detainees' wives due to a convergence between knowing the Palestinian predicament as trauma, on the one hand, and local ways of acknowledging suffering by the criteria of event and relation, on the other.

As we shall see, however, these criteria are not equal. Event is given emphasis in the convergence of Palestinian and psychological ways of understanding suffering, while relation is considered secondary, or at least derivative. In the second half of the chapter, I analyze how these criteria and their internal hierarchies fail to recognize the less clear-cut aspects of Palestinian affliction.

The Criteria of Event

In their book *The Empire of Trauma* (2009), Fassin and Rechtman map out how knowledge production about suffering and interventions in the occupied territory have altered in scope and focus since the second Intifada in 2000–2003. The orientation of international donations has shifted from providing medical assistance to people who were wounded in direct violent clashes, during the first Intifada from 1987 to 1993, to the broader, all-inclusive category of conducting psychosocial interventions with the people affected by, for instance, house demolitions, violent clashes, home invasions, and the loss, wounding, or death of family members. Rather than following the precise diagnostic criteria for evaluating a client's mental state, interventions and representations of suffering slide into a witnessing of the general situation of the Palestinians. Fassin and Rechtman term this phenomenon "humanitarian psychiatry" (209).

Against this backdrop, Fassin and Rechtman suggest that a focus on direct violence and the events that cause traumatization have been replaced by an emphasis on the clinical narratives of clients, their general life circumstances, and mundane suffering (2009: 201). While their analysis brings to the fore central tendencies in how adversity is understood in the occupied territories, I would argue that the notion of "event" has in fact retained its centrality. As will become clear in the ethnography that follows, "event" serves as a marker for suffering across diagnoses, narratives, and representations, even when the suffering is not related to an actual event. This was brought to light early in my fieldwork: When I asked the staff in the Prisoners' Support Center to meet those among their clients who were wives of prisoners, the therapists instead urged me to meet with widows and mothers whose relatives had been martyred and who were therefore able to express their experiences in terms of "events."

The lure of violent events as markers for suffering emerges clearly in the Prisoners' Support Center, where documentation of the physical consequences of torture and detention occurs in tandem with the psychological diagnosis and treatment of ailments. Since the early 1990s, in similar zones of protracted conflict across the world, emphasis on the psychological effects of violence has perpetuated psychosocial theories and practices of alleviating the effects of violence (Fassin 2008; Pupavac 2001; Summerfield 1999). As an employee of a Swiss development organization said about the omnipresence of psychosocial intervention; "Is it not what we all do these days?"

One expression of this "empire of trauma" is the sheer number of scientific articles, studies, and statistics, written and collected by both Palestinian and international scientists, about the prevalence of traumatic events and posttraumatic stress disorder (PTSD) among Palestinians (Peltonen et al. 2010; Abu Hein et al. 1993; Salo et al. 2005). In the main office of the therapists at the Prisoners' Support Center, a faded photocopy on the wall displayed the *Diagnostic and Statistical Manual of Mental Disorders* fourth edition (DSM-IV) checklists for PTSD, anxiety, obsessive compulsive disorder, and depression—which is remarkable, given that none among the staff were clinical psychologists or psychiatrists. The presence of the DSM-IV photocopy next to ads for favorite takeout restaurants and Naje al Ali's iconic drawing of Handala encapsulates how therapists imagine their clients' suffering: it is about a violent event that is direct and detectable through psychiatric diagnosis, despite the fact that the aim of the interventions and the mandate of the organization were more along the lines of local support to prisoners and their families. In a similar vein, the former director of a major health NGO, Dr. Issa Nejmeh, told me how the trope of traumatization was a mode of imagining the plight of the Palestinians and the mental effects on the wounded victims of the first Intifada from 1987 to 1993: "The notion of trauma was related to the people injured in the Intifada, and is completely different from what was later called PTSD. It was a direct physical pressure or manifestation, say, if a resistant lost an eye or ended up in a wheelchair. It was a psychological phenomenon related to a physical happening. Secondly, people became aware of physical problems that were a result of psychological problems." Nejmeh's drawing attention to how PTSD in Palestine was related at its inception to a physical phenomenon indicates that the move from physical injuries to psychological distress was circular rather than linear. PTSD was crystallized as a mode of presenting the suffering of the Palestinians (and those in other conflict zones around the world) as on par with human rights violations (see Young 1995; Fassin 2008; Allen 2012), to both the political world and to "eager, but uncaring donors," as Nejmeh said dryly. Elaborating on the counterintuitive lack of care among international institutions and organizations that channeled large amounts of funding to the Palestinians, Nejmeh offered the well-known fact that, whereas projects concerned with the effect of the conflict are sure to attract generous funds, the political will to change "the situation" have evaporated with what he saw as the post-Oslo depoliticized relationship between Palestinians and their donors.

During our conversation, which started in his clinic in 2007, continued in his living room, and was taken up again in a Bethlehem café in 2011, he elaborated his point by analyzing the main Palestinian actors who work under the umbrella of trauma and psychosocial interventions as a response to violence. These were centers established to help those perceived to have been most severely afflicted by the occupation, namely, the detainees, the torture survivors, or those suffering from physical disability caused by what are considered heroic acts of resistance. It is violence, and thus events of radical negative change, rather than general health, that preoccupies all these local institutions.

Western donors and experts, and their financial aid and knowledge, have been instrumental, though not exclusively so, in shaping how the Palestinian psychosocial organizations have grown, and have set the benchmarks in the Middle East and internationally (Hanafi and Tabar 2005). Though the Psychosocial Bill was pushed by the Ministry of Health in 2009, there is little doubt as to where the best counselors go: to the generously funded NGOs. Therefore the Ministry of Health looks to them, as well as the World Health Organization in Palestine, when it wants to establish so-called best practices.

The infrastructure of psychological care in Palestine is thus remarkably different than elsewhere in the Levant or the Middle East in general. There is most certainly a space for the local sheikhs in offering assistance to the distressed, at least in the countryside and in the more conservative parts of the West Bank and Gaza. But such traditional healers arguably play a less significant role than, for example, in the contemporary Egypt that Amira Mittermaier and Paola Abenante describe in their powerful work (Mittermaier 2011, 2014; Abenante 2012). In Palestine, there is a general familiarity with Western psychology due to Palestine's colonial past and the ways that European and American concern about the Palestinian plight has been expressed in psychosocial interventions for a traumatized population. Consequently, there is a receptivity, however minimal, to understanding the effects on the psyche that the military occupation may have had. One might go so far as to say that psychology, counseling, and psychiatry have become close to household terms due to the massive effort to raise awareness about the psychological consequences of violence. The largest effort was spearheaded by the late Palestinian psychiatrist Eyad al-Sarraj, whose Gaza Community Mental Health Program has educated and provided services to many a Gazan since the 1990s (Fischer 2007; Perdigon 2011). More than any other, Sarraj's approach embodies Fassin's notion of a humanitarian psychiatry, and his approach to the effects of the occupation on Palestinians has been tremendously significant in terms of how the language of trauma, like that of human rights, has become the language of Palestinian victimhood (Allen 2012).

Organizations with a psychosocial mandate thus employ an ever-growing number of the educated Palestinian middle class of health professionals. Nejmeh nonetheless pointed out that indicative of these professionals is "a lack of human resources: we don't have psychiatrists. Instead we have people who study psychology and then they act as psychological consultants. And we have social workers who have had some training in psychology and sociological behavior." Whereas therapists have earned BAs in psychology and education, generally from Birzeit University, specialized training is given within the NGOs. These courses are funded and negotiated by the centers' donors. As the research coordinator of the Prisoners' Support Center told me, "We follow the fashion. We might want a course in family therapy, but in Europe or the US, EMDR or CBT is on everybody's lips and thus on the list of training courses that, for example, the EU want[s] to fund because it is evidence based." The bulk of Palestinian therapists I spoke to described their therapeutic approaches as eclectic, comprehensive psychosocial programs that take into consideration the entire human being and his or her lifeworld. However, access to the treatment and services offered by the centers mentioned above are allocated according to clients' scores on the Harvard Trauma Questionnaire and other mental-health-ranking instruments. These scores determine whether the client shows symptoms of anxiety disorder, depression, or PTSD. Hence, what seemed initially to be peripheral to the psychosocial services available to prisoners and their families—namely, trauma—proved in fact to be at the very center of such services.

The complexity of diagnostic practices dawned on me when I joined the newly educated therapist Ahmad at a school in Salfit, where he was to undertake psychosocial interventions. The visit to the school is part of the so-called outreach work, which recognizes that many clients are not able to come to the center's offices for treatment due to financial constraints or fear of stigma. Outreach work is popular among psychosocial organizations, among the target group of clients, and not least among the donors. It is taken as a sign that the organizations, far from being elitist, are committed to helping beneficiaries who are most in need. At the Prisoners' Support Center, well over half of the consultations took place through outreach work. The work is often done by the newest employees in the organization and thus often by those who have the least clinical experience. In the morning, the therapists travel to the village targeted for that day's outreach work. Either they are driven by the center's driver in its car or they take *as-servīs* (a minibus). Upon arrival at the villages or refugee camps, the therapists are dropped off at their clients' houses. The driver then waits for two or three hours while the therapists finish their work.

Therapists often dread outreach work. It involves the hassle of a long journey, few or no breaks, and the frustration of not being able to do proper therapy. When the therapeutic space is the home, the client's family, children, and guests frequently walk in and out of the sessions. At the end of the day, the weariness of the car full of therapists is palpable, and the ensuing hours of recovery long. Many of the therapists I spoke with doubted the efficiency of the outreach work, but donors like it. Given the pressure of being able to prove that services are effective and reach as many people as possible, the outreach teams I met were often under pressure to see as many clients as possible during their trips. Thus after a long car journey on the Palestinian byroads, Ahmad, the driver, and I reached the school, where we went straight to the director's office, outside of which three children were waiting. Ahmad asked one of the children to join him, and the other two had to wait. The case concerned a young boy who had witnessed his father being injured by Israeli soldiers in the street. The father had survived, but apparently the child suffered from concentration problems. Closing the door behind us, Ahmad took out his papers and went through the checklist for symptoms for around twenty minutes, during which time curious children constantly banged on the door and pushed it open with roars of laughter. The boy then left the room and Ahmad told me that he had PTSD and listed the symptoms from the DSM-IV. The examination of the two other children followed the same procedure. After the three consultations, we left the school and got into the car to go back to Ramallah.

The point here is not to expose Ahmad as a therapist who is not quite at home with the difficult work of diagnosis, but, rather, to reveal how the notion of trauma is, in practice, employed under the umbrella of psychosocial interventions. Psychosocial intervention is common, and would not raise eyebrows in the West Bank and Gaza, but it is worth underscoring that in its combination of an individual and social approach to the suffering person, it is based on a conceptualization of suffering as an individualized and bio-medical trauma. Ahmad's translation of the boy's concentration problems into the language of trauma was a way for the therapist to know the boy's affliction and therefore help ameliorate his distress. Trauma here serves as a useful proxy of suffering, and one that is a result of the many factors that influenced the therapists: donor pressure, the lack of clinical training, burnout, and the fact that the therapists often share the experiences of their clients.

With an eye to current and potential donors, the diagnosis of posttraumatic stress disorder is therefore important to Palestinian organizations because it allows them to document their activities with so-called evidence-based therapy, among them cognitive behavioral therapy (CBT). The effectiveness of CBT and narrative exposure therapy have been tested through randomized control trials of victims of rape, American Vietnam War veterans, victims of terror attacks, and British victims of traffic accidents (Bisson and Andrew 2009; Bisson 2008; van der Kolk and Blaustein 2005; Gersons and Olff 2005; Basoglu 2003). Hence, donors assume these methods will be effective among traumatized Palestinians, too.

The fact that Palestinians have to have experienced a traumatic event in order for their distress to be acknowledged goes beyond the issue of therapy. Consider Maryam, whose life figures in more detail in Chapters 4 and 5. She is the mother of three children, and her youngest son was only three when we first met. Maryam recounted how he caused her endless distress, to the point where she actually had to have him on a leash in his room in order to take care of her other children and household chores. Her mother-in-law scolded her, saying that his behavior showed she had failed to discipline her child appropriately. Two years later, she told me with relief that her son had been diagnosed with autism and that he had made fantastic progress with a new program for autistic children that Maryam herself had helped establish. With the diagnosis of her son, everyday life for her and her children had become much easier. Socially, the countless visits to her son's doctor were no longer cause for gossip about the whereabouts of a woman with an absent husband, but rather the actions of a concerned mother caring for her child. Nonetheless, autism and other forms of congenital illness, in particular mental disorders, fail to attract anywhere near the same attention or funding as do disorders and traumas that are results of the occupation. And despite the historical presence of a language of psychology to acknowledge mental distress, congenital mental disorders are considered a stigma in Palestine. This uneven recognition is evident in the difference between the glitzy premises of the Prisoners' Support Center and the "clinic" to which Maryam took her autistic son for day care, and where she volunteered three times a week: a small, shabby room adjacent to the nursery for the other children. The contrast reveals how event-based trauma is acknowledged and addressed, as opposed to the lack of recognition afforded what is described by Povinelli as the painstaking uneventfulness of chronic suffering, such as that caused by stigmatizing mental disorders (2011: 146).

Importantly, the contrast between the two is specifically owing to the presence of a violent event that enables the recognition of suffering (for an elaboration, see Mittermaier 2014). This brings to mind Das's identification of a critical event after which "new modes of action came into being which redefined traditional categories such as codes of purity and honor, the meaning of martyrdom, and the construction of a heroic life" (1997 6). Violent events in occupied Palestine offer precisely that nexus of new modes of action and the acknowledgment that comes with being either a hero of political resistance, a martyr's widow, or a traumatized victim.

The Force of Eventful Suffering—Immediacy and Immediation

> Priority in allocating grants is given to projects providing direct medical, psychological, social, economic, legal, humanitarian, educational or other forms of assistance, to torture victims and members of their family who, due to their close relationship with the victim, were directly affected at the time of the event.
>
> —United Nations Voluntary Fund for Victims of Torture (2007)

Alongside the European Union, the United Nations Voluntary Fund for Victims of Torture (UNVFVT) is a major global funder for centers that offer assistance to torture victims and their families. In its 2007 round of funding, the UNVFVT had a total budget of USD 9 million. The above excerpt about the criteria for receiving funds forms the basis for the evaluation of applications and, as two members of the UNVFVT staff said during a meeting in Palais Wilson in Geneva, they continuously stressed these criteria when they had meetings or missions to visit or evaluate projects. The

UNVFVT workers repeatedly emphasize to beneficiaries that the assistance must be directly allocated to the actual, immediate victims of torture.

During fieldwork in the West Bank, I joined a meeting between the Prisoners' Support Center and a representative from the UNVFVT. The communications manager of the center initiated the meeting with a PowerPoint presentation that displayed numbers of violations and of people treated at the center during recent years. According to the tables and graphs, a growing number of clients were the relatives of detainees and martyrs. The presentation ended with pictures of the physical wounds on the bodies of torture victims, dead children, and lamenting women. After the presentation, there was a discussion about uncertainties concerning the identity of the organization's clients. The representative from the UNVFVT said, "I need numbers of how many of your beneficiaries . . . are actually torture survivors or direct family," to which the director firmly replied, "All of them are survivors of torture—they are captives in Israel!" This point was ignored for the remainder of the meeting. However, the representative of the fund said again in front of the employees of the organization, "It is important that when you make projects for the families, it has to be families who were directly affected. For example, ordinary domestic violence is not torture or to be directly related to it. It does not count."

During the meeting with UNVFVT in its European headquarters, I asked the representatives how they identify direct victims affected at the time of the event. One answered, "No one can distinguish between someone who is tortured and the one who witnesses torture." Both the fund and its beneficiary projects are thus intimately aware of the pitfalls and permeable boundaries of the definitions they constantly draw and redraw. It is interesting here to think in terms of Deleuze's idea of convergence, described earlier. Within this line of reasoning, there are at least two points of convergence between the language of the European donor and the Palestinian center's mode of expressing the suffering of its clients, the detainees, and their families within a framework of the Palestinian plight: immediacy and relation.

Immediacy is the first and primary point of convergence. Immediacy saturates the language of the representatives of the fund in their invocation of the terms "direct" and "directness" in the UNVFVT guidelines. "Direct" refers both to those who have undergone an event of torture, limited in time and space, and also to the insistence that the relation to that event must be "direct." Immediacy was further expressed by the Prisoners' Support Center through the director's outburst that imprisonment equals torture, and the graphic portrayal of physical wounds and lost limbs in the PowerPoint presentation. As Allen asserts, a "politics of immediation" currently permeates Palestinian political discourse and social relations as well (2009: 163). The "politics of immediation" is an affect-driven discourse that is embedded in the Palestinians' call to the world to pay attention to the immediacy of suffering—to the visceral aspects of the conflict—by insisting that images of fragmented bodies be displayed in the Western media, in addition to the Palestinian Maan News, al-Aqsa channel, or pan-Arab channels like al-Jazeera. Allen (2009) underscores that visualization plays a crucial role in the representation of the Palestinians as deserving victims who are worthy of recognition. In late summer 2014, for example, international news and social media were dominated by images of corpses, wounded children, and weeping mothers from Gaza during Israel's Operation Protective Edge. Displaying the human body, Allen (2009) argues, is a way of sidestepping the mediating elements that are thought to obscure the message of the humanness of the Palestinians. Of particular significance here is that such visual displays are imbued with invocations of violent events as a cause for suffering, and in this way can be seen as an imperative call to action on the part of witnesses.

A focus on immediate suffering also figured at a women's mosque meeting initiated by the Prisoners' Support Center. The counselor opened the meeting by introducing the center and its services, after which she said, "I want to start with a new subject today: 'Azme [crisis]. I want to know what *sadme* [shock] means to you." Various women quickly responded, "a disaster," "problems and worries," and "mašākil fi d-dār" (problems in the home). To these responses the counselor said, "Let me tell you what 'azme or ṣaḍme mean: if I knock on your door, how will you respond to that? You will open the door, right? It's a reaction to a particular event. When I knock on the door, you will respond to this action by reacting to this event. . . . Who else has something to say? Imm Amjad, tell us what happened when you got the news that your son had been killed?"

Addressed so directly, Imm Amjad replied, "Oh, you want me to cry now?" The counselor replied that she would feel better if she cried. Imm Amjad began to describe the death of her son:

It was the twentieth day of Ramadan, so I was fasting and praying all the time. So on that day when they killed him, my brother came

to tell me about it, he was telling gradually. He told me that my son
was in the hospital, so I asked him why, and he told me that the
Israelis had shot him. I told him, "Please ask them again, maybe you
are not sure, or someone told you that he died, but we are not sure.
Let's wait to be sure," but he told me, to be sure, and that he saw
him. Then I felt like I was unable to stand up, I couldn't even cry.
But at the same time, I was saying that everyone wishes to die as
a martyr, so my son got it and I shouldn't feel bad. Thank God
anyway."

The counselor approached the sorrow of the bereaved woman as well as the
other women's experiences of affliction through a language of acute crisis.
Moreover, she tied their experiences to the onset of an event to which the
women respond with immediate affect. The therapist's decision to focus
on a woman who lost her son to martyrdom illustrates how the emphasis
on immediacy permeates psychosocial intervention, as it does the manner in
which this woman shares her grief with the other participants. During
the session in the mosque, a focus on experiential wounds that are discrete,
visceral, and delineated in time and space eclipsed long-term suffering. The
converging point of immediacy is an expression of the assumption that an
event occurs in a moment. It is directly experienced by a victim or a witness,
and it can only be ameliorated by the presence of an other, in this case the
specific other of direct psychological, medical, psychosocial, or legal assistance.

There is a similarity here to the ethics of immediacy that, according to
Mittermaier, suffuses the "Tahrir Square state of mind," the hopeful in-
tentionality of the demonstrators in the square in Cairo during the Arab
Spring as well as the *khidma*, a Sufi place in which a meal is offered free of
charge to those in need in downtown Cairo (2014: 55). Based on fieldwork
at the height of the Arab Spring, Mittermaier says that an ethics of immediacy revolves around a set of embodied practices that call for tending to
those in front of us and around us (55). The politics of immediation in
occupied Palestine are not the same as an ethics of immediacy in contemporary Egypt, but it seems that they share the appeal of that which is
right before us—for example, a tortured person or a human being in need
of a meal—and how that person calls forth action on the part of an other.
Immediacy has an inherent urgency and as such immediacy surfaces as a
crystallization of the forceful lure of life marked by events, albeit tragic. In

contrast, the lives that lack this eventful, immediate criterion are easily missed.

The Criteria of Relation

The second point of convergence in the grammar of suffering is "relation." This point is reflected in how the fund representative emphasized that a relation to the event of torture, either through witnessing it or by "being directly connected" to the torture victim, is the most significant criterion when choosing projects to fund. For the Prisoners' Support Center, the importance of relation is premised on the fact that the relatives of torture survivors form a major client population. Emphasizing a relationship to the torture victim or the detainee includes this client population among the deserving victims through a language of secondary victimhood or secondary traumatization.

The DSM-IV diagnosis of PTSD emphasizes both the occurrence of a traumatic event and the ensuing emotional response of traumatization (APA 2000). It is considered a fact, and a source of puzzlement, among researchers and mental health professionals that women universally and in the occupied territory display higher PTSD scores than men, despite the fact that women rarely experience so-called traumatic events of torture, detention, direct violence, or the like (Helweg-Larsen and Kastrup 2007; Giacaman et al. 2009). Women are admitted to rehabilitation programs due to their classification as secondary victims because of their relationships to the primary victims (Solomon et al. 2004). An Israeli study of wives of prisoners of war by the well-known psychologist Zahava Solomon (2007) and her team showed that compared with women who had lost their husbands, the wives of prisoners of war showed higher degrees of traumatization.

The challenges of working with secondary victims were the topic of a conversation with the Palestinian therapist Muna, introduced earlier. I asked her why she employed cognitive behavioral therapy in her group intervention to the detainees' wives. She replied, "They need CBT, they need many things during the day, they are under the pressure of society, or they suffer from traumatic events and maybe there are irrational thoughts in their minds like, 'I'm a wife of a detainee, I can't go out, I can't do anything.' This is irrational beliefs. With CBT we can work with these beliefs through working with relaxation techniques." Noting Muna's description of the wives' afflictions as traumatic events, I asked her which precise events she was talking about. She replied, "I want to remove the traumatic events from their lives. During the session, the women said, 'Oh, I am not alone, there's another woman like me.' When some of them said, 'I feel like this and like this, another one said I feel the same, I suffer like you, I am not the only one who feels that.' They learn from each other, how to deal with problems like the children and the family-in-law."

How Muna frames the distress of her female clients as the result of traumatic events that have befallen them illuminates how a relation to a direct victim–political hero is a criterion for having one's suffering acknowledged, in addition to the occurrence of a traumatic event. That these criteria are at times indistinguishable was revealed when Muna explained to me what she meant by "traumatic event": she recounted intricate, ongoing situations of relational injury from the women's social relations, rather than singular happenings. Significantly, these at times implicitly wounding relations do not include the secondary victim's relationship to the primary victim. This confounds the criteria for the recognition of suffering, as well as the fit between therapeutic measures and the kinds of suffering these measures attempt to describe and ameliorate. The discrepancy between the language available for knowing suffering and the experiences the therapist tries to heal is evident with individual therapists. It is also evident in the institutionalization of a psychosocial approach to suffering in Palestine. Muna's comments point to two parallel concepts of suffering: one in which the immediacy of the traumatic event and a relation to a primary victim are the criteria of knowing suffering, and a second that is an acknowledgment that the object of amelioration is actually not the reliving of a traumatic memory of a violent event at all. Rather, it is the uneventful everyday life as a detainee's wife, folded into potentially harmful or challenging social relations.

How to think about the apparent incomprehension of what it means to be in the shoes of a detainee's wife can be aided by paying further attention to the notions of knowing and acknowledgment respectively. To know, argues Cavell, means to read others and to allow oneself to be read by others. It is "a process of being read, as finding your fate in your capacity for interpretation for yourself" (1988: 16). Being known as a human being thus allows for a language for speaking and thinking about oneself and one's experience. Cavell, however, underscores the discrepancy between knowing (reading) and experiencing. Following Cavell this leads us to Martin Heidegger, who in *Being and Time* argued that, although language straightens out experience, experience can never be straightened out "except through existing itself" (1962: 33). This process of straightening out experience unfolds, in this example, with reference both to the global psychological discourse and a Palestinian moral discourse on suffering. Through resonance between the two, the criteria of violent events and relations are concretized and become the criteria, per se, on which knowledge about bereaved women rests. Importantly, "knowledge" here is not the same as "acknowledgment." Cavell argues that acknowledgment goes beyond knowledge. It includes a moral dimension formulated as "recognising what I know" and acting upon it (Cavell 1979: 428). This distinction figures in Kelly's recent work (2011) on torture. He concludes that our failure to acknowledge the event of torture and the marks it leaves on its victim is not a result of the inexpressibility of pain. Rather, lack of acknowledgment comes from our failure to see and listen to the pain right in front of us (4).

The distinction between knowledge and acknowledgment helps us get closer to what is in fact lost in the "straightening out" of the experiences of prisoners' wives. Relation as the second criterion of suffering, to be sure, includes and acknowledges detainees' wives. Yet this is a frayed, partial inclusion. In the straightening out of experience, not all relations are valued: the grief of mothers who have lost someone through a violent event is recognized, whereas that of wives who experience only absence is eclipsed. Desolation is recognized only through relations to the figure of the hero and primary victim. In fact, however, the relations that seem to distress the wives of the detainees most are those with the people who help make do during their spouse's confinement: the family and the husband's family. This gestures toward a hierarchy of the two criteria, in which event is privileged, and relation downplayed.

Revisiting Muna's Tears

Let us return here to Amina, for whom Muna shed her tears. Amina was included in the category of the secondary victim, and on this premise was admitted to the therapeutic group for detainees' wives described earlier. Amina was present when the Israeli Army detained her husband fifteen years ago in their home. Her family home was destroyed due to her husband's violent acts of resistance against Israel. She raises their four girls and lived with her mother and sister for ten years until she moved to a single-unit family home. Amina is under close surveillance by the village community because she is married, yet living as a single woman. Amina embodies the idea of a secondary victim because her husband is in prison. The question worth posing, however, is the extent to which her actual experience is knowable through the criteria of "event" and "relation." At first glance, Amina's life is translated by counselors so that it overlays the criteria by which suffering in Palestine is known through relation to a violent event or as a direct victim of a violent event. Amina's experience, in other words, is "straightened out" so that it matches the criteria necessary to know and acknowledge it for fellow Palestinians as well as therapists. In Amina's case, however, an apparently inclusive language of acknowledgment does not in fact enable one to read her experience.

The misreading occurs because the criteria of acknowledgment are imbued with the eventfulness of violence. They emphasize how some relations are intrinsically more wounding than others, as is true in the difference between a mother's loss of a son and a wife's experience of an absent husband. Interestingly, such understandings of suffering mesh with how physical injury was known in the wake of the first Intifada.

Muna's frustration with the lack of progress in the group therapeutic project suggests a gap between the experiential realms of the detainees' wives and the available therapeutic method. This gap is what made Muna pose the question to the teacher during the workshop on group therapy: what could she do to help her client, who did not feel better after several months of therapy? The teacher interpreted Amina's case in the following way: "She reacts like she expects her husband to prefer that she is not OK." His framing of Amina's feeling of victimization may suggest a failure on his part to acknowledge that the circumstances of Amina's life might actually be enough for her to feel anguished, regardless of whether her husband agrees. The teacher's comment resonates with the use of an event as a criterion for the recognition of affliction: he tells Muna that Amina's life is "not staying the same; life changes." Implicitly, the teacher compares Amina's situation with that of her husband. Seen in that light, Amina is out of prison, whereas her husband is the one whose liberty has been taken away. The words of the teacher therefore suggest that Amina can quite easily break free of her victimization, whereas her husband is the one who is still marked by a violent event—his incarceration.

The teacher's assertion that "things change" resonates further with the criterion of a traumatic event, something that is limited in time and space. His advice to Muna assumes that suffering eventually ends. One of the criteria to be fulfilled in the diagnosis of PTSD is the experience of a traumatic event. Were we to think about Amina in purely psychiatric terms, she shows the symptoms of a disorder, but she lacks a traumatic event to explain her symptoms.

Muna embodies the resonances and convergences between the thera-peutic and nationalist modes of framing affliction. Her representation of Amina's case converges between her position as a therapist trained to think within a psychological mode of reasoning and her status as a Palestinian who also thinks about her clients within the national notions of suffering outlined earlier. By posing the question to the teacher regarding Amina's claim to victimhood, Muna presents Amina's reactions as excessive. However, at the moment of her breakdown, Muna appears to reconsider, as she herself feels the excess of suffering that is not supposed to be there. In other words, Amina's relationship with her husband does in fact allow her suffering to be translated into the grammar of suffering in occupied Palestine. Notably, though, her experiences fail the criteria of event-based suffering. It is at this point that we need to attend to the internal connection and hierarchy among the two criteria, which help explain why Amina is not "supposed" to feel like a victim, despite the apparently straightforward translation of her situation into the grammar of suffering: The criterion of relation is an optional crite-rion, whereas the temporal criterion of event is in fact obligatory. This is why Amina's experience is not fully acknowledged, either by Muna as a therapist or by Muna as a Palestinian.

The moment of Muna's identification with Amina is one in which Muna reads Amina and thus acknowledges her. By allowing herself to read Amina's experience, Muna comes to know her suffering on different terms than the available grammar of suffering by which affliction is known and acknowledged in occupied Palestine. Acknowledgment requires a moral in-clination to act on one's knowledge, which is what Muna does by addressing it during the course, and by breaking down when she recognizes her inability to effect change in Amina.

Muna's recognition invites us to think further about an anthropological wording of experiences of hardship that do not fit into the grammar of suffer-ing in contemporary Palestine, even though this grammar does, indeed, encompass a wide range of experiences, as this chapter has shown. The criteria for the recognition of suffering are in fact so powerful that they constitute what I think of as a standing language. I propose the idea of a standing language in order to acknowledge, along with Khalili and Sylvain Perdigon, that the Palestinians themselves have developed a fine-grained vocabulary to articulate the diverse experiences their statelessness imposes on them. Yet I hesitate to assume that such a language offers a wording of suffering truer to the Palestinian experience than, as Fassin and Rechtman argue, a Western language of trauma, because of the circumstances of post-Oslo Palestine and the criteria of suffering described here.

A standing language is not simply psychological, national, and religious representations of suffering that morph into a grammar of suffering. That grammar includes the tripartite set of heroic, tragic, and sumūd narratives that Khalili finds among Palestinians in Lebanon and the psychological discourse of traumatization that has proliferated in Palestine. In order to flag the difference between this grammar and a standing language, I turn to Wittgenstein and more specifically Das's reading of him (2011; see also Han and Das 2015). The premise of a standing language includes agreement over criteria as to what forms of life are human. What makes such an agreement about criteria relevant in the context of gendered expressions of suffering in contemporary Palestine is the question of whether all forms of suffering experienced by Palestinians can actually be seen to belong to a particular form of life reflecting agreement about the criteria of what it means to be human. How the experiences of prisoners' wives fail both knowledge and acknowledgment in the grammar of suffering in contemporary Palestine reads to me as a reformulation of that question. The experiences of the prisoners' wives cannot be embodied in the standing language: There are simply no words for what it means to be in their situation. Muna cries when she realizes the inadequacy of the standing language to allow her access to the slow grinding of Amina's lived life, a grind so finely textured that it slips away from the criteria that have been put in place to know and acknowledge it. Amina's feelings reflect the unsettling, continuous situation that is a predicament for all the women who are married to long-term detainees in contemporary Palestine.

The question is how the slow grind of Amina's life relates to the slow grind of ordinary life for the majority of Palestinians (Kelly 2008), a condition eclipsed by the standing language of suffering, but that produces adversity, nonetheless. The argument I make in this book is that the unsettling effects of everyday occupied life are in fact so grave as to bring Palestinians to profoundly question the national project and the cost of endurance (see also Buch Segal 2015).

How do a grammar of suffering and the idea of a standing language help us better conceptualize distress? Why not simply analyze the complexity of the idea of trauma, as has been done sensibly by, for instance, anthropologist Rebecca Lester in her merging of anthropology and psychotherapy? I am hesitant to employ the language of trauma as an analytics of ethnography, but not because I am suspicious of the notion of trauma laid out by Fassin and Rechtman. The resonances between a psychological discourse of trauma and a Palestinian moral discourse of suffering lead me to think of the grammar of suffering in contemporary Palestine in terms similar to Nils Ole Bubandt's (2008) work on psychological distress in North Maluku. Bubandt argues that "the introduction of trauma to north Maluku has given rise to new forms of meaning that make perfect sense to people, even if they are patched together from global flows of media narratives and development practices" (293).

It is precisely this merging of the global and local in language and action that constitutes the grammar of suffering in contemporary Palestine. We thereby see that there is no "authentic" language in which distress can be vocalized, either through a discourse of trauma or through the words available in Palestinian moral discourse. Not only do internationally circulating discourses rooted in trauma naturally fail to cover all forms of global affliction, so, too, do the local vernacular discourses. This is perhaps the most radical conclusion of the book, since there is a strong tradition in anthropology that documents how local vernaculars of pain encompass and console by providing words to talk about difficult circumstances that the Western trauma idea does not. As will be clear in subsequent chapters, Palestinians have a reason to make ineffable particular experiences that occur as a consequence of the struggle for national recognition, and this discourse is therefore not all encompassing of suffering, either.

However, the fact that Muna, as both a therapist and a Palestinian woman, at one point acknowledges Amina's suffering may suggest the potential of shifting from a register based on distance, heroism, and objective diagnostics to an affective register that eschews the comforting armature of scientific and national terminology alike. As Das observes, this alternative vision requires that the eye be not an organ that sees, but an organ that weeps (2007: 62). Only in Muna's tears was Amina's suffering acknowledged in a way that transcended spoken expression. This could be read as corroboration of a point that underlies both notions of trauma and an anthropological literature indebted to Elaine Scarry's argument that some forms of pain defy language (1985). What I have tried to show is in fact the opposite. Wittgenstein writes on the relationship between pain and words: "So are you saying that the word 'pain' really means crying? On the contrary: the verbal expression of pain replaces crying, it does not describe it" (1953 [2009]: §244). Muna's tears and the words she uttered simultaneously force us to think closely about the imbrication of language and the suffering it tries to describe.

CHAPTER 2

Domestic Uncanniness

Heimlich becomes increasingly ambivalent, until it finally
merges with its antonym *unheimlich*. The uncanny is in
some respects a species of the familiar.
—Sigmund Freud, *The Uncanny*

This chapter explores how the affective world of the ordinary unfolds for
detainees' wives once the imprisonment of their husbands becomes part of
the tapestry of everyday life. I focus on how feelings are configured in the
realm of the domestic in relation to normative Palestinian responses to bereavement and incarceration, and how those who are subject to these norms
experience them. The quotation above from Sigmund Freud's work on
the uncanny gestures toward the chapter's concern with what Kelly and
Thiranagama think of as "the tension among intimate personal relationships, the demands of the states, and the hard moral choices that these
produce" (2010: 1). My subject here is how these tensions unfold in the
heart of Palestinian homes.

Nadia's Salon

A significant space in a Palestinian household is *as-salon* (living room).
Emotional labor and financial resources go into decorating this room, since
it serves to represent the family, its relative prosperity, and not the least its
ability to receive and host guests. As elsewhere in the Middle East (Bille 2010;

Shryock 2004; Abu-Lughod 1986 [2000], 1993 [2008]), hospitality is a key value in the occupied territory, no matter what a family's circumstances. The way the living room is arranged expresses how a family wishes its guests to perceive it.

Families who either temporarily or permanently have an absent male member often arrange *as-salon* carefully to express and display graphically the absent figure. The arrangement of the living room in the house of a young female interlocutor, Nadia, is a poignant example. Nadia's salon is located to the right of the hallway in her flat, which is a new extension of her in-laws' house, situated in a quiet area of Bāb aš-šams. In as-salon two grandiose, plush sofas dominate the walls, and across from the bigger one are two chairs made of the same material in black, cream, and gold. A small coffee table occupies the middle of the room, which is moderately airy due to the thin curtains hanging in front of the two windows close to the ceiling. Whether equipped with expensive furniture or cheap copies that are sold along the approach roads to Bāb aš-šams, a salon such as Nadia's is typical of a Palestinian living room. Aside from the sheer size and pomposity of the furniture, the décor of Nadia's tidy living room is dominated by one thing; a one-hundred-by-eighty-centimeter poster in a gold frame occupying one corner. The photostat displays a portrait of a young man in profile posing for the camera. He is wearing a combat uniform and holding an AK-47, the most common weapon in the occupied territory and one used throughout the first and second Intifadas. The background of the photostat is a clear, blue waterfall set among rocky cliffs and green pine trees. In the lower right-hand corner is a passport-size photo of another man, a simple portrait that could easily be overlooked, showing only a face. The big photo displays Nadia's first husband, who was killed by Israeli soldiers and who is therefore considered to be *as-šahīd* (a martyr). The smaller photo is of Nadia's second husband, her late husband's brother, who is *al-asīr* (a detainee), sentenced to twenty-two years in an Israeli prison. The contrast in size and ornamentation between the two photos of Nadia's former and present husbands and the location of these national objects in the heart of a Palestinian home expresses materially this chapter's theme.

The difference between the presentations of the prisoner and the martyr, between al-asīr and aš-šahīd, may help to clarify how the experiences of detainees' wives are perceived in radically different ways, depending on the duration and character of their husbands' absence, than the life of the widow of as-šahīd.

The precise differences and how they give shape to everyday life become clear when we compare the affective worlds of the wives of detainees with widows of martyrs. The difference between being the wife of a detainee and the widow of a martyr may be thought of in terms of how absence and loss, respectively, are woven into the intimacy of practices that appear ordinary. Living with the absence that being married to an imprisoned husband entails can never equal the sharp poignancy and immediacy of the loss experienced by a martyr's widow. At first glance and from afar, it seems that absence is in fact included in the grammar of suffering. The difference is indeed as easy to miss as the photo of Nadia's second husband in the corner of the photostat. For wives of detainees, however, the lack of a place in language to settle the unsettledness of a husband's absence reverberates in ways that create uncanny configurations of hearts and homes.

The Domestic as a Site of the Ordinary

My contemplation of the domestic as a site of the ordinary is anchored by close attention to how people sustain the domestic in the wake of violence. Suffering that is mundane, rather than an event that befalls a subject, poses a challenge to anthropology: how should we conceptualize suffering without a moment of original violence that provides a beginning and an end?

Historically, the occupied territory is a highly problematic site for understanding loss. The uncertain character of life in occupied Palestine may best be described as a "non-linear permanency": it neither moves toward a resolution nor is it, by now, understood as a temporary state of affairs (Kublitz 2013:117). The permanency of latent conflict makes it necessary to think of violence not as a discrete event or as an *interruption* of the ordinary, but as an essential part of the ordinary. While violent events do indeed occur in the occupied territory, they tend to be concentrated around certain periods, such as Israeli military incursions. Such violence took place, for instance, during the two Intifadas and Operations Cast Lead and Protective Edge in Gaza during the winter of 2009 and the summer of 2014 (see Allen 2012 for an analysis of Operation Cast Lead). As destructive as these acts of explicit violence are, they often hide the permanent structures of violence that have been established as part of the security apparatus of the Israeli state, which require most Palestinians to confront, negotiate, and work around Israeli bureaucratic procedures (Buch Segal 2013). Palestinians face ongoing restrictions on mobility and live under the constant, almost default suspicion of terrorism (Kelly 2006, 2007). The deformation of most ordinary activities through the constant need to negotiate the Israeli military and police presence seems extraordinary from the outside, but to Palestinians in the occupied territory, it has become part of ordinary, everyday life (Kelly 2009; Buch Segal 2013).

That such repetitive practices of structural violence are "to be expected" makes the notion of the ordinary poignant.[1] We should remember that the ordinary does not exist a priori: as Das puts it (2010), the everyday is not a given, but something that should be thought of as an achievement. The Palestinian term 'ādi and the way it is accompanied by a shrug of the shoulder makes a fine case for what can be said to belong to the ordinary in the occupied territory. Palestinians evoke 'ādi—a local theorization of the ordinary—as an aspiration that is neither given nor abstract (for comparison see Blom Hansen 2013). It is a realm of affective politics, characterized by constant evocations of heroism with regard to aš-šahīd and al-asīr, that is anchored firmly in the everyday rather than in an understanding of the ordinary as an esoteric idiom of transcendence.

Heroic Politics: The Difference Between the Martyr and the Prisoner

> Open your arms you Qassam people because you are the
>   heroes
> Detainees, martyrs and injured, a revolution with a
>   flame of struggle
> From Nafha[2] the victory was, it is like a stone of will and
>   persistence
> And everyone can see how strong we can be
> Oh you who can go to al-Jalboo,[3] please pass our salam
>   to our beloved detainees
> Our hunger and sufferance will continue forever till we
>   see free Palestine.

This verse is from a song entitled "Al-Asra" (the detainees), written by a detainee in an Israeli prison (Ramadan 2005). Songs and poetry in the same political vein circulate across occupied Palestine (Nashif 2008; McDonald 2013; Kanaaneh et al. 2012), and are an intrinsic part of Palestinian culture

(Khankan 2009; Swedenburg 1990; McDonald 2013). The univocal praise for the Palestinian resistance fighters, put in what appears to be portentous language, can only be understood in the historical and current circumstances of the occupied territory. Sara Roy has termed these circumstances a state of "de-development" (1995, 2007). The term defines Israel's policies of closure and restriction of access to export infrastructure as a strategy aimed at bringing the Palestinian economy to a standstill. One result of this is an estimated poverty rate of 57.2 percent in 2008 (UNDP 2011: 17). Lacking the financial means to secure either education or migration, Palestinians find social status and upward mobility difficult to achieve unless one participates in activities to oppose the Israeli occupation and its pressures on Palestinian economic, social, and political life (Allen 2006). Historically, acts of both nonviolent and violent resistance have merited national, local, and domestic acknowledgment. However, in contemporary Palestine, the rhetoric of heroic recognition rings hollow and the material compensation is far from adequate for the labor that goes into political activism (see Khalili 2007).

Despite contemporary fatigue with yet another case of affliction among Palestinians, martyrs and detainees stand out because of their heroic deeds and extraordinary suffering, even though all Palestinians consider themselves to be living and suffering due to the occupation (Khalili 2007: 107). However, not all forms of affliction are considered equally torturous or worthy of attention. It is here that the difference between martyrs and detainees and their respective places in Palestinian moral discourse becomes significant.

To explain in deeper detail these differences, it makes sense to ponder the difference between the martyr and the detainee with regard to three salient elements of investment in the Palestinian cause: religion, temporality, and ambiguity.

The martyr who has lost his life in the struggle for Palestine has made the ultimate sacrifice (Khalili 2007). Significantly, this is a political sacrifice imbued with a religious vocabulary (Mayy Jayyusi qtd. in Asad 2007: 47). As Talal Asad writes, this should be interpreted in light of the fact that martyrdom in Islamic theology is not a sacrifice, for its literal meaning is an act of witnessing (2007: 47). This meaning of the term may partly explain why Palestinians often refer to themselves as a collective of *aš-šuhada*; they testify collectively to the violations brought upon them by the Israeli state. Meanwhile, my interlocutors also invoked *aš-šahada* (martyrdom) as a religious sacrifice in everyday conversation among each other and with me. The meaning of *aš-šahīd* extends beyond a form of national sacrifice, and this allows us to understand the pivotal difference between a martyr and a prisoner and, therefore, between being the relative of a martyr and one of a prisoner (Asad: 2007: 47).

Sacrifice in the occupied territory then is simultaneously a religious and a national act, undertaken in the hope of creating a Palestinian state (Khalili 2007: 114; Allen 2006, Johnson 1982). This dual meaning is significant to understanding the difference between the martyr and the detainee. In her studies of the commemoration of heroism among Palestinian refugees in Lebanon, Khalili notes that, at the onset of the national struggle for a Palestinian state, the *fida'yi* (guerrilla fighter) was the embodiment of heroism (2007: 114). With an increase in violent events in Lebanon, among them the infamous massacres at the Palestinian refugee camps of Sabra and Šatila in 1982, this position was superseded by the martyr's deceased body, with its capacity for displaying suffering for the world, according to the politics of immediation. The politics of immediation has been called a discourse permeated by human rights, visuality, and the call to affect (Allen 2009: 262). Within this discourse, the plight of the Palestinians is presented as unmediated, raw, human suffering in order to appeal for the inclusion of Palestinians in the category of the universal human being with a right to integrity. The deceased body becomes emblematic of this discourse because it displays unintentional victimhood (Khalili 2007: 114).

Mamphela Ramphele has observed that freedom fighters' widows in South Africa are ambiguous and liminal figures: "The widow in mourning having lost her spouse and yet still considered married is in a special kind of ambiguous, transitional state typically involving pollution and related beliefs" (Jacque Pauw qtd. in Ramphele 1997: 99). In the context of the occupied territory, however, the martyr is an unequivocal figure, whereas the detainee is ambiguous in his detention. Esmail Nashif has described the detainee as a liminal figure (2008: 96). He argues that the liminality of the detainee occurs because he is "deported from Palestinian society, only to be transplanted into a foreign land/space, and not any space but a liminal one, the prison of the colonial metropolitan" (95).

The martyr and the detainee are further distinguished by matters of temporality and closure. For the former, his death finalizes his life and turns him into a martyr, a transformation that allows him to take on a different presence in the social world. A detainee is still alive, simultaneously absent from the domestic sphere and present as a celebrated national figure. By his "only" giving up his freedom and not his life, his sacrifice does not belong to the religious register as does the martyr's. An analogy I encountered in local vernacular was that of a ladder upon which the martyr figured at the top, and the prisoner just below him.

The unsettledness intrinsic to the category of the detainee can be thought of in terms of space and temporality. A detainee's absence is temporary and spatially undecided due his simultaneous presence and absence in his relatives' world. His spatial indeterminacy is underscored by the common Israeli practice of transferring detainees from one prison to another during incarceration. The unresolved temporality is illustrated by Israel's widespread use of the administrative detention of Palestinians, where people are detained in custody without trial for long periods.[4] Even when a sentence is handed down, the detainee's situation is unresolved because of ongoing and often-suspended Israeli-Palestinian negotiations over the potential release of detainees.[5] There is thus always a hope that a deal between Israel and the Palestinians will bring about the release of one's son, husband, or father. These conditions unsettle the figure of al-asīr.

The ambiguity of an asīr in contrast to a šahīd also rests on uncertainty about what might be taking place during detention in an Israeli prison. This uncertainty allows people to spread rumors, and to worry, or suspect, that the detainee has surrendered to interrogators' pressure and provided Israel with information, thereby potentially stooping to treachery against the nation and, as importantly, against himself and his intimate ties (see Kelly 2010; Talebi 2011: 82). As Das writes, the power of rumor lies in how experiences can come to life through the act of telling (Das 2007: 208). Through rumor, the heroism of the detainee always has one foot in the doubt that allows intimates, neighbors, or comrades to question the legitimacy or anticipate the illegitimacy of his captivity (Talebi 2011: 82). The way a detainee circulates in the world of rumor molds the status of his wife as simultaneously settled and unsettled. Potential allegations notwithstanding, aš-šahīd and al-asīr epitomize the heroism of agents in the struggle for a Palestinian state. They are praised in popular national discourse for having been willing to pay the ultimate price for a greater common good (Allen 2006; Nashif 2008).

In a conceptualization of the difference between aš-šahīd and al-asīr, these distinguishing features do not become fully clear if we think of this difference only as one of degree, or grade (see Deleuze 1988: 38; Bergson 1912 [2004]). On a first reading, the difference between aš-šahīd and al-asīr may seem like a difference in degree analogous to the vernacular representation of their difference by way of a ladder. But it is precisely with regard to temporality and spatial presence that the two categories of hero differ in kind rather than degree. Temporally, the martyr's life has ended, and he is gone rather than absent. The detainee, on the other hand, although physically absent from his relatives' lifeworlds, is still alive and made present through his family's practices to make him part of their everyday lives. Spatially, the martyr has been transformed from a man into a martyr, whereas the detainee is still both a man and a husband, albeit an absent one (Bille, Hastrup, and Flohr Sørensen 2010; Buch 2010). Hence the difference between *aš-šahīd* and *al-asīr* is a difference in kind.

Inspiring a line of progressive thinkers Marilyn Strathern has argued that ethnographic objects are not exclusively analyzed by the ethnographer (Strathern 2004: 25; Henare, Holbraad, and Wastell 2006; Pedersen 2009). Rather, every object contains our informants' analysis already. The analysis of Palestinian comprehensions of aš-šahīd and al-asīr accordingly conveys what it is in the experience of being married to a detainee as opposed to being the widow of a martyr that escapes the discourse of acknowledgment in occupied Palestine.

We can think about the different ways that detainees' wives and martyrs' widows are perceived and live their lives through an exploration of the meaning of absence and loss, respectively, in the local context. We can see what evades the standing language by looking at how the husband's absence materializes in the everyday existence of the women as a simultaneously intangible and tangible presence. To this end I cross the threshold of the Palestinian home as the site of the personal and impersonal affect implicit in being related to national heroes.

Politics of Loss in Palestine

Among historians and social scientists alike, the occupied territory seems to crystallize a place in which the past is not past but present (Kublitz 2013; Abu-Lughod and Sa'adi 2007). Every personal and collective story that is told about loss, violence, or death in Palestine is always already inscribed within the larger story of the Palestinians as a people defined by their losses: loss of a homeland, loss of physical homes, loss of family members, loss of human dignity (Khalidi 2006). The vital point in this metanarrative is the 1948 al-Nakba. According to Israeli historian Ilan Pappé, more than seven hundred thousand Palestinians were displaced as a result of the establishment of the Israeli state (2006: xiii). This event has affected generations of Palestinians because al-Nakba placed them in the exceptional category of "Palestine refugees"[6] and resulted in the establishment of the United Nations Relief and Works Agency for Palestine Refugees in the Near East (Rubenberg 2003: 13). Loss, bereavement, coping, and making sense therefore form part of everyday life and public discourse in the West Bank. Every family has experienced sudden deaths, disappearances, and violence.

The public display of mourning is paralleled privately by the families and widows of martyrs. During my fieldwork, wives of detainees and widows of martyrs spoke willingly and extensively about the martyr in a manner similar to Luma. The narrative about the martyr is an often-told story about his deeds, the detailed, visceral circumstances of his death, and a description of the emotionally straining loss of a father or a husband. One such narrative was provided by Nadia's mother-in-law, who lost her son to martyrdom. Six months before I met her she lost her husband to a heart attack. In addition, she has three sons incarcerated in Israel. We spoke on a beautiful morning in her sunlit living room where her daughter ('Uht Hazem) and her daughter-in-law Nadia joined Imm[7] Hazem, my assistant Mayy, and me after a while. The extract is long and the account is meticulously detailed, as is common for commemorative stories in the occupied territories:

> *Lotte:* Are your family, your father and mother, from Bāb aš-šams?
> *Imm Hazem:* Yes, actually my father is blind, he is always near the mosque explaining people's dreams;they come to him and say what they dreamed about and he explains the meanings of these dreams to them.
> *Lotte:* Did you have a dream that he explained to you and which came true?
> *Imm Hazem:* Yes, when my son Hazem died. I had a dream before my son died, a dream that my father refused to explain to me; the only thing he said about it was, "Something will happen to one member of your family," and nothing else, he refused to continue. . . . Yes, he refused to say what it meant.
> *Lotte:* Do you remember how long ago before your son was killed that you had that dream?
> *Imm Hazem:* Two to three weeks, I saw a black angry horse that entered my room and since that time I did not feel good about

that dream, I couldn't feel optimistic at all. . . . It was the strangest dream of my life, I have not dreamed of anything like it before.

Lotte: Did you know what it meant? Did you have any idea when your father told you that, "I don't want to tell you what it is," did you then know what it was?

Imm Hazem: I felt that something was wrong, but I did not know what it was. . . . I was always holding the holy Qur'an and said to myself that everything that is going to happen to me is from God and God wrote it for me, and I accept it, and that actually gave me patience and strength to handle all that happened to me. When my son died and when they told me that he had been killed I actually did not believe it, but after like a week I started to understand it. I couldn't cry at that time, my tears simply dried, all I could say was "Thank God."

Lotte: I'm so sorry to hear that.

Imm Hazem: It's difficult, but God gives me faith and strength. Actually I was more patient than my husband: it influenced him so much, he was so sad and kept all those sad emotions in his heart, because my son never said no to him, he was such a great son who took care of his father and mother, all my sons are, but he was kinder than the others, he never smoked a cigarette, he kept the money to build his house and when he died it wasn't complete.

Lotte: Yes, he was in the middle of his life with his wife and had begun a life with his family.

Imm Hazem: Yes that's true: it was only the start for him and for his wife. . . .

Lotte: You were saying that you had a dream that something bad was going to happen, did you know from what your son was doing that he might be imprisoned or die?

'Uht (Arabic term for sister of) Hazem: No she didn't. Tell her about the story when you prayed to God that you want to smell "the scent of the martyr" from one of your sons!

Imm Hazem: You tell her about that!

'Uht Hazem: When a neighbor was killed by the Israelis, we went to his house to console his mother, there were some napkins that had the martyr smell, that smell was great and when we

smelled it, my mother spontaneously prayed to God and said, "Oh God I wish to smell that beautiful smell from one of my sons," which means that one of them will be a martyr, and it happened.

Imm Hazem: If I knew that it would happen, I would never have said it.

Mayy: Well, God made you say that because it's written for you and to your son.

'Uht Hazem: Yes, that's indeed true.

Imm Hazem: My sisters-in-law remind[ed] me about that incident when my son got killed!

Mayy: Lotte, do you know the scent of the martyr?

Lotte: No, please tell me.

Mayy: Well, we believe in that and it's really true, that when someone has been killed and he becomes a martyr, he will have such a great smell, of musk and amber.

Lotte: Where does this smell come from?

Mayy: It's just there! When he dies he will have that smell, and really, it's true.

'Uht Hazem: And it is different from the commercial ones that the companies tried to produce and fake.

Lotte: Yes, I know.

Imm Hazem: When my son died his face was so beautiful, he shaved that morning, and he was well dressed that day, like he was preparing himself to die. We will all die.

Mayy (assistant): We will, but we pray to God to die as martyrs rather than to die in a natural way because it is a more honorable way to die.

Imm Hazem: Yes, and the martyr can ask for forgiveness for seventy people whom he used to know when he was alive.

Lotte: Forgiveness for things that already happened or also for things that will come? Can you tell me what a martyr is, if you have to define it, I mean if you are telling somebody who did not know what a martyr is, what would you say?

Imm Hazem: A martyr is an honor from God. [After a moment's thought:] It is somebody good.

'Uht Hazem: Somebody chosen by God to go to Paradise.

Lotte: Please take your time; I know it's difficult to say what martyr is.

'Uht Hazem: A martyr is not dead in the real meaning, his spirit is alive and we believe in that as Muslims. He gets a guarantee of entering paradise, and no one gets that guarantee otherwise.

Imm Hazem (interrupting): And the martyr's body stays the same after his death, he does not rot or stink, it stays fresh and warm.

'Uht Hazem: If anyone did something wrong or is guilty about something and did not ask forgiveness he will be punished, but a martyr will be forgiven for whatever he did in his life.

Lotte: And do their souls become saints?

Mayy: No, their soul stays theirs, but they live in heaven.

Imm Hazem: When Hazem was killed, I told everyone that we have to celebrate everything to its extreme! Whether it is the happening of a birth or someone dying, we have to celebrate. And even when people used to come and console me, every few minutes I used to go to do anything other than talking about what I experienced. I always kept myself busy.

'Uht Hazem: Yes, she did and still does so. I remember that two weeks after Hazem's death there was a wedding that all the family was invited to, and we [the sisters and sisters-in-law] were extremely sad about our loss, but my mother said no don't be sad, we have to go and celebrate the wedding with the family. It is a wedding, and we have to be happy and we are Muslims and Islam says that mourning is three days and it has been fifteen days, so we have to celebrate the wedding! And after that she asked us not to mourn her after her death.

Imm Hazem: It is the will of God. Sometimes, when I remember, I can't handle it and start crying for a whole day, and no one can help to make me stop. But it only happens to me periodically, not all the time.

Lotte: Did many people come to you and support you in the situation?

'Uht Hazem: Yes indeed, and it's not only the people that we know: anyone, everyone, from the city came to console us and to support us.

Nadia: The consolation of any martyr is different from anyone else, everyone comes to the martyr consolation, to support his family and to tell them that they have to be proud of the martyr. People came from Nablus and many other places outside Bāb aš-šams. Maybe because people feel for the martyr's families more than any other family that has lost someone dear.

Imm Hazem here depicts the loss of her son as meaningful by evoking the martyr as a religious figure, against the backdrop of his valorization in Palestinian moral discourse. The presence her son assumes after his bodily death is construed as a gift, rather than a loss. The invocation of loss associated with martyrdom as a sacrifice indicates the ambiguity at play here: even though martyrdom is not a sacrifice according to Islam, sacrifice is a powerful trope in occupied Palestine.

One way to think of this trope is through what Hans Lucht has termed "existential reciprocity." In his work on West African migrants, Lucht considers the idea of sacrifice as he looks for proof of existential reciprocity (2008: 232). Were we to think of the above narrative through the perspective of existential reciprocity, Imm Hazem's invocation of sacrifice appears as her testimony to the existence of God. Remembering that in Islam aš-šahada literally means "witnessing," Imm Hazem's narrative is one way in which the local vernacular of sacrifice converges with Islamic theology.

The deep meaning of Imm Hazem's loss is made physical in the scent that is believed to emanate from the martyr's body. The same day that I spoke with Imm Hazem, I drove with Mayy and Wesam, our driver in Bāb aš-šams, to the Ibrahim Mosque in al-Khalil, where Mayy asked me to smell the bloodstains on the carpet from the Goldstein Massacre (Collins 2004: 248). Still hesitant about my own sensual impressions upon kneeling in front of those burgundy, if faded, stains on the worn carpet, the sense in which something had violated this sacred place was palpable. On the morning of February 25, 1994, Baruch Goldstein, an Israeli settler and known extremist, opened fire on Palestinians praying in the mosque, killing twenty-nine (248). The deceased were Muslims performing their morning prayer when they were killed, so their status as martyrs was indisputable. For both Mayy and Imm Hazem, the scent emanating from the stains of blood was a sign that the men had indeed become martyrs.

The martyr's bodily and spiritual transformation mirrors the closure reminiscent of a mourning process (Freud 1917 [1957]). Through its recognition of the finite nature of death, mourning brings about the transformation not only of the deceased but also of the bereaved. Freud contrasts mourning with melancholia, a state in which bereavement is never fully processed and thus goes on indefinitely, whereas mourning ends after a certain period.

Any researcher, academic or otherwise, who has spent time in the West Bank or Gaza will have heard numerous, almost interchangeable stories like that of Imm Hazem (Jayyusi 2007: 108; Allen 2006, 2009; Kelly 2007). As in her narrative, the dramatic events leading up to a martyr's violent death initiate the story. Next comes the emotional response of the martyr's mother, accordingly embellished as sweet despair, in keeping with the religious meaning available to interpret violent death as martyrdom. As someone who has heard similar stories before and after Imm Hazem's narration, I read a certain stability into accounts like the one above, a stability based in repetition, on how it has been told and retold to many a listener. The story appears to lack the gaps and silences that are naturally a part of life stories and personal narratives. Nonetheless, Imm Hazem's story is marked by affective cracks where her personal loss seeps through the containment of religious and patriotic meanings; for example, when she says that she sometimes cannot stop crying, but reassures us that this only happens periodically. Admitting to such feelings is contrary to the effect such a loss is supposed, and assumed, to have on several intersecting levels: first, on the level of Palestinian moral discourse, which praises sumūd;[8] second, on the level of Islam, in which hardship and suffering are intrinsic to life and feature as a test given to the believer to verify that her faith is unwavering; and, third, on the level of international observers, who claim to "know" that Palestinian human losses are incommensurable with loss of a life in the West due to the alleged meaningfulness ascribed to aš-šahada in both Islam and Palestinian nationalism (Allen 2006; Khalili 2007; Fassin 2014). In contrast to the consoling effect of heroic, tragic, and sumūd narratives that Khalili finds among Palestinians in Lebanon, Imm Hazem's account in fact raises questions as to the efficacy of the available narratives to offer consolation. Her unresolved emotions of loss mirror what Paul Saint Cassia's study of the missing in Cyprus stated so clearly; namely, that in anthropology we tend to think that ritual channels emotion (2005: 153), and here I would add, *all* emotion. What can be gleaned from Imm Hazem's story, however, is that even powerful tropes of political sacrifice and martyrdom can only partly lay her loss to rest.

Imm Hazem's story may be understood in a different light if we pay closer attention to language. I contend that language is a prerequisite for social intelligibility. By this I mean that I do not assume that some experiences are inexpressible, per se, due to an intrinsic gap between experience and language.[9] Rather, whether the speaker manages to achieve intelligibility depends on whether there are words available in the standing language by which the experiences in question can be expressed, and heard. In such a reading, Imm Hazem's narrative is an attempt to communicate her feelings of loss within a language that does not acknowledge the martyrdom of her son *as* a loss. The narrative shows how language is a tool to make oneself and one's experience intelligible, but simultaneously an instrument through which affect that does not belong in the standing language is made alien from the very narrative in which it appears.

To further our understanding of what is at once personal and political, we may look at Imm Hazem's mode of speaking vis-à-vis philosopher John Austin's thoughts on illocutionary acts. An illocutionary act is an act of language in which the utterance of words is the action in and of itself (1962 [2009]: 102). The way in which Imm Hazem narrates suffering as a gift from God rather than a personal loss can be seen as an illocutionary act, since she enunciates loss as positive, leaving aside the unspoken feelings. Her articulation is political, drawing as it does on the positive connotations ascribed to martyrdom in Palestinian moral discourse. In light of Lucht's notion of existential reciprocity, Imm Hazem's illocutionary act bears witness to the existence of God by giving her son to Palestine in the hope that God will repay her sacrifice through the redemption that is intrinsic to martyrdom.[10]

The simultaneous inclusion and exclusion of affect concerning loss appears in both national and international vocabularies of Palestinian suffering as well as in private conceptualizations of bereavement. For instance, images circulate of the "Palestinian Mother" who, like Imm Hazem, mourns and suffers proudly the loss of her sons either to death or imprisonment, and they are recognized in formal and informal social forums. Along this vein, the Palestinian Mother was the topic of the closing comment in one issue of the widely read local cultural guide *This Week in Palestine* (2008). The framing of a mother's loss in the national and religious registers appears in yet another detainee's song called "Oh My Mother," written by a former detainee, Ayman Ramadan (2005):

Oh mother, if they forbid you from visiting me, I will send my heart
     to you
And I will ask my heart to gently kiss your hand and take care of
     your flowers and garden.
Oh mother do not be confused. . . . All Palestinian men are eagles.
Please mother, I ask you to stay as I always knew you
Free and strong with your faith in God.[11]

In the verse a generic Palestinian mother epitomizes the plight of the Palestinians. We may thus conclude that there is acknowledgment of the
complex feelings that arise in the nexus of motherhood and heroism, yet
without this acknowledgment necessarily containing the full spectrum of
how this condition is in fact felt. This leads me to ask which markers of suffering are associated with these mothers, alongside and in contrast to widows
of martyrs? And in what sense, if any, can their experiences find a home in
the standing language? I therefore turn to how the presence and absence
of these markers of suffering enable or disable widows and mothers to render their suffering socially intelligible.

Homely Loss

During my fieldwork there was a notable tendency on the part of my interlocutors not to make explicit the difference between being the wife of a detainee and the widow of a martyr. This void in the data can be explained by
something intrinsic to the situation of living with an absent husband while
not having experienced an absolute loss. To further juxtapose these circumstances: the wives of detainees live with an absence that defies both verbalization and graphic materialization, yet is no less a part of the everyday. The
absolute loss experienced by a martyr's widow, on the other hand, is in stark
contrast to the elusive nature of absence that detainees' wives endure. I visited the living room of one of my interlocutors, Fardoz, and the décor of the
room indicates the fundamental difference between the two.

Fardoz is the widow of a martyr. In her home, the relative splendor of
as-salon contrasts dramatically with the rest of the threadbare, sparsely
furnished concrete house. Fardoz's damp, dark living room has as its main
attraction two centerpieces, each standing on a pedestal. One displays a pair

of men's spectacles together with a photograph of Fardoz's deceased husband. The other exhibits his plastic digital watch. The watch is still running: "I cannot bring myself to stop it, so it still has its alarm set for eight o'clock in the morning. In that sense my husband lives on with me, may God be with him. I know every morning that the alarm will go off. You see, he is still part of my day," Fardoz said.

The way in which Nadia's and Fardoz's martyred husbands stay with them through artifacts alludes to their ability to materialize their losses and their commemoration. The objects serve as personal metonyms for aš-šahīd. For instance, the watch of Fardoz's deceased husband used to be an instrument that helped him structure his everyday routine. Since his death the watch has lost its instrumental meaning and become a metonym for the husband. It is, however, not only through such manifest objects that the women's husbands stay with their families. In these particular families' interpretation of Islam—an interpretation that some other Palestinians consider traditional and somewhat extreme—the martyr's physicality is thought to stay with him. This appeared from Imm Hazem's evocation of the scent of the martyr. The absence of decomposition and decay that she observed in another martyr even made her wish for her son to become a martyr. As the above conversation with Imm Hazem also shows, although bodily deceased, the martyr remains present through his eternal soul. Fardoz's and Imm Hazem's stories illuminate how a man's martyrdom yields his eternal presence in the lives of his close kin.

Revealing a possible difference between affinal and consanguine kin, the martyrs' widows I spoke to used a language remarkably different from that of Imm Hazem. Recall, for example, Luma's story. She is the mother of four children and the widow of a martyr. Together with her children, she lives in a spacious house on the outskirts of Bāb aš-šams. In her backyard, her deceased husband's horse grazes. My first encounter with Luma took place during the initial phase of my fieldwork. While serving us homemade tiger cake and chocolate cake, she recounted the graphic details of how her husband had died in an Israeli air strike. Luma cried, weeping her way through her story, but insisting that she would go on, although we did not press her to continue, and tried to comfort her. Yet during the tearful narrative there was simultaneously a sense that the words were available to her—she did not have to search for them. Her story had been told before. She knew it intimately, its details, its dramatic peaks, its ending. One day Mayy and I stopped by Luma's house because she had shown us a rash during our last visit, and we had offered to take her to Mayy's father, who is a physician. While waiting for our driver Wesam to arrive, she started again speaking about the loss of her husband. Her account, though, was distinctly different, and didn't feel like a remnant of mourning. Luma seemed to come to life when talking about her husband. She was flustered, her cheeks blushed, and she was clearly filled with adrenaline when she narrated the last hours of her husband's life and how his death made her feel. Like Imm and 'Uht Hazem, Luma evoked the sensuous if not physical presence of her deceased husband.

At the same time as the martyr's presence is conjured among his bereaved family through objects, memories, and sense perceptions, the widows I spoke to all stressed that their lives with their husbands were closed chapters. The men's absence from their lives, even though it ensured their souls' eternal presence, was certain and unequivocal. Although martyrdom returns the martyr from the dead by conferring on him eternal life, thus giving him a presence in the lives of the bereaved, this presence is definitive and distinct from the unsettled presence of a ghost. Often marshaled in anthropological work on war and violence, ghosts deserve some comparative attention (see, e.g., Talebi 2011; Das 2007; Bear 2007).[12] Ghosts, argues W. G. Sebald, are caused by an excess of grief that haunts everyday lives (Sebald qtd. in Carsten 2007: 10).

Without doubt, the violent deaths of many a martyr is a ghastly experience for the bereaved. Why, then, are experiences of losing a loved one to martyrdom not ghostly? The Palestinian martyr, being dead yet simultaneously present, lets his relatives reorganize their lives without him, which, according to Freud, is proof of a completed process of mourning (1917 [1957]). A martyr's relatives know where he is, and this sense of closure allows them to mourn him through practices of domestic commemoration such as photos, personal paraphernalia, and, not the least, the storytelling that takes place in the home. Similarly poignant is the fact that the inescapable political meaning of the martyr's death makes it hard to rally ghostliness. The martyrs have died due to the political conflict, their deaths are documented, and in contrast to Saint Cassia's (2005) description of the missing bodies in Cyprus, the Palestinian martyr bodies, however broken, are buried and brought to rest. Saint Cassia argues that funerals do not end mourning. Here I want to complicate his assertion and argue that funerals may actually end the public process of mourning, but fail to contain the personal grief experienced by the martyrs' relatives, which is not laid to rest by the collective narratives of political and religious sacrifice. Just as important, however, the widows I met tried in different ways to move on, to find a way of being herself as a widow rather than a married woman. For some, this included even attempts to build a new house, complete their education, and find a job. Their lives were not haunted by how the martyrs were present in them, because this presence was not ghostly. In the same vein, the widows of Palestinian martyrs are not ambiguous figures. The death of a Palestinian martyr draws on religious interpretations that make his death definitive (Johnson 1982: 77). In contrast to that of the South African widows, the definitive status of the martyr is what allows a martyr's widow a settled and, derivatively, honorable social presence (see Allen 2006). Below I explore how ambiguity in the occupied territory attaches to incarceration rather than to violent death.

Unhomely Absence

One martyr's widow expressed herself differently than others: Nadia, whose second husband was at the time of my fieldwork detained in Israel. He has since been released and deported to Gaza, a place that he cannot leave and to which Nadia cannot go. As applies to other women too, for instance Yasmin (whom we will meet in the next chapter), the premises of their relationship—that is separation induced by imprisonment—are still deeply relevant to my analysis. Nadia only spoke about her detained husband when I probed her directly. I encountered Nadia for the first time in an unpleasant room in a branch of the Prisoners' Support Center, where she had formerly taken part in a project for bereaved women. She had suggested that we meet there. When she arrived, she was escorted by her sister-in-law. I had imagined this encounter as an occasion to present myself and my project and to see whether, at a later stage, she would allow me to visit her in her home for longer conversations about her life. I did not envision a substantial conversation with her then and there, and definitely not about emotional issues. Nadia appeared hesitant, sad, and somewhat "empty," in Mayy's words. Our conversation unfolded in a calm atmosphere in which, quietly and matter-of-factly, she told me about the circumstances of her life. After that I spent many hours in her house with her and her female in-laws, among them her mother-in-law, Imm Hazem; the following lengthy, detailed conversation from our first encounter illustrates how she expressed herself differently from both her mother-in-law and Luma:

Nadia: I was born in Bāb aš-šams, where I still live, in a separate part of the house of my family-in-law with my children. I married twice: my first husband became a martyr, and the second is in prison. The house I now live in is where I moved with my first husband just before he was killed . . . God be with him. We had three children together, a girl, who is ten, a boy of seven, and a girl of five. With my second husband I have a son who is four.

Lotte: Do all of your children live with you?

Nadia: Yes.

Lotte: Is that OK both with the family of your late husband and of your present husband?

Nadia: Yes, they were brothers: my second husband is my brother-in-law.

Lotte: And he is in prison now? That's not easy; how long is his sentence?

Nadia: Twenty-two years, but we are hoping for an exchange of detainees.[13]

Lotte: Are you allowed to see him?

Nadia: Not at the moment, but I get letters from him every three or four months. It is a bit difficult since they move him to different prisons without informing us. We get the information later.

Lotte: And your first husband, God be with him, was he in prison too?

Nadia: No, he was killed. I lived for two months with him in the house we had just built before he was killed. Before the year was over, I had married his brother.

Lotte: Did you know your first husband's brother well at that time?

Nadia: No, I only got to know him better after he was imprisoned. He is far away from my heart. But he is a good man, he took good care of the children when my husband died.

Lotte: Who do you consider to be your husband of the two [when you use the term like that]?

Nadia: My first husband.

Lotte: Why?

Nadia: The entire situation with him. My marriage with him was beautiful, and after our engagement we became really close, even though I did not expect that. At first, when we got engaged, I did not feel anything, but after getting to know him, I began to feel really happy.

Lotte: Can you describe him for me, as a man?

Nadia: He had a great personality, he treated me well, and his way of dealing with people was nice.

Lotte: So it must have been a great loss when he was killed and you had to marry someone else.

Nadia: At first it was tough and very strange. But after a while it began to feel OK, he handled the children very, very well, so it was better than being alone. I am lucky, because he is not jealous of my husband, he loves my children and he does not favor his child over the children of my husband, and I can speak about my husband in front of him without him minding. But due to the situation and the time I got to spend with my husband, there is another man in my heart. In the beginning it was very tough being alone with my children, but it is OK now, even though I am also alone now.

Lotte: I am so sorry for your loss. And on top of that you have had to deal with a lot of challenges to keep you and your children going after he died.

Nadia: It is a loss. My children lost the word "dad"; to me it is the loss itself, losing him. Most people want me to have a good life, and some were just plain intruders.

Lotte: How did people intrude in your life?

Nadia: My mother did not intrude. At first my father-in-law wanted me to marry my husband's brother: you see, everyone is just looking after his own interests. My own family supported me, and after a while my in-laws stopped pressuring me. But people said to me, "You cannot live without a husband." But I was so young, and so confused.

Lotte: How did you figure out what to do?

Nadia: I spoke to my mother's cousin and then I made my own choice. Now I am married, but not in practice. . . . But when people intrude, there is protection.

Lotte: Yes, I see, it must have made things easier after you married again?

Nadia: Yes, but it is not good, it is not a good life.

Lotte: I think I understand, but can you tell me why?

Nadia: It is on the inside, there is an empty space, a hole in me.

Lotte: Do people around you know about how you feel?

Nadia: No, not all people recognize it, but those who know me do, my friends, my mother, my sister, and my cousin, the people that feel with me.

Lotte: Which one of them do you feel understands you the most?

Nadia: My cousin, she is the one who asks about me, how I am, others ask about my husband, how is the detainee.

Lotte: I know. How do you imagine the day when he comes out of prison?

Nadia: I do not have any ambitions with my other husband; he comes out of prison when my children have grown up, so he cannot really help with the burden of raising them.

Lotte: No, twenty-two years is a very long time.

Nadia: Yes, four years feels like forty. I am twenty-six, but I feel older than that.

Although this began as a martyr's widow's story, Nadia's account has more than a slight resemblance to the conversations I had with women who could unambiguously be categorized as detainees' wives. Conversely, it differs from the often-told stories given to me by martyrs' widows, complying as they did with popular templates at the nexus of national sacrifice and religious martyrdom.

The similarity between Nadia's story and those of unambiguous detainees' wives might better be understood with the help of Wittgenstein's notion of family resemblance (1953 [2009]: 36). The term refers to instances where there are multiple constellations of similarity between two or more phenomena, but not one overarching, shared feature. Despite being the widow of a martyr, Nadia has no martyr's story to tell. Reminiscent of accounts from detainees' wives, the story of her incarcerated husband is not closed. It is a story without an ending, and thus does not allow for a claim to suffering or for a spectacular materialization of her loss. Adjacent to how national discourse of loss and mourning delineated the words she could not voice ran a story that was as important: Nadia's description of her second husband also had to do with her relative lack of feelings for him. Whereas her first husband became someone she loved, in her own words her second husband was simply "nice, polite and a good father for the children." In the conversation she speaks of him loyally, but at a remove. He was never the one she thought or dreamed about. From her words we learn that to talk about life as the wife of a detainee is to talk about a void: about places, times, and situations that are not quite right because something was and still is missing.

A Community in Its Own Right?

Aisha was an esteemed and respected community leader from Dar Nūra. I frequently came to her office in the afternoon, and from there we would drive back to her flat in her workplace's old Mercedes, listening to scratchy recordings of Fayrous. One afternoon we spoke about the occupation, and she said, "People in Dar Nūra were responsible for a lot of important stages of the Palestinian revolution.[14] . . . Even though it was not good for the families, people from all over Palestine respect us because of it." Aisha spoke with pride about having participated in the struggle against the occupation. Simultaneously, she revealed how the heroic deeds had not affected the families of the men only positively. Her words show her familiarity with the limited efficacy of the national discourse in the domestic sphere. Aisha knows this not only because she is a Palestinian: her husband is serving a life sentence.

This severance of her marriage was also why she too was part of the three-month group therapeutic project for five detainees' wives in Dar Nūra initiated by the Prisoners' Support Center discussed in Chapter 1. The center offers therapeutic services to the detainees and the ex-detainees. Yet by far the largest group among the clients are the violently bereaved families and the families of detainees, all of whom are grouped together under the heading of the so-called secondary victims. In these therapeutic sessions, the women in the group would talk at length about how their neighbors and families were keeping their whereabouts under close surveillance, "as if we are under a microscope," as one woman said. The therapists facilitating the group wanted to promote strength and empowerment by telling the women to stay well but not to care too much about the comments and the rumors circulating about them behind their backs. An explicit goal of this therapeutic group was the creation of a support network among the women. In the beginning of the project, the lead therapist invited the women to speak about their feelings in relation to their captive husbands, their families, and the village. This invitation was largely ignored because of the potent forces of kinship and social relations at play in Palestinian society.[15]

This points to a difference between the significance of the social relations that constitute these women's lives and how these are imagined within a Bion-inspired notion of group therapy, the model employed here. Wilfred Bion is one of the European founders of group therapy (1961 [1996]). His background was in psychoanalysis, yet in his method, individuals, their concerns, and their problems are secondary to the group as a whole during therapeutic sessions. Bion's premise was that the therapeutic group is a forum that reflects social interaction outside the therapeutic space. Emphasis is therefore on the actual group process rather than the social relations in which group members participate outside the therapeutic space. Bion's aim for group therapy is for the social relations of the group's participants to become a social forum in its own right throughout the duration of the group, a forum in which the participants can momentarily suspend their habitual social ties. Below I consider why this did not happen in the therapeutic group project in question here.

Dar Nūra is known to originate from one prominent West Bank family,[16] which continues to dominate the village both in population and political influence.[17] For instance, members of this wealthy, educated, and politically engaged family often occupy major positions in the local council and the wider community. This, in tandem with the preferred Palestinian form of marriage[18] to patrilateral parallel cousins (in which brothers' children marry), implies that the women in the therapeutic group were related to each other through either consanguine or affinal kinship, or both. In light of the social significance of containing information that could harm one's family, it is not surprising that the ideal of a therapeutic group in which regular social bonds are suspended by the ties formed in that group was hampered, if not impossible, from the outset.

Early in the therapeutic process, one of the women in the group, Amina, broke the news of her daughter's engagement. Amina is thirty-nine years old and has four daughters. Several years before I spoke to her, the Israeli Army demolished her house as a punishment for her husband's role in violent activities of resistance against Israel. He is currently serving a multiyear sentence and figures at the center of one of the thousands of different posters of heroes and martyrs of the second Intifada that adorn buildings in the occupied territory. Speaking about her daughter's engagement made Amina simultaneously proud and sad. Amina rued the loneliness she would feel without her daughter in the house. But she was also sad that her husband could not discuss the engagement, the suitability of the groom, or the party, or share any of the responsibilities of a marriage that traditionally belong to the father of the bride. The other women in the group showed their understanding, saying that Amina had to go ahead anyway, and not worry about the gossip. They told her that she was still alive even though her husband was in prison. Amina invited them to attend the wedding, as a wedding is considered a joyous occasion for all villagers. The women responded vaguely to Amina's invitation, saying *inshallah*, God willing.

On the wedding night, Amina looked elegant, wearing makeup and the exact same subtle and respectable clothes as her younger sister, Layla, with whom she shared the practical and moral responsibility for her household. The wedding was held in a party hall in the center of town. Because this was a traditional wedding, men and women celebrated separately, and the only man allowed to be among the women was the groom. As with many such weddings, however, the gender separation was permeable. Adolescents and laughing kids constantly made sure they kept the door open between the men's and women's areas. Amina handled the role of the hostess for the women's part of the wedding well, yet her usual air of quiet sadness lingered even on this night. After dancing for a while, she came over and chatted with me. When I asked her if she was happy, she looked away and said, "There is something missing." Amina's husband, though, was not the only one missing. None of the members of the therapeutic group project, who were also Amina's near or distant kin relations, were there. The only guests from the group were the two psychologists from Ramallah and me. When I later asked Amina where the other women from the therapy group had been, she said she did not know. When I posed the same question to the women of the group on the next few days, they all made excuses.

Their absence from the wedding reveals the lived, actual shortcomings in the omnipresent national and local discourse of support and strong social ties in the village, a discourse that connotes a social ideal by which all the women should have attended the wedding. Although Amina is the least educated and least wealthy of the women, she is well liked and has a good reputation, partly due to her husband's perceived heroic deeds. According to the discourse of collective pride about the village's heroes evoked by Aisha, a marriage within one of the most heroic families would have been an appropriate place to display support for Amina and her family.

The incident of Amina's wedding suggests that the bonds established via the therapeutic group were not sufficient to quell her fellow group members' fears of the intense and uninterrupted social control to which their behavior was subjected. It shows how the detainees' wives' fears of social control are felt subtly but unmistakably. Rather than subjects of honor, the women seem to have become potential sources of offensive behavior, a position feared by the women themselves and their families. The wedding thus testifies to how affect is configured when a husband is incarcerated. Part of this affective configuration is how support, loyalty, and praise that extend to the detainee's relatives coexist with social control that is apparently so powerful that it can keep otherwise obvious guests away from an event as important as the wedding of Amina's daughter.

Another example illuminates the gaps and absences in the social practice of honoring detainees' families within this affective configuration. Public appearance and social control were recurring topics of conversation among my interlocutors, both with each other and with me, whenever we spoke about their lives after their husbands had been detained. People in the village, as well as the women's close and distant relatives, kept an eye on them. As my interlocutor Mervat said during a conversation I had with her and another interlocutor, Weeam, next to the heater in Weeam's living room: "It is as if, when her husband is in prison, a woman has to kill herself and she must put herself in the prison too. And at the same time, my husband is saying, if I tell him how I feel, about my sadness, why are you crying, you must be proud of me, that I am in prison." Weeam added that her husband was always calling the house from the prison to see if she was at home or out of the house. If she was out, he would say, "Where are you," "Where have you been," "Why are you going out," "Who are you with," and "What are you wearing?" No matter whom she was with or where she went, there would always be someone who claimed to have seen her in the company of someone improper, wearing something inappropriate. "After my husband was detained I stopped being a woman; now I am just a mother," she said.

A few days after the conversation with Weeam and Mervat, I called Weeam to see if I could stop by for a chat with her one morning. She welcomed me, and when I arrived with Rawan a few days later, Weeam looked different. Usually when she was at home she wore a casual tracksuit. But now she was wearing her gold jewelry and an elegant blouse with a low neckline. In fact a neckline so low that it nearly fell down her shoulder when she gestured with her hands. During our chat she constantly attempted to cover herself up until her oldest daughter purposefully entered the living room with a safety pin, which Weeam awkwardly used to gather up her clothes. A reference to our discussion about womanhood the week before,

Weeam's materialization of her female identity was for Rawan's and my eyes only. Any sign of femininity, sensuality, or the like was confined to her home and could be displayed only to a close circle of female friends, like Mervat. This applied to all the women I got to know. The first times I visited, the women were dressed up. But even after my first few visits they did not bother changing into something different, since when I went to see them I gradually came to be perceived less as a guest and more as a friend. If one of the women in a group meeting wore mascara, the others would comment. Some complimented, while others exchanged disapproving glances.

Practices of social control and perceived appropriate behavior for women—particularly women without the company of their male kin—are not abstractions, but a lived orientation in the world, directed toward others and the self (see Abu-Lughod 1986 [2000], 1993 [2008]), as demonstrated in the fact that among my interlocutors, the wearing of makeup even in female-only forums was a contested issue.

To relate Weeam's display of her femininity to Amina's daughter's wedding, I suggest that, to detainees' wives, a wedding is more than the traditional joyful event. A wedding is normally an event where Palestinian women are allowed to let their hair down and wear festive, even sensual clothes and makeup and display femininity outside the domestic, albeit gender-separated, realm. To the detainees' wives in Dar Nūra, however, the wedding represented an occasion for villagers to scrutinize the women's appearances and behavior, evaluating their social presence, as if they were displaying their sensuality and femininity inappropriately in public. The event of the wedding and Weeam's enactment of femininity in her home suggest that, to detainees' wives, the public and the domestic realms are less distinct than is often assumed in the anthropology of the Middle East (see Eickelman 1998). Indeed, the way in which kin and community evaluate the detainees' wives seems to indicate that the women's domestic realms are, to a large extent, public.

The social mechanisms at play in Amina's daughter's wedding can be illuminated through Das and Addlakha's contention that the domestic is actualized as "the sphere in which the family has to confront ways of disciplining contagion and stigma" (2001: 512). If the wedding constitutes a displacement of the domestic into the public sphere, then it is no less a place in which Amina's family had to "confront ways of disciplining contagion and stigma." One reason why the other detainees' wives refrained from attending is because a wedding constitutes a space where they, like Amina, must confront the rumors that circulate about them. The wedding may thus be construed as a site where intimacies are configured by politics—politics that permeate both the public and private realms (Goodfellow and Mulla 2008). The home is also revealed as a site where politics configure intimacy in the ways that Weeam's detained husband is the one to monitor whether she is behaving like the proper wife of a detainee. The absence of the women's detained husbands, which ostensibly does not change anything because it is not recognized as a loss, proves to have caused a distinct configuration of affect that saturates the women's self-perception, as well as their entire lifeworld.

Like the difference between the prisoners and the martyrs the affective configuration of the detainees' wives' lives is different from the transformation of the martyr's widow on the occasion of her husband's death. Corresponding to the unsettled status of the detainees, the wives have become unsettled, derivatively, due to their husbands' absences. For the detainees, part of their unsettled presence in a social world that otherwise salutes them as heroes is the fact that their heroism can always turn to treachery. It can be called into question, or revoked: nobody knows whether the detainees are informing the Israeli authorities about their political comrades. This ambiguous status reverberates in the lives of their wives. They, too, are considered legitimate targets for rumors, the mere potential of which, in this example, kept them from participating in the wedding of Amina's daughter.

This indeterminacy runs through the entirety of the women's lives and was instantiated in a conversation I had with Aisha over a casual Friday lunch in her house. Aisha had insisted that Amina and I join her in her flat to have the opportunity for a more private talk. After the meal had been eaten and cleared away, we sat in silence and watched the sun set over the hills surrounding Dar Nūra. I commented on Aisha's new short haircut. She replied, "I am so frustrated, I did not know what to do, so after my visit to Anwar's [her husband's] lawyer I cut my hair short—Anwar can't see me anyway, so it does not matter what I look like or how I appear."

She continued, "It's not a loss, it's something else. It's living without my soul mate. We used to share everything, but then I suddenly lost him, [and] there is something missing in my life. No, it is not a loss because loss is a negative thing, whereas missing someone is more romantic. And he does not want me to be lost. And I do not accept having the feeling of loss in my life, because he has to be with me. Whenever there are important decisions around our new house, I postpone them until Anwar is out of prison." Aisha's frustration illustrates the ambiguity of permeable boundaries between loss and absence. Since Anwar is not dead, she has not lost him: he is "just" absent. In line with the Palestinian moral discourse, her feelings are supposed to be dominated by romantic longing and desire, as well as by pride that stems from playing a part in the national struggle. However, this is clearly only partly the case. In the reality that is Aisha's life, feelings of loss are clearly at work, but Aisha must struggle against them, as illustrated by her explicit refusal to accept having them. We may think of her husband's absence not only as a temporal suspension of his physical presence in her life but a suspension that, in comparison with the martyrs, does not transform the relationship between him and his wife as a proper, definitive loss would, thus allowing the bereaved to turn their lost ones into people who can be commemorated.

An alternative analysis of this commemorative void might invoke Wittgenstein's idea of language going on holiday (1953 [2009]: 38). This happens when there are unresolved metaphysical problems of which language cannot speak, or which defy a solution. The problem of absent husbands is both metaphysical and mundane. As we saw in Chapter 1, and in these examples, there seems to be a difficulty in the standing language to accommodate the effects of detention. Aisha speaks in terms of the standing language, yet it fails to make the precise nature of her experience intelligible, either when she speaks in her public voice of the Palestinian moral discourse or, interestingly, when she sits at her kitchen table with friends who all understand her experience. What becomes of the domestic when experiences cannot be voiced, even in the privacy of the home?

Domesticating the Uncanny

The gravely distorted everyday lives of detainees' families invite anthropological thinking about absence, loss, and the ordinary in the Palestinian context. With reference to the work of Freud Cavell offers a way of thinking about the almost imperceptible changes that can seep into the ordinary and that, rather than distorting it, become familiar (1988). To help us understand such subtle changes that mark the ordinary in Palestine, I follow Cavell in his reliance on Freud's notion of the uncanny. Freud alludes to how the familiar can become unfamiliar, because the familiar and the unfamiliar are less oppositions than changing surfaces of the same ground. Analyzing the uncanny in his essay of that title, Freud employs the German terms *heimlich* (homely) and *unheimlich* (unhomely): *heimlich* becomes increasingly ambivalent, until it finally merges with its antonym *unheimlich*. The uncanny is in some respects a species of the familiar (1919 [2003]: 133). We can think about the differences between martyrs' widows and detainees' wives through the notion of the uncanny. I conclude by discussing the respective transformations of the domestic realm for widows and wives, and argue that the uncanny is uniquely and exclusively part of the domestic for detainees' wives.

As appears in the cases of Nadia, Fardoz, and Luma—all martyrs' widows (although Nadia is also a detainee's wife)—the commemorations of their husbands are at the heart of their homes, in as-salon. The organization of this room is saturated with national and religious politics. This is no less the case in the homes of the detainees' wives, but their status differs from that of the martyr's widow because of the unsettled ambiguity of the detainee's heroism. The photos of detainees in their families' homes signal a wish to keep them as part of the domestic, and to keep them intact.

I want to dwell on detainees' wives' efforts to keep the other intact. In the case of the martyrs' widows, the photographic displays of as-šuhada' may be thought of as a quite straightforward practice of commemoration. In contrast, the superficially similar but substantially different visual display of the detainee, striking a heroic pose and wearing combat attire in the heart of the domestic may be thought of as an attempt to keep him intact as a heroic figure. Due to the significance of displaying loyalty and support for the resistance against Israel in the domestic sphere, the photos of the detainee might also be an effort to keep the home intact in the wake of absence and the rumors and intense social control—"as if we are under a microscope"— that this absence invites. But the effort fails, precisely because of the detainees' unsettled status, which allows for rumor. The failure to keep the domestic intact is illustrated both in the case of Weeam's husband, who is constantly on the phone to check up on her, and in the way that fellow detainees' wives skipped Amina's daughter's wedding. The domestic is often presented as a space separated from the public realm in which the expression of female self and sexuality is encouraged (Abu-Lughod 1986 [2000], 2002; Eickelman 1998), but the two "domestic" cases here were imbued with national politics, in which sexual modesty is a key value. One could argue that a wedding is not part of the domestic realm, but a semipublic event. Yet insofar as the domestic is actualized through social relations, a wedding is an extension of the domestic. Under normal circumstances this extension is unproblematic— but the wedding was judged insufficiently domestic by the detainees' wives because they knew that their femininity was seen as potentially unsuitable for public display. This is why none of them attended the wedding. It is changes like these, when everything appears normal on the surface, but is in fact transformed, that we may think of as uncanny configurations of the domestic. The detainees' wives' feelings of being at home in the organization of space and social relations is affected to such an extent that the familiar becomes unfamiliar; the home itself becomes uncanny.

Before these women became inscribed in these two categories, they were Palestinian women. And in the occupied territory a woman's presence, if not existence, is denoted by the presence or absence of the man who, at any given time, is her primary male relation. Suad Joseph suggests that the Western notion of self is inappropriate in Middle Eastern countries, because the ideal self in Arab societies is not a bounded, unique individual but, rather, a relational person, configured according to patriarchy, and with permeable borders between self and other (1999).

In the context of the analysis of women who are related in different ways to heroic men, patriarchal relationality can be inferred from the term used to designate these women: it was not *armale'* (widow) but *'zoge aš-šahīd'* or *'zoge al-asīr'*: "wife of a martyr" and "wife of a detainee." In the women's own speech, the issue of relationality figures in how the women most often refer to themselves using *wa'di*, which refers to "my situation" (as married to detainee or martyr) instead of *ana or* "I."

Martyrs' widows and prisoners' wives diverge in an important way around the duration of their husbands' absences. Absence in the form of a permanent loss is markedly different from the absence that is allegedly temporary, its duration equal to the prison sentence. This is partly because it is recognized that, when a man dies, his family and his wife experience a loss. Consequently, because the widow of a martyr has derivatively sacrificed her own life for a greater cause, her loss is acknowledged. Religion is salient here, because of the meaningful frame of interpretation, justification, and legitimation of loss allowed for in Islam (Lindholm Schulz 2003; Allen 2006; Johnson 1982). To lose a husband in a way that complies with the available religious parameters is, in fact, a gain. Whether this applies on the emotional level varies from woman to woman, but socially—that is, in public discourse—losing a son, a father, or a husband to martyrdom is considered honorable, a loss that has its place in the vocabulary of the standing language. This does not exempt martyrs' widows from having to face many of the same issues of public gossip, speculation, and surveillance that beset detainees' wives. But the acknowledgment of martyr's widows and their affliction has to do with the transformation in their social status that occurs when their husbands die, a transformation that, through their close relationship to the martyrs, places them at the heart of the standing language in which victimhood merges with heroism (for an alternative view see Perdigon 2014). This transformation distinguishes them from detainees' wives, and not merely in degree, but in kind. Detainees' wives are included, but not acknowledged, in the standing language, and their experiences evade its vocabulary.

The failure to acknowledge detainees' wives returns us to the matter of temporality as it connotes loss and absence, respectively, for the martyr and the detainee. For the martyrs' widows, their transformation in social status and their loss are both permanent. If the widow chooses to stay unmarried, the chapters of the widow's life as a wife are closed, and whatever remains of the husband-martyr's personal belongings and memorabilia ensure his eternal presence, but, significantly, in a new chapter in their lives. The widow's transformation thus meshes with that of her deceased husband.

A detainee's wife, by contrast, lives with an absence that is perceived in public discourse to be temporary, regardless of the fact that it may last for the rest of a woman's life. Because of the hope for a peace agreement with Israel by which "the detainee question" will be solved, the issue of captivity remains within the realm of the temporary, no matter how many life sentences the detainee in question has been given. Because of this, the absence of the detainee-husband is considered nationally to be a pause, and thus not something that triggers the permanent transformation of a husband's death. We saw the ambiguity of losing versus missing in Aisha's comments. Part of the ambiguity resides in the fact that a detainee's wife's social status is not supposed to change, or, if it does, it does so presumably for the better because it is an honor to be married to a hero. Despite this, nothing stays the same: her social status does indeed change. From being treated as a respectable housewife, she moves into a suspended state of being married, yet dangerous and unrestrained because her husband is absent. In contrast to this ambiguous presence, the martyr's widow becomes a person in her own right because of her loss, and because of the value of that very loss: it is the ultimate sacrifice for Palestine.

The detainee's wife's situation evades the vocabulary of the acknowledgment of sacrifice and loss, because what she is living through is considered neither. The detainee is also a potentially ambiguous figure, though perhaps not to the same degree as his wife. Ambiguity unsettles the validity of a public, well-known discourse about the relatives of the detainee as subjects who gain social status and honor. The double ambiguity of a detainee's wife comes first from how the wife's social presence is derived from her detainee husband's absence and second from the potential ambiguity intrinsic in the figure of the detainee that infiltrates the wife's presence, derivatively.

No Place for Mourning

I have focused here on the ambiguities surrounding the honor ascribed to or withheld from detainees' wives. While I am not suggesting that these ambiguities render the honor given altogether invalid—indeed, I would argue that there is no reason to doubt that detainees wives do feel, and are, honored by their kin and in their communities—my concern has been to investigate how the standing language at once configures the affect around the incarceration of Palestinian men and simultaneously fails to acknowledge how the absence of a detained husband alters the ordinary, to the extent that the ordinary of the detainee's wife becomes uncanny.

What are the consequences of this uncanniness? Skepticism is appropriate here because of how issues of loss and absence become, in different ways, part of the social relations that actualize the domestic sphere, which is often described as the safe haven, a tower that stands tall through hardship. I have attempted to convey in this chapter that the ordinary is never to be taken for granted. Rather, in Cavell's words, "The world must be regained every day, in repetition, regained as gone. Here is a way of seeing what it means that Freud too thinks of mourning as an essentially repetitive exercise. . . . Freud regards mourning as the condition, that is to say, of allowing its independence from me, its objectivity. Learning mourning may be the achievement of a lifetime" (1988: 172). The uncanniness of the domestic is the slight change that prevents detainees' wives from mourning, in contrast to martyrs' widows, for whom the everyday is the site where postviolence recovery is possible. The difference cannot be quantified. It necessitates a perspective so focused on subtle difference that we can discern the uncanny within the ordinary of the detainees' wives.

CHAPTER 3

===

Enduring Presents

I do not think about the future. Maybe one, at the most
two days ahead. That is all I can think of.

—Yasmin

Yasmin's husband was serving a life sentence in a prison in Israel. He belongs
to a political faction that does not fall under the heading of "moderate," and
he has been convicted of activities that place him in the category of "security
detainee." This category is defined by the Israel Prison Service as fitting "a
prisoner who was convicted and sentenced for committing a crime, or who
is imprisoned on suspicion of committing a crime, which due to its nature
or circumstances was defined as a security offense or whose motive was
nationalistic" (Baker and Matar 2011: vii; Francis and Gibson 2011). Yasmin's
husband was in fact released as part of a prisoner exchange in 2012, and like
Nadia's, Mervat's, and Fatemeh's, he is one of my interlocutors' husbands to
be freed. This would seem to cast Yasmin's story in a different light, but the
fact that he was returned not to his home in the West Bank but to Gaza,
where Yasmin is not allowed to go and which he cannot leave, makes his
release mockingly irrelevant. Due to his classification as a security detainee,
Yasmin was not allowed to visit her husband during the last four years of his
imprisonment, nor has she seen him since his release. She is thirty-one, was
married at fourteen, and lives with her six children in the top flat of her
mother-in-law's mansion in a posh district of Bāb aš-šams. Given the still
tense relations between political factions in Palestine there is little chance
that Yasmin will be able to see her husband anytime soon. However, to bring

about even a slight feeling of still being part of a conjugal relationship, she has to keep applying for a permit, even though she knows that it is futile.

I take Yasmin's words as an invitation to explore the temporal consequences of imprisonment that derive from Israeli securitization procedures toward Palestinian detainees and their relatives. In this chapter, I elucidate, first, how the specific Israeli securitization procedures of incarcerating Palestinians structure the everyday life of detainees' wives temporally. Second, I analyze how, contrary to the assumption of a linear, redemptive aftermath intrinsic to notions of trauma, the securitization procedures never permit the absence of the women's husbands to fade into a past. Third, I convey how the absence of a linear progression through trauma and its aftermath plays out in every practice the women have to engage in if they wish to stay in touch with their husbands. Consequently, the women become captives of the immediate present, a present that never becomes a future because, as soon as the women's practices are completed, these practices must be repeated. In this sense the entire orientation and movement of time for the wives of detainees is structured by and around securitization measures undertaken by Israel.

My contemplation of the derivative effects of the Israeli incarceration of Palestinians gauges two major tropes of thinking about violence: securitization and trauma. First, a vital premise of securitization theory is that the state, under threat, is what secures the lives of its citizens (see Holbraad and Pedersen 2012: 170). In the case of the Israel-Palestine conflict this holds true for Israeli citizens (Ochs 2011). Given that my analysis places emphasis on those who are perceived to be a threat by the state of Israel and its Jewish citizens—namely, the Palestinians—this relationship between a state and its citizens is unsettled (for more on this topic, see Baker and Matar 2011). Conceptualizing the different ways in which Israelis and Palestinians relate to the Israeli state, Kelly distinguishes between Israeli citizens "whose relationship to the state is governed by legal rights and the rule of law" and Palestinian subjects, "on the other hand, [who] are subjected to the administrative and coercive power of the state" (2006a: 13). Securitization is here employed as a concrete instance of "the administrative and coercive power of the state" rather than as a theoretical concept. By "securitization procedures," I refer to the procedures laid down by Israel that detainees' families have to comply with in order to stay in touch.

Second, the focus on how such procedures of securitization structure the everyday temporality of detainees' wives seriously questions the psychological notion of an "aftermath" that follows a trauma. In contrast to an everyday life that comes together after violence and offers a potential space for recovery, exactly what kind of ordinary existence is possible for the families of detainees through the Israeli securitization procedures that they must comply with is the focus of this chapter. The practices required for women to stitch together connections with their husbands are time and attention consuming, and continuously so, such that Israeli securitization structures their everyday life. Whereas repetition can in some cases create a routine and banality that decrease the tension and uncertainty of such practices, this is far from the case for my interlocutors. The securitization practices are repeated, but always with variations and unpredictability that make the practices at once familiar and unfamiliar—they can never be completely sure of the result of their actions. One consequence of this duality of knowing and not knowing is that the detainee's absence, his incarceration, and the violence that preceded it never transform the present into the past, rendering moot the idea of an "after." The simultaneity of past and present contracts the women's temporality into an inescapable "now."

I have found Bergson's notion of "duration" useful to understanding this kind of temporality (Bergson 2010). In Deleuze's work *Bergsonism*, "duration" has a dual meaning. Duration includes first the length of lived experience or the temporality of a subjective life. Second, duration here is understood as the "condition of experience" that is made up of multiplicities of time and space (Deleuze 1988: 37). These multiplicities hinge on Bergson's distinction between "the virtual" and "the actual." The virtual is thus a temporal multiplicity. In Deleuze's words, "The virtual is (therefore) real without being actual, ideal without being abstract" (1994: 264). The actual covers multiplicities of space, which occur in what Bergson terms the process of "actualization." Whereas the virtual allows for actualization, it is not the virtual that is actualized. Actualization emerges through virtual lines of differentiation whose numerical differences correspond to the differences that are exterior and that therefore become part of the dimension of the actual.

Intrinsic to the notion of duration is the opposition between "contraction" and "dilation" (Deleuze 1988: 21, 75). "Contraction" refers to the relationship between the past and the present when the two of them conflate (1988: 75). "Dilation," on the other hand, refers to matter as "the most relaxed degree of the present" (75). These contractions and dilations of temporalities hint at what the everyday means to detainees' wives. Das (2007) notes that the everyday both holds the potential for recovery and is the site in which violence is woven into domestic intimacy. For instance, visiting, narrating, being oriented toward a lawyer's appointment are activities that stitch together family connections that have been severed by the general Israeli securitization procedure of incarcerating Palestinian men. Whereas these practices may seem extraordinary, they are repeated again and again over the course of a lengthy prison sentence, thereby belonging to a quotidian rather than an extraordinary register.[1] These differences create a lived time for detainees' families that is suffused by uncertainty and a lack of progress(ion) of time. This is what constitutes both "aftermath" and the ordinary for detainees' families. Being securitized is ʿādi.

A Prison Visit

The television screen in the front of the bus repeats the same cartoon show for the fifth time: an Arabic-dubbed version of Donald Duck as a cowboy. The cartoon lasts for twenty-five minutes. After a short break on the flickering screen, when the passengers of the bus glance out at the lush orange groves rolling by, all heads return to the screen when the introductory tune begins. The passengers have been on their feet since four in the morning, eager to make it from the villages in the southern West Bank to the central pickup point in Ramallah at seven. Though the prison visits are organized by the International Committee of the Red Cross, through its Family Visits Office in Jerusalem, the coach belongs to a local Palestinian bus company. When all the families have gathered in Ramallah, the bus drives the few miles to the checkpoint of Qalandia, the biggest terminal for moving between the occupied territory, the West Bank, and Israel. To be allowed to pass, people normally need a blue Jerusalem identification card, proof of permanent residency in Jerusalem. None of the passengers have this. They hold a green Palestinian ID and a temporary permit to enter Israel, for the duration of the visit to their sons, fathers, or husbands, detained in an Israeli prison. Despite the permits, it takes two and a half hours before the passengers are all in place on the bus in the parking space on the Israeli side of Qalandia Terminal. Present, too, are the discreetly armed Israeli police officers who will escort the bus through Israel to Bersheva Prison in Ashkelon. The police officers observe the bus drivers getting the passengers on to the bus, making sure that none of them skips the visit and instead enters a Jerusalem that is prohibited to them. A main task of the police officers is to make sure that no one gets off the bus during the trip. Whether the trip takes two or five hours, the bus is not allowed to stop.

Even though people are impatient for the remaining passengers to be allowed through the checkpoints, everyone knows the routine. They know that the bus eventually will go on, but they do not know if it will be in ten minutes or two hours. The atmosphere on the bus seems to be one of resigned impatience and lingering dissatisfaction. The sound of occasional sighs fills the air, yet there are no signs of any intention to try to influence the situation.

Thus, when the bus finally moves off, the relief is almost tangible. Passengers breathe easy again and talk, and for a while the bus comes to life. The boys and girls have been munching on cookies, chocolate, and potato chips for the last few hours. Their mothers restrict their drinking. The children speak, but after a while the cartoon occupies them. There is little talk among the women on the bus. I am sitting next to Fatemeh, an interlocutor of mine on her way to visit her imprisoned husband. She has not visited him for four years. Only her son Hassan, who is now almost seven, has seen his father regularly, together with Fatemeh's mother-in-law. Over the years, Hassan has brought back letters from his father to his mother from the prison visits. Hassan never carries letters back to his father. Fatemeh cannot be asked to write back anymore. "To tell him what?" she said to me. "Nothing new happens here." Fatemeh is twenty-eight years old. The other women in the village say she is different—you can tell she is from Amman by her ultrasmart clothing, her slimness, and, for a village woman and the wife of a detainee, her plentiful use of black kohl around her eyes. She is in a new green *jilbab*, with a matching light yellow *hijab*.[2] Her clothes and her comportment are often the topic of conversation among the other women of the group of five detainees' wives from Dar Nūra. And glances are exchanged when her name is mentioned in the company of the women's families. Mervat, for instance, likes Fatemeh but refrains from socializing with, her due to Fatemeh's reputation for being suspiciously overly preoccupied with her looks, for a detainee's wife. Fatemeh does not speak a lot on the trip; she is nervous, bored by the long drive, and by Hassan's demands for sweets. She looks out on the Israel she is not allowed to be in. Her only way of being here is in the bus, on the way to the prison where her husband is being detained for political activities that threaten the security of the state of Israel. His sentence is seventeen years, of which he has served seven. Hassan was three months old the night the Israeli Army detained his father.

Reaching Ashkelon, the women pack up their bags busily, checking their looks in the reflection of the bus windows and scolding their children for looking scruffy already. When the bus stops in front of the prison blocks, the passengers get off the bus and enter the visitors' entrance to the prison, escorted by the policeman. Fatemeh's cheeks blush, she smoothes out her jilbab and straightens Hassan's hair. I am not allowed to enter the prison with the families, so I wait in a dreary café across the road from the prison. The nervously excited voices of the women and children in the visitor's hall reach across the sleepy road.

A couple of hours later, the families return to the bus, accompanied by the sound of a siren because Qassam rockets launched from Gaza are nearing Ashkelon. The passengers seem disoriented. After a while the siren stops, and the drivers inform us that the rockets did not hit a target. There is an awkward feeling of relief, as well as guilt at feeling just that. The faces of the women and their children display different suppressed emotions: tiredness, disappointment, joy. One woman is very quiet. Fatemeh nods in her direction and says in a whisper that it was the woman's turn to see her husband just when the siren sounded. Due to the security threat of the rockets, the remaining family visits were cancelled and the families sent back outside to the bus. The bus ride back home is quiet. Nobody speaks, and the air is heavy with emotion. Fatemeh and I speak only a little, she being her usual private, observing, and silent self. Fatemeh falls asleep shortly after the bus moves off, every now and again looking at the cartoon show or out of the window. Asking her how it was to see her husband's face, she says with a shrug and smile, "ḥilu" (beautiful, lovely). Then she adds, "'ādi."

Back in the village, over the next few days when Fatemeh goes to the grocer or meets other detainees' wives, she will be met with questions like "kīf al-asīr" (How is the detainee?), "gaddeš sana" (How many years?), "wēn-o" (Where is he?). These questions indicate the familiarity among the families of detainees with the proceedings of the visit described above, and the steps leading to those forty-five minutes of personal connection that constitute a prison visit. These steps and what they achieve is one instance of contraction of time that incarceration brings to the lives of the detainees' wives. If we try to think about these contractions using Deleuze's points, we may want to remember the paradox of simultaneity, which implies that each contraction of time is a simultaneous dilation.

Seen in this light, the contraction of time created by Fatemeh and the other women's practices to stay in touch with their husbands can also be seen as a potential refuge from a future they are obliged to believe in, yet whose bleakness they must also live with. Fatemeh therefore remains oriented toward the demands of the present. Whereas these demands may seem exterior to Fatemeh, they are at the heart of her personal affect, because the practices are what allow her to stay close to her husband.

Emblematic of how personal life in Palestine is always already political, the quotidian act of answering a neighbor's questions concerning her visits to the prison allows Fatemeh both a degree of conjugal intimacy and a part in the struggle against Israel through her insistence on visiting her spouse despite the difficulties. In a sense this allows her to form a relationship with the Palestinian collective in which she can figure as the loyal supporter of her heroic husband. The conjoining of conjugal and national bonds is a tangible example of how the duration for Fatemeh simultaneously contracts and dilates. Contraction ties Fatemeh to the present, whereas movements of dilation stretch her present before and beyond the immediacy of the now.

The neighbors' questions about the prison visits, then, illustrate the derivative effects of Israeli securitization procedures for Palestinian detainees in Israeli prisons. Through the practices involved in either trying to get the detainees released or arranging to visit them, the lived time of the detainees' families illustrate the conditions wrought by the ongoing Israeli security measures. The questions about the detainees suggest how the Israeli securitization procedures are embedded in everyday interactions and concerns in detainees' families. This supports Kelly's contention that mundane bureaucratic practices dominate life in the West Bank: life is not all blood and violence (2007: 5). Significantly, these procedures are disputed, volatile, and negotiable. Capriciousness does in fact generate the violence and tensions that mold everyday life for Palestinians in the West Bank (15). The particularity of Israeli carceral measures, however, shows how bureaucratic procedures punctuate the sense of temporality. This temporality appears changeable or negotiable, because there is always the possibility of mounting a lawsuit against Israel or an appeal to have a husband released. Nonetheless, for detainees and their relatives, such apparent legal possibilities are rarely successful.

In the following, I ponder three instances of temporal contraction arising from the women's questions to Fatemeh concerning her husband, the detainee. Because how particular questions refer to the relation of time to the ordinary is significant, the questions emphasized here are: how is the detainee, how long is his sentence, and where is he? I then ask what the "future" can be taken to mean for the women of this book.

Kīf al-asīr (How Is the Detainee)?

The most widely used phrase in Palestinian vernacular when you meet someone is "kīfik, šu akbārik," ' which means "How are you, what is your news?" The answer to this question if a person is feeling well is "mnīḥa," meaning "good," or "tamām," which can be translated as "all right." If someone is feeling so-so, the reply would be "māši il-ḥāl," which literally means "it goes." When people are close to each other and find themselves in an appropriate social space, deeper probing into the well-being of the other can take place. Mostly, however, the conversation is closed then and there, no matter what the answer.

Among the detainees' female relatives and people they encounter who know of their situation, it is a courtesy always to ask as the first question after "kīfik, šu akbārik," "kīf al-asīr," meaning "How is the detainee?" This question may be asked of either a wife or a mother. The answer to the question varies, but can be said to follow an almost formulaic set of sequences, which includes an account of how bad the food is in the prison, as well as if and how the detainee was tortured during interrogation or ordinary prison procedures. An issue that is always mentioned is the family's challenges in finding a way to ensure that the detainee actually receives the gifts of clothes, shoes, and cigarettes they send to him. These accounts end with the speaker shrugging while she asks "Šu mn-sawwi," which translates as "What can we do?" or "What do we do?" This question is rhetorical, of course, indicating instead the resigned acceptance and recognition that there is nothing that can be done about the occupation as a whole or about the particular detainee's situation. The obligatory practice of inquiring as to how the detainee is and answering as described entails a most significant acknowledgment that the detainee is suffering more than anyone else, and for the collective of Palestinians.

However, the appeal of revolution has decreased within the detainees' movement and the Palestinian population, due to the general deterioration of Palestinian institutions after the second Intifada, factional splits, and the evaporating hope of change for the better (Buch Segal 2015). These issues are increasingly recognized and formulated, if only in intimate or "safe" social forums. As Kelly has pointed out (2007), post-Oslo Palestine is haunted by tensions that create violence, not only toward Israelis but also internally among Palestinians. This was clear in the way in which my interlocutors' narratives about their imprisoned kin were composed differently from the narratives constructed by the interlocutors of Nashif's research (2008) on education among Palestinian prisoners in Israeli detention. Rather than being stories about the collective and the community, the narratives about the detainees, across political factions, are stories that contain lead parts and supporting actors. The lead part is taken by the detainee himself.[3] The national struggle is his context only, as illustrated in the narratives below. First is Amina's story of the precarious days in which her husband was captured, then an extract from a conversation between Mervat and Weeam about how their husbands think about their political activities during incarceration:

The day after they had demolished our house we turned on the radio because we didn't have electricity to watch the news on TV. We wanted to understand why all of this was happening. They said [on TV] that four houses had been destroyed in Dar Nūra and they arrested Basil, my husband, so when I heard that, I do not remember what I did. And the next day I kept laughing, I don't know why, and then I started crying, you know, they destroyed my house and they took my husband and my brothers. I have small kids, and his family is not here, so I did not know what to do, it was a very big shock. I want to forget what happened, but I cannot. After that we went to our destroyed house to see if we could find anything, but nothing was there, everything was gone. And then my husband tried to call the Salib al-Ahmar [Red Cross] to tell them that he is OK, and that he wanted a lawyer, and to not be worried. And then he stayed in the prison for five years where I could not see him, just once in the court, I saw him once. And I tried a lot to get a permission to visit him, but it is not working, it was difficult, but now I can visit him, it is getting better.

Mervat: They care about Palestine, and for fighting for it, but after that, when they are in the prison, they feel it. He [her husband] told me, "When I am released I will make it up to you." I told him, "When you get out you are never going to be able to make up one day of those days that you left us alone."

Weeam: Yes, they regretted all those days not being with us. And
because he experienced a life without a father before, he now
feels with his kids. And his mother, she was so sad about him,
she would look at his picture and start crying.

Amina's story begins on the day after the Israeli Army captured her husband and demolished her family home. She mentions her husband's transfer
between different prisons in Israel, which is a practice that causes families
much despair, since they do not know where their family members are, if they
are alright or harmed during their flight and ensuing capture by the IDF. Often a story about a detainee will also include a list of the ailments inflicted on
him during incarceration. For instance, when I visited Weeam, from time to
time she would brief me on the pain in her detained husband's ears. Similarly,
the mother of a detainee from a village nearby recounted in detail to Rawan
and me how her son's teeth had deteriorated alarmingly during his imprisonment in Israel. It was due first to torture,[4] she said, and then because of the
lack of medical care available in Israeli prisons. In Weeam and Mervat's conversations, political activities slide into the background, subsumed by reflections about the costs of imprisonment for both detainees and their families.

The individual detainee as a center of gravity for his family's narrative is
underscored by the way that he forms part of every family conversation, as
illustrated by the ubiquitous question "kīf al-asīr." Sympathetic to Nashif's
analysis, I contend that individual narratives about the detainees draw on and
feed into a collective genre of detainees' narratives. But the content of these
shared stories emphasizes the acts and whereabouts of the individual Palestinian detainee. Nashif's analysis and my own diverge because of the different
historical context of his particular interlocutors, who were imprisoned before
the second Intifada, and the current context, characterized by a collective
fatigue with which Palestinians register yet more suffering, more martyrs,
and more detainees. Additionally, the collective struggle is a figure in detainees' stories, but not the basis of the families' stories. Whereas the discourse of
the national cause is meaningful inside the prison, among my interlocutors,
it seems that over time this meaning has become secondary to the difficulty
that the detainee's absence causes his family—emotionally, socially, and
financially. Exercising so much influence in absentia, the detainee, not the
national cause, inevitably appears as the focus of his family's narrative.

The narrative of the detainee belongs, as Nashif notes (2008), to a certain
narrative genre of suffering. In a sense the story of a single detainee can be

seen as one family's claim to the Palestinian collective's shared history of affliction (Pappé 2004; 2006). Since the family of a detainee repeatedly encounters and answers the same questions, and because the narrative of the detainee belongs to this particular genre of bodying forth the Palestinian plight, the narrative event causes the family's temporality to evolve around that of the detainee: when did he last see a lawyer, when was he interrogated, when is the next time they can bring him presents? A detainee's absence thus makes him present in the everyday temporality of his family through the way in which his family repeatedly narrates his incarceration. In this manner, every narration actualizes his absence and, through this, returns to the violent event that caused him to be imprisoned in the first place. We may therefore think about narrations as contractions of past and present that thereby unsettle the idea of an aftermath in the wake of violence.

Relations and Cut Connections

Analyzing the narratives that the wives of the incarcerated share in response to "kif al-asīr" shows that the effects of the enduring absence do not recede over time, as would occur with an "aftermath" during which a family moves on. Rather, absence is continuously flagged: every time the women answer this question they must reaffirm the disappearances of their male relatives. The narration also reaffirms that a detainee's family, wife, and children are the relatives of a detainee first. Vitally, if banally, such practices take time to perform. They fill relatives' time—particularly the detainees' wives' time, because they are classified as the primary relations of the incarcerated, by the International Committee of the Red Cross Family Visits Office in Jerusalem.

Strathern's work (2004) can help us think further about how a husband's incarceration changes conjugal relations. For Strathern, a relation is not only an actual connection; it may also be a connection that has been severed. For instance, a person may be dead, but his family is still related to him. Of importance here is that every cut to a connection elicits a new relation (81). In this light, Israeli securitization procedures thereby act as things that cut connections, but not relations, between detainees and their wives. Meanwhile, the acknowledgment of only a particular fraction of a woman's identity—her relationship to a detainee—means that all the other aspects of her person are eclipsed.

A woman then is known only as a detainee's wife, rather than, say, a female head of household, the mother of four children, or the best seamstress in town. Importantly, the practices with which she fills her time may amount to what Wittgenstein terms "aspect blindness": seeing one figure in a drawing, Wittgenstein asserts, means being blinded toward another (PS: §xi). The blinded aspects can be made to appear yet under other circumstances. Thinking about the narrative practices of detainees' families, we may say that the aspects that dawn through narrative practices are only the family or the individual woman's relationship to a hero. Accordingly, aspect blindness confines women in this situation to a particular social role.

Gaddeš Sana (How Many Years)?

What kind of temporality, we may ask, emerges amid the time-consuming activities involved in caring at a distance for an imprisoned family member? Since imprisonment is a premise of the quotidian lives of my particular interlocutors, the everyday may be tainted by uncertainty, but it is not an uncertainty that numbs action. Quite the opposite, because detainees' families know which office to apply to for visitors' permits, what to worry about, and what to talk about with other people. These specific practices to sustain contact with a family member structure the everyday chores and therefore the orientation of the subjects who engage in these chores, thus forging an absolute commitment to the present.

With sentences for detainees varying between fifteen years and life imprisonment, existence for their families is structured the same way for many years on end. Yet receiving a sentence means something else than a life that falls into structured, set practices. For Aisha, the day her husband was sentenced in the high court in Jerusalem was a blow. Soon afterward, I was sitting with others in the living room in Amina's house, my home in the village, chatting with Amina, when we heard the sound of Aisha's old Mercedes. Aisha came in and kissed us all hello. But at the moment of her peck on our cheeks she did her utmost to avoid eye and physical contact. This happens among strangers or people with little liking for each other, but the crowd in the living room, including me, consisted of people who knew Aisha, whom she cared about, and with whom she could relax. However, Amina and I also knew about the feelings that Aisha took great care to hide from visibility in her otherwise public figure. Today she was different, and we knew why. We asked about her father-in-law, who had been admitted to a hospital, attempting to avoid the sensitive topic of the sentencing of Aisha's husband. Instead of avoiding it, however, we jumped straight at it. Everyone knew that her father-in-law's heart attack happened the day after his son had received his sentence: life. To Aisha, the sentence changed everything. Any hope of a future together with her husband and the father of her two children evaporated. Whereas a sentence for a certain number of years can appear to have a finite end—though it may not—the infinity of the sentence for Aisha's husband cut her off definitively from the future she imagined. Starting anew is not a possibility for women who are married to political detainees. Legally, it is possible to divorce one's husband, but if a detainee's wife does this she loses the right to her children. She will then depend on her consanguine family to take financial care of her, which, on top of the shame involved, is a burden for them.

For Aisha, however, the difficulty is not financial, since she can provide for herself, or a desire for divorce. She has great affection for her husband, and theirs is a companionate marriage. Their friendship goes back to when they were around fifteen years old and politically committed. At that time it was not proper for her to marry exogamously, since then, as now, patrilateral parallel first-cousin marriage is considered the ideal marriage in the occupied territory (Muhawi and Kanaana 1989), as noted earlier. As Johnson, Abu Nahleh, and Moors (2009) note, the years around the first Intifada witnessed a new form of marriage, the so-called political marriage, which is based on the political status of a potential spouse rather than his or her agnatic line. The marriage between Aisha and Anwar is a political marriage. They finally obtained the agreement of both their families and shared their time at the local university, as well as working together politically. Anwar was detained many times because of this work, and this last time for life. Though he is physically absent from her everyday existence, Aisha can still do all the things she would with him—travel, build a house, take good care of the children—but she will do them alone. In spite of her relatively high social position, she is nonetheless as vulnerable to rumor as any of her peers. And, due to the sentence, even intimacy is bound up with the rules regarding prison visits laid down by Israel.

Her husband's sentence, conveniently perhaps, also demands that she be entirely oriented toward lawyers' appointments and the hope of release that is always present because of chronic Palestinian-Israeli negotiations over the fate of detainees. In this regard there is no difference between a long-term prison sentence and a life sentence.

This speaks to Kelly's (2007) argument that it is the volatility and uncertainty of law in Israel and the occupied territory that render the everyday unpredictable and tense, even the everyday in light of a life sentence, like that of Aisha's husband. Although life for Aisha and the other wives is saturated with uncertainty, this uncertainty, as noted, is not unpredictable. In the case of detainees' wives, uncertainty itself is solely predictable. The everyday is also repetitive, albeit in a unique repetition. For instance, Anwar is a security detainee like Yasmin's husband. Although he is being detained for life, the uncertainties involved in his captivity, such as the appeal to shorten his sentence, his current location, and the negotiation of visitation permits, demand that Aisha, like other detainees' wives, repeat the described practices to stay in touch with him. If his case is dismissed in court, she has to start all over again, not knowing whether there is any chance of release. But she knows the procedures. Due to Aisha's required involvement in such practices, Israeli carceral procedures repeatedly summon the aspects of Aisha's person that relate to her heroic marriage, rather than the multiplicity of her identities and roles.

The important conclusion here concerns temporality. The lives of Aisha and of detainees' wives in general are oriented toward Israeli securitization procedures. They live within a "now" that presumably might end, for example, when they receive permission for a visit. When permission is received, this may appear to be a milestone of progression. But in the case of detainees' wives, the fact that these practices need to be constantly repeated hampers temporal progression, or the creation of an aftermath (for comparison with other situations of prolonged conflict see Sørensen 2012). The present does not turn into the past, because at the instant that permission is granted for a visit, Aisha has to begin repeating the entire set of practices, such as applying for the next permission to visit.

Instead, the circumstance of lengthy incarceration contracts time: the lives of detainees' wives remain in the repetitive present. Due to this temporal premise, the lives of detainees' wives can only in a limited fashion be illuminated through anthropological understandings of narrated time as progressive (see Peacock and Holland 1993; Ochs and Capps 1996). For instance, central and influential works on narrative and temporality by Cheryl Mattingly are based on the idea that the narrator's emplotment of the past allows a sense of closure, so that narrators can move on and inhabit the present (Mattingly 1998). In contrast, the temporality at work for detainees' wives requires us to think differently about the relationship between past, present, and future in the sense that, for these women, the one does not follow the other. On this premise the next section examines the implication of living a life that is ensnared in the present rather than progressing along a linear temporality.

Wen-o (Where Is He)?

The forty-five-minute visit to a prison can be the culmination of months, sometimes years, of preparation. For example, Amina showed me photos of herself taken on the occasion of her daughter's engagement. The photos were intended for her husband: she was not wearing the hijab, and she glanced coyly into the camera. Amina was excited: she was going to show them to her husband on the next prison visit. Since the prison visits take place in a big room where the detainees are lined up in a row behind glass, the families stand shoved together on the other side. The photos are thus as close to physical intimacy as a husband and wife can get. When I saw Amina a couple of days later, I asked her how the visit went. She answered with a "tsk," the culturally familiar shrug and lifting of one's head. She explained that he was not there, that he had been moved to another prison, which she and allegedly (she did not believe it to be true) the International Committee of the Red Cross did not know. The trip, the photos, and all the expectations had been in vain. "Šu- basawwi?" (What can I do?), Amina said, returning to kneading her dough. She knows, tacitly, that she can do very little to bring about change. To find out where her husband is, Amina must go through the International Committee of the Red Cross. Detainees' families have to inquire at the local office in the West Bank, whose officers then get in touch with the main International Committee of the Red Cross Family Visits Office in Jerusalem. The Family Visits Office then contacts the Israeli prison authorities, who, according to the families, may or may not inform the committee. Sometimes, though, the families communicate about detainee transfers among themselves. Aisha's husband wrote this to her after he was sentenced:

My love Imm Ahmad,
I have the feeling that the way we visit each other will change, or
that this is going to be the last, and I can't hide that this will be
really difficult for me. I used to talk to you without barriers, I got

used to your visits without you actually visiting me because your
letters made me feel happy, and I was feeling that you visit me when
I got a letter from you.

How will I feel when I move far into the desert and will have no
connections with you? It is going to be a black desert, and how can
I feel my heart beats when I do not read your words?

Aisha told me that although the Israelis had informed neither the International Committee of the Red Cross nor the family that her husband had been
transferred to another prison, her husband had a hunch that this would
happen and told her by letter. He wrote that the visits would change, and
he wrote about isolation and a black desert, clear allusions to the prison of
An-Nafha, situated in the Negev. This is a prison for those security detainees
whom the Israeli authorities often move because they are suspected of creating strong communities around them in the prisons, as Nashif has con-
vincingly confirmed in his analysis (2008). Knowledge about where Aisha's
husband is and when he will be there is therefore restricted. Aisha must
keep herself thoroughly updated and always be ready to change her applications for permissions to visit him in another prison.

The cases of Amina, Fatemeh, and Aisha show how the temporalities of
families and individuals, their "now" and their orientation to the future, are
structured by Israeli securitization procedures and the corresponding practices the women must perform, whether in conversation with the family or
with strangers. Their now is structured by the fact that next month one must
go back and forth to the local International Committee of the Red Cross office in order to check whether permission has been granted; or borrow the
neighbor's slow Internet connection to see if new lists have appeared showing who has been released in this round of negotiations between Israel and
the Palestinian National Authority. The sum and multitude of these practices
constitute the temporality of the everyday to the detainees' wives, tying that
everyday inextricably to the present, without the chance to leave behind a
past or have a future emerge.

Captives of the Present

What does it mean to be tied to the present? First, the everyday temporality
of detainees' wives is structured around attempts to stitch together the

severed connections of the captive marriage by maintaining their relationships. The key here is to repeat the procedures of applying for permits to visit,
arranging bus trips, and finding a better lawyer when the final sentence has
been handed down. Through the wives' repetition of these practices, future
horizons are suspended. The acts required to maintain a connection with an
absent husband are repeated in the very instant they are completed. In this
regard, such practices can never be completed. Moreover, detainees' sentences are simultaneously temporary and endless, because "the detainees
question" between Israel and the Palestinians has been and remains perpet-
ually futile and unsettled. This makes the women captives of the immediate
present. Consequently, the lived time does not pass, but figures as a crude
instantiation of what Deleuze (1994: 81) terms "the paradox of contemporaneity" (cf. Hodges 2008).[5]

The paradox of contemporaneity seems to resonate with the particular
ways in which the part of the detainee's wife's past that began with her
husband's detention has a permanent hook in her present. This furthers our
understanding of what detention does to conjugal relations and temporality
in Palestine. It ties them to the present, enduringly.

Being a captive of the present is by no means a situation exclusive to wives
of Palestinian detainees. As Day, Papataxiarchis, and Stewart (1998) point
out, living for the moment seems characteristic of marginal people: living for
the moment is a result of the insecurity and instability of the future inherent
in life as, say, a prostitute on London's Preet Street (Day 2009). Pedersen and
Holbraad, on the other hand, calls for an alternative conceptualization of
the different modes of presentism (2013: 13), in regard to which they call on
Bergson and Deleuze to explain how living in the present does not mean
living only in the now (2013: 15). Rather, they argue that any moment always
extends to the past and the future and is extended to them. Pedersen and
Holbraad's understanding of the present resonates with the argument I am
making in this chapter that being tied to the present is not a deliberate wish
for the detainees' wives. Rather, it starkly undercuts the Palestinian ethos of
sumūd—the ethos of a bearing, moral aspiration of standing tall until the
Palestinian state becomes reality, come what may.

The ways that wives are captives of the present is a precise example of
how Israeli carceral procedures have in fact insinuated themselves into the
very temporality of Palestinian families. The practices that the wife of a detainee must engage in require her absolute attention. This is so not only the
first time around, but at every subsequent attempt to maintain the conjugal

relationship, because the necessary practices are never entirely the same. The procedures change, if only slightly, at every repetition. This happens when parts of the bureaucratic process change; for instance, when the place or deadline for handing in a request for permission changes, even though the formula is the same. Or when suddenly a detainee's son can no longer visit because he has become fifteen or has responsibility for seeing his younger siblings through the visits, or making sure that letters are passed between his mother and his detained father. Because of such expected variations, the anticipation[6] created by a coming visit, a plea for permission, or a date from one's lawyers absorbs the subjects engaged in such practices. This keeps wives focused on the conditions created by Israeli securitization measures, and grounded in the immediate present. In Yasmin's words, there is no future; she is caught up in the present. As she later said, "If I think about the future, I'm lost."

For the wives, the future is itself an aspect of time that remains hypothetical. Thoughts and hopes about it are never realized. Because detainees' wives never know when or where a prison visit will actually take place, from where the bus will depart, or whether they will be granted permission again, they are repetitively oriented toward the practices in and of their present. Through this repetitive cycle, the future never replaces the present, and the present never fades into a past. This creates short-sighted subjects, whose worlds end and begin with the next permission or the next visit. In a sense all that is left is the present, added, perhaps, to a distant future of the state of Palestine, which "in sh'allah" will come true. The portrait in this chapter of an everyday existence is what the standing language of knowing suffering in Palestine cannot read, and therefore fails to acknowledge. Yet this is what constitutes "aftermath" and the ordinary for detainees' families. Uncanniness is ordinary. It is ʿādi.

CHAPTER 4

On Hardship and Closeness

Among Palestinians, in the occupied territory as well as in the diaspora, *al-ʿāʾila* (the family) is the stronghold against the occupation (Perdigon 2011; Taraki et al. 2006: xii). Different forms of labor, care, and heroic investment are required to keep that stronghold intact under occupation, as can be seen in political cartoonist Naji al-Ali's drawing of a wife who hands her husband a gun in the name of Palestine. The woman's gesture conjures an ordinary atmosphere in the sense that she might as well have handed him a packed lunch as he left for work, while she cared for their infant. The scene is depicted by one of the Palestinians' most cherished cartoonists, who is known for his satirical drawings that comment on Arab regimes and the Israeli-Palestinian conflict, in particular (Political Cartoon Gallery 2008: 4).

The satire of this particular drawing nonetheless eludes me.[1] Sharif Kanaana asserts that the jokes and myths he has collected about the Intifada depict an alternative, coexistent, and antagonistic reality (1990 [2005]: 20). What is interesting in this drawing by al-Ali is how he paints a reality that is in fact neither alternative, coexistent, nor antagonistic to the women of this book. Rather, the drawing depicts a version of the real that is uncannily familiar to every single one of my interlocutors: the obligation of women to support the resistance fighters, and reproduce. This family resemblance implies that the drawing is not satirical. Rather, and given that it is created by a man, it may be interpreted as an even stronger call to show support for the male fighters because the women are the ones handing them the guns. Al-Ali's drawing therefore depicts the complicity of both men and women in the struggle for freedom from occupation, connoting the place of the Palestinian family at the heart of national politics.

I take the husband's absence, among the conditions of the relationships that make up al-'ā'ila, as a prism through which we can understand how conflict works itself into the most intimate of relationships. The questions that guide this exploration concern the kinds of emotional labor that go into keeping the dispersed family together. Given the discourses of stability and strength evoked in both public discourse and social conversations about the Palestinian family, I here subject to scrutiny the actual effort and talk of how to sustain closeness among kin in order to try to keep the family intact. I ask how the family is made close, and what kinds of care are made possible or necessarily severed in this attempt. The chapter thereby opens a conversation the Palestinians consider toxic, a conversation about how prolonged suffering works itself into the way in which people offer care and kindness to those closest to them. This testifies to the fraught nature of endurance as it is lived on an everyday basis with, and sometimes in conflict with, close kin.

Withholding of Knowledge

For the women of this book, the Palestinian family is endogamous and village based, even though in the case of Dar Nūra a large part of the village's population has migrated to Jordan. The women here have married their cross-cousins, as is the custom, and however diluted the families can be said to be, many of the women are in fact related through both consanguine and affinal relations (see Granquist 1926; Bourdieu 2001). Marriage preference in Dar Nūra then is both endogamous and, if at all possible, territorially anchored in the village. As we shall see, however, lives and labor make this collective attempt at kinship normativity a living relation rather than a stale, unchanging set of rules (see Das 1977 for a discussion of this). In Palestine kinship continues to be the primary anchor of belonging, yet it binds people equally to the Palestinian collective, in the absence of a viable territorial state. This junction of family and national belonging, however, deserves closer scrutiny. Despite the family's status as a strong, long-standing institution keeping the collective of Palestinians together, there is little public talk of the costs of the occupation for the family dynamics of close kin or talk in confidential conversations in contemporary Palestine. What goes on in families is kept within families.

The inarticulability of problems internal to families strikes me as evidence of the inadequacy of the standing language to articulate experiences that question the criteria of "forms of life." It is, however, an inadequacy that must be seen in light of Palestinian understandings of kinship, in which kin abstain from mentioning problems internal to the family as protection against shameful gossip (Kanaana and Muhawi 1989: 15). With reference to Das's work, we might call that which is contained "poisonous knowledge" (2007: 54). Das's study about the partition between India and Pakistan in 1947 included an analysis of women who had been abducted but, "rather than bearing witness to the disorder they had been subjected to, the metaphor that they used was of a woman drinking the poison and keeping it within her" (2007: 54). Without assuming any kind of similarity between the experiences of the women in Das's work and those of this book, I see the metaphor of drinking poisonous knowledge as an evocative image of how to think of Palestinian families' withholding of knowledge regarding the implications of being married to a detainee—knowledge that would compromise the family and its members if it were verbalized—as a dual act of protecting the wives of the detainees and trying to mend the relational cracks caused by the Israeli-Palestinian conflict.[2] Palestinian families must show sumūd in order to interpret defeat in light of national pride.

Containing Trauma

The image of the family as a place to contain knowledge and emotions so as to project resilience and homeostasis toward the outside is consistent with how the Palestinian family is imagined in studies of the psychological effects of the occupation. My entry into Palestine has been through (and beyond) the idea of traumatized victims of violence, and the majority of the families I was in touch with had at some point received counseling services from one or more organizations or doctors in regard to their or a relative's mental health. In that sense, one could posit the tentative notion of therapeutic citizenship as one of the unifying bonds for the women featured in this book (Vinh-Kim Nguyen 2005). The languages in which the families of detainees are spoken about as matters of concern for a wide range of psychosocial interventions in the occupied territory are therefore also languages of psychology and psychiatry. Although the disciplines informing this discourse have multiple sources, the theoretical framework of psychosocial interventions is anchored in the notion of traumatization by violent events (see Thabet et al. 2014; Thabet et al. 2011; Salo 2009; Khamis 2008). Here I would add that the family members of the victim are seen both as those who heal traumatization and as those who are affected derivatively.

The studies of traumatization in the occupied territories focuses largely on the prevalence of post-traumatic stress disorder among parents and children. The family is thus imagined more as the nuclear family than the notions of al-ʿāʾila and *qarabah* (closeness) connote. The Palestinian psychiatrist Abdelaziz Thabet's general interest, for instance, is in the individual and how his or her trauma affects other members of the family (Thabet et al. 2014; Thabet et al. 2011). Violence or malign events that befall the family are here understood to single out one member as the primary victim, and others as secondary or tertiary victims. Within this framework, individuals take precedence over the family as an extended unit, and the relationship with the social world surrounding the family is thus imagined through the individuals composing it. This mode of understanding how families are affected by violence is an example of the criteria for knowing suffering that constitute the standing language. Thus in instantiating the standing language, Thabet's work focuses on the individual who has experienced an immediate, violent event. Secondarily, he is concerned with those who are not directly afflicted, but whose experience is imagined through the position of the indirect witness of a given event of traumatization (Thabet et al. 2011).

Clinical psychology, however, considers suffering in a variety of ways. An alternative perspective to Thabet's is that of Punamäki, one of an international group of doctors that has published extensively on the mental health of the Palestinians (Punamäki et al. 2005). Punamäki and her coauthors argue that there is a system of balance among individual family members in how suffering is distributed. In more practical terms this argument implies that if a man, for instance, is suffering from severe trauma and displays little resilience, his wife is likely to display hope, resilience, and coping strategies that enlist the entire family. And if both parents are affected negatively, the sum of negative and positive attitudes is kept in equilibrium by their children. Such a focus on the nuclear family unit and homeostasis in this conceptualization of the violently affected Palestinian family meshes with the Palestinian notion of the family as the container, and processor, of the malign events that befall it. Although their work uses a psychodynamic model of a family as relational, Punamäki and colleagues interpret the family as a unit comprising individuals, each with his or her own emotional response to trauma, a view that reflects Joseph's point that there seems to be a limit as to how "relational" the individual can be within the discipline of psychology (1999: 1).

Juxtaposing the two modes of imagining the Palestinian family—a Palestinian notion of al-ʿāʾila as a unit of stronghold against Israel on the one hand and, on the other, the theoretical framework undergirding institutionalized attempts to deal with the psychological effects of incarceration—makes clear the differences and interesting convergences between them: in either perspective the family is understood as both the proud supporter of a hero and a group of secondary victims of the husband's heroic imprisonment. How may we think of the braiding of strength and vulnerability differently? Ethnography is one such perspective that allows precisely the fluid reality rather than the normativity of kinship to come to the fore (see Carsten 2000).

Kinship Normativity in Palestine—Up Close and Personal

When evenings fell in the home of Amina, Layla, their mother, and Amina's children, Layla and I would push aside the sofas in the living room, pull two mattresses to the center of the room, and sleep there while Amina slept with her children in the kitchen, her mother in one of the bedrooms, and if a brother was visiting, he in the other. With the others sleeping, no one could overhear the words that could prove harmful for Layla, who was already in a delicate situation as the old, unmarried daughter of their mother's household. One night we spoke about dreams and future hopes. Layla brought up the topic of marriage herself:

> I know you think it's strange with a second wife [i.e., polygamy], but as we talked about at the playground in Ramallah yesterday, it's just as strange for us that you are not married to your boyfriend, you see. . . . I do not want to be the second wife. A man came and proposed to me but I could not, he was nice, but I could not imagine having to . . . having to be his wife, ouf. I said to my mother and to my brothers that I could not, I do not want it. They said to me, OK, enough, that's OK, but we think you should do it. But I could not. Another man came to our house; his wife was in Jordan, but he was here in Dar Nūra with the children, and he could not get

permission to go there, and she was not allowed back in. He needs another wife to take care of his children. I could not.

Layla's words convey the equivocations by which patriarchy is simultaneously evoked and sidestepped, out of her family's concern for her well-being. Accordingly, Layla both understands and rationalizes the practice of polygamy, though she would do everything in her power to avoid it. Layla did avoid it, but at the cost of remaining unmarried until she was nearly forty, which is socially awkward for a woman from a village in the West Bank.

Although it is tacitly known, her sisters do not mention the fact that Layla was close to Mahmood, the son of her oldest sister, Khuloud. They came of age together, were friends, and talked together about everything, Layla recalled. He was engaged to another woman before he was detained, but she broke it off when she learned he had received a life sentence. According to the notion of endogamous patrilateral kinship, relatives on Layla's father's side are preferred as suitable spouses for her. This means that the *ibn ammi* (father's brother's son) is considered an ideal husband. However, since Mahmood is Layla's sister's son, he is out of the range of men available for Layla to marry for different reasons than marriage preference: both have nursed from Layla's sister Khuloud, Mahmood's mother, something that is still practiced in many Levantine families (Clarke 2007). According to Levantine notions of riḍāʿ (milk kinship), this means that Layla and Mahmood are "milk-siblings," which renders them *nasab* (connoting a consanguine relation) and thus barred from marrying (Clarke 2007: 382).

However, Layla did marry. She got engaged in January 2011 when a widower from the village who had emigrated returned in order to find a spouse to replace his first wife, who had died of cancer after twenty-one years of marriage, leaving six children behind in a large city in the United States. He proposed, Layla accepted, and the engagement party followed shortly thereafter. A couple of months later he returned for the wedding and a few weeks before my next visit, the newlywed couple had returned from a lavish honeymoon in Turkey. Layla was not to follow him to the United States until four months later, when the paperwork came through. Layla proudly showed me the photos from Turkey and sported a new *jilbab* with a matching head scarf every time I saw her during my two-month visit. Little gestures told me that her status in the family had changed substantially. Her niece Ibtisam, who is the daughter of her older sister Khuloud, lived with Layla, Amina, and their mother, was now the one who served the guests, cooked, and cleaned, while

Layla was treated like a guest of honor. She was also the one who gave the children a few shekels to go to the shops and would time and again discreetly make arrangements to pay for her sister's and niece's phone cards when credit on their phones had run out. Layla was glowing and exited to move to America. One night when we walked together to Amina's new house, I asked her how she felt about leaving behind her family in Dar Nūra. She said she was happy to marry, but given the choice she would have stayed. She assured me that her fiance was a good man who treated his family nicely. He had a job as a supervisor in a large company. Layla went out of her way to introduce him to me on Skype, via her new laptop in her bedroom in her mother's house. She was well aware that he was grieving and that she would not be a new mother to the bereaved children. But she said that she would try to stand by the oldest daughter, who was about to get married, like a friend or a cousin. Layla delivered a baby boy in the spring of 2013 and when we last exchanged photos of our boys, he had become a cherubic toddler.

This glimpse into Layla's situation illustrates how patriarchy is the overarching kinship norm among Palestinians, setting the signposts for kin relatedness among my interlocutors. The patriarchal norm comes to the fore in the way in which Layla's family continued to nudge her into marrying so that she could establish a household on her own. The fact that Amina's husband is incarcerated, however, complicates kinship normativity: One could argue that for Layla and Amina's mother, it was in fact both convenient and necessary that Layla help out in their maternal home in Amina's husband's absence. This was only possible because Layla was unmarried. By the customs of patrilocality, she would, upon her own marriage, have to move to the house of her in-laws, who would then become her primary obligation, thus leaving Amina alone to be the sole caretaker of her mother. Yet despite the convenience of Layla's presence in the domestic scene of her mother's household, the family still urged Layla to marry, even though she did not find the proposals suitable. This indicates the importance of expressing support for kinship norms. One may speculate as to whether the effort to arrange Layla's marriage gained additional urgency because the detention of Amina's husband forced Amina and Layla to take responsibility for their mother's care, which was already at odds with Palestinian kinship norms that dictate that the youngest, unmarried daughter stay in her parents' house. Layla was at that time unmarried, true, but she was too old to occupy that category of womanhood. Thus the household of Amina, Layla, and her mother was already on the periphery of kinship normativity in Palestine, and Layla's marriage became ever more urgent.

Layla's failure to marry until 2011 meant that she was obliged to live with and care for their mother, Amina, and Amina's children. In practical terms this meant that for the first ten years of her husband's sentence, Amina shared acts of nurturing and care with Layla according to their respective strengths and weaknesses. Amina, for instance, had a hard time reading and writing, whereas Layla tried to use her university education in history to earn a position tutoring English in the local school. Or at least this was how she jokingly responded when I asked her precisely what topics she taught in school. One day she said, "Lotte, you know, I am not a teacher. I am only helping, making coffee for the teachers and helping in the club where Reema is working. I never finished the degree and we can't afford to pay the tuition fees. And, I have to help my mother and Amina." She did this by studying every afternoon with Amina's three youngest girls, who also had difficulties grasping reading, writing, and arithmetic, according to Layla and the psychologists heading the group therapeutic project for prisoners' wives in Dar Nūra. In their view Amina's children suffered derivatively due to Amina's unresolved feelings of victimization, as discussed in Chapter 1. Under these circumstances, Amina nonetheless took up work periodically so as to earn a living for the family, including Layla, and bring in income on top of the meager amount they made from their olive groves.

Shortly after Amina's move to her new home adjacent to her older sister Khuloud, the daughter of Khuloud, Ibtisam, moved in with Layla instead of Amina to help take care of her grandmother (Layla and Amina's mother) because Ibtisam was divorced from her children's father. He had a Jerusalem ID, which meant that Ibtisam could not go to see the children in their father's family house. And since he refused to bring the children to the West Bank, half an hour's drive from his home, Ibtisam confided in me that she had not seen them for seventeen months in the early summer of 2011. She told me this while we were doing the dishes after a festive lunch for me, my mother, and my oldest son, who was nearly a year old when we visited the family. "I love them as much as you love your son, but I can't see them and I do not know when I will," Ibtisam said. In one sentence she made it clear how she and I were both alike and living worlds apart.

An older daughter unmarried, the younger one with a heroic husband in prison, and a niece who had lost the right to see her children—whereas these three women's lives seem to be at odds with the rules of kinship, a different reading brings to light how each of their lives was unfolding according to Palestinian ideas about kin relatedness. What also transpires in the ethnography above are the labors of care by their close relatives, mother, aunts, and sisters. These gestures of care in different ways constantly include women once more, even where they seem to have departed from normative ideas of kinship in contemporary Palestine. Janet Carsten urges us to think about substance, about the stuff that makes up kin relatedness, things such as blood, letters, household objects, and ghosts (2007, 2011, 2013). The preceding sections have shown how occupation works itself strongly into the everyday registers of how consanguinity is lived among sisters, mothers, and their daughters. It reminds us of the importance placed on consanguine relations in Palestine, as well as the work—emotional, social, and economic— that sustains these important relations. Yet it has also outlined the contours of how even these consanguine relations are under pressure from the constant strain of occupation and, as specifically attended to here, the Israeli practices of detaining Palestinian men. In the following sections I focus on consanguinity by attending to the concrete rearrangements of domesticity that followed the imprisonment of Amina's husband, as well as those of other women in similar situations.

Enclosing Family Homes

For the majority of my interlocutors, the capture of their husbands meant few changes in actual living arrangements, since at the time of the detentions the women were already living in the houses of their families-in-law, in accordance with the principle of patrilocality. Alternatively, if they had been living in a smaller conjugal household, the women would have moved back into the houses of their families-in-law upon their husbands' incarceration. The absence of real change in actual living arrangements, however, is counterbalanced by other realities of Palestinian kinship. This applies to Mervat, whose husband was building their new house some three hundred meters away from his parents' household in Dar Nūra. When her husband was caught by the Israeli Army, Mervat became anxious and moved back in with her husband's family , despite already-escalating conflicts with her mother-in-law. These conflicts had inspired Mervat and her husband to move out of his family home and build their own house in the first place, despite strong protests from her husband's family. Mervat only stayed a short while in her mother-in-law's household. She felt that she was being asked to undertake all the household chores, while her sisters-in-law merely watched. When Mervat's own house was half-finished, she moved there with her six children. How her mother-in-law was in fact still too close for comfort she explained to me once when I visited her house: "I am a detainee's wife, everything is illegal for me, I cannot go out, I have to stay at home. You know, if my mother-in-law sees me like that [Mervat was wearing a trace of mascara that day] she will say, 'for whom are you doing this?' Once she came in the morning and found me sleeping and told me, 'Why are you wearing this?' I told her, 'I am sleeping.' She told me that the neighbors could see me like that."

Like other women in her situation, Mervat was in a bitter conflict with her mother-in-law over the detainee's subsidy. Her mother-in-law believed that, as the mother of her incarcerated son, she was entitled to the money since she did not have her oldest son to take care of her financially, as he is obliged to do. To Mervat this seemed outrageous and a threat to her efforts to make ends meet for herself and her children. Money problems between wives and their families-in-law were a recurring concern in more than a few families I encountered, though not due to legislative ambiguity. According to the rules of the political organizations that administer allowances to their activists' families, the official entitlement belongs to the wife, due to her role as the primary caretaker for the detainee's children. However, in many families the women do not have their own bank accounts, nor do they have the funds to open one. Therefore they rely on their in-laws to receive the money and pass it on to them. And since the children are supposed to care for the older generation as soon as they acquire an income, according to Palestinian notions of kinship, Mervat's mother-in-law was entitled to financial support from her son, Mervat's husband. This still applies in the absence of her son because, with the detainee's salary of then NIS 1,200 a month (the equivalent of USD 309 at the time of publishing this book), the son is in fact providing an income, which must be used to take care of his parents. Mervat is therefore only partially entitled to the money necessary to sustain her life, which makes her quarrels with her in-laws even more stressful. Her financial ability to care for her children relies on the sympathy of her mother-in-law. For a meal including meat, the family had to go to Mervat's parents. Significantly, though, the situation was less a string of dramas than a tritely discordant element of the ordinary, enmeshed within tacit claims as to whom the imprisonment of Mervat's husband had affected the most, and whose affliction was therefore most worthy of compensation. Mervat would often say, "I am so bored, Lotte, I am glad you came, I have been waiting for you. Why were you so long a time at Aisha's house?" Having almost finished building and decorating her house, Mervat filled her days with cooking for the children and cleaning her house. Repeatedly she has said, "Just give me something to do, I would love a job where I could get out of the house, do something and not only exist for the children. I go crazy inside these walls." My assistant Rawan and I decided to ask Rawan's sister, who works as a counselor in the YMCA in Ramallah, if the organization had a vocational program to which Mervat could be admitted on the basis of her status as the wife of a detainee. Participation in the program would give Mervat an income from the profits of the sales of the handwork she would produce. When Rawan and I told her she had been admitted she thanked us and changed the subject. Rawan's sister called Mervat and arranged a start date. Rawan offered to walk with her to prevent gossip about where she was going and what she was doing away from her house. But Mervat did not turn up. She excused herself and said the day was not good for her. She did the same when Rawan's sister called next time. When we asked her why she had not taken up the offer, she shrugged her shoulders and said, "Inshallah, I will someday." Mervat repeated these words whenever I asked afterward if she would be interested in taking up the standing offer of a place on the project. Her boredom did not cease, and she did not stop needing the money. I can only guess why Mervat ignored the offer. Perhaps she feared becoming the subject of rumors in the village. Due to the already-described ambiguities that surround the detainees themselves and their wives and families, rumors, true or not, circulate constantly. Simultaneously, Mervat's example connotes a permeable boundary between showing sumūd and resignation at the hand of the occupation.

Things also changed, albeit less conflictually, for Aisha, who had been living with her sister in Ramallah for two years while she was studying and her husband was imprisoned. After a while, she accepted her husband's advice that it would be better if she moved back to Dar Nūra to be closer to his family. She did move back, but lived in a flat with their two children away from both her family's and her husband's family's houses. After eight years, she finally finished the process of building a home next to her in-laws' house. The house is situated at an oblique angle so that its windows are visible from the courtyard of her husband's family home a few meters away. Before her home was completed, Aisha spent many of her days and nights in her in-laws' house and received her guests there, if not in her former office at work, thus circumventing local principles of conduct. According to such principles, if a man visits the premises of a single woman or a woman who lacks a man in her immediate presence, this violates the codes of honor and shame and is an invitation for others to question the woman's honor and decency. The reason for this is the notion of qarabah, in which the situation dictates whether a man is either *ġarīb* (close) or *ajnabi* (a stranger) (Clarke 2007: 383). Strangers are those who are eligible spouses, a category that includes not only men from other lines of descent but also men who are nasab (part of the agnatic line). Living with an absent husband makes any act by Aisha that involves male strangers a rationale for questioning her morality. Due to how honor and shame fold back into the closeness of her relations with kin, the virtual suspicion permeating her existence makes Aisha's family and her husband's family deal with her presence as an actual "single" woman by, for instance, offering her the space to meet her acquaintances in their own home. The only legitimate men surrounding a woman are her brothers and the children of her close kin. How women, married and formerly married, relate to their brothers-in-law on the other hand points toward the changeable configuration of qarabah, since, these men are obliged to protect their sisters-in-law in the absence of their husbands, but according to the norms of leviratic marriage they are also obliged to marry their brother's widow in the case of their brother's death. This is mostly practiced in the more conservative areas in the West Bank, yet the structural ambiguity of the relationship between a wife and her brother-in-law remains, as is revealed in the two cases of Fatemeh and Yasmin. When her husband was captured, newlywed Fatemeh was living with him and their three-month-old baby above her n-laws' house. They had finished building the new flat during their first year as a married couple, after living in a room downstairs in her in-laws' house. When Fatemeh's husband was imprisoned she stayed in the flat, alone with her son, just above her mother-in-law and next to her sister-in-law. In the absence of her husband, it was her brother-in-law whom she had to ask for help, and whom she would ask for permission before leaving the house. She described to me how they became close and how some people would gossip about how much time she spent with her unmarried brother-in-law.

The ambiguous relation to a brother-in-law during the absence of a husband is an aspect of kinship that also permeates Yasmin's life. She too lives on the top floor of her husband's family's house, together with her six children, a home her husband has yet to inhabit. Together with Mayy I visited her four times, and each time either her brother-in-law would let us into her flat (even though he did not live on the premises) or he would turn up at some point, bringing with him cookies, soft drinks, or fruit, or calling her on her landline and cell phone. Financially privileged due to her in-laws' significant role in the city's money-changing industry, Yasmin had a second house in Jericho where she went with her children during weekends and school holidays, always accompanied by her husband's family. Fatemeh, Yasmin, and other women living in *ad-dār* (the house) of their in-laws each had their own, separate flat with as-salon, a family living room, a kitchen, and at least one bedroom, which they often share with their daughters, while the boys stay in a separate room. For Aisha the site of habitation changed when her husband was captured, but for my other interlocutors their residences did not change. Crucially though, their sense of home and homeliness *did* change yet perhaps more subtly than one may think, given the violent circumstances under which the husbands had been captured by the Israeli Army. What happened for the women in the wake of their husbands' captivity was a contraction of the closeness surrounding them: they literally moved closer to their in-laws, were more often accompanied by a brother-in-law, and their whereabouts were monitored by their entire affinal kin network more than before the capture. One house, then, may be the site of changing domesticities that follow the pattern of its inhabitants' presences and absences in the home.

A House, Not a Home

Just after Amina had described to me the demolition of her mother's family house and the capture of her husband, I asked her what she did in the following days. "In the first two weeks we were living in a tent," she replied. "People, the press came to visit us, and we have lots of pictures of us sitting on top of our destroyed house, and after those two weeks we lived in my brother's house, but each day we were coming to the house to visit it."

During the first weeks after the destruction of their house, Amina and her family watched and waited for a new house to be constructed from the rubble of the old family house. Shortly after the demolition, Amina's household, including her sister, mother, and four daughters, as noted, moved into her brother's house, next to the house in which they had all been living. After a short while the family moved on to the house of Reema, Amina's second-oldest sister. Amina's situation of staying in her mother's house until it was destroyed is uncommon due to the principle of patrilocality. Amina did so because her in-laws live in Amman, even though they are part of Amina's agnatic line. Theirs is therefore a patrilateral parallel cousin marriage. Right after their marriage, when Amina was twenty, she moved with her husband to Amman to live with her husband's family, as is the norm. Even though Amina did not thrive in Amman, partly because, according to her, people are not "close" there, the couple did not return to Dar Nūra until sixteen years later. At that point they moved into Amina's maternal home, which, according to Palestinian notions of kinship, would be the next best place to live. With the destruction of the house due to her husband's political activities, Amina in a sense returned fully to the realm of her consanguineal family after having been away, to being the responsibility of her brother and older sister, despite her marital relationship. Normally her absence from her consanguineal family would become permanent with the onset of her marriage, which on the day-to-day level removes both her and her kin's responsibility for her from her consanguineal to her affinal family. Although both families belong to the same agnatic line, this is a matter of organizing everyday chores in the households. Thus, while they were staying in her mother's house, Amina's husband was responsible for the livelihood of the entire household. Adhering to patriarchal kinship normativity, Amina is also remaining closest to her consanguineal family despite her marriage (see Joseph 1999). She and her close relatives are reciprocally obliged, as shown by how Amina's brother and sister opened their homes to them.

After a year in her sister Reema's household, Amina's new house stood erect on the grounds where the destroyed house had been. The new house, provided by the organization with which Amina's incarcerated husband is involved, has never become a home to the family. The arrangement of the space in the house is culturally awkward, since the first room one enters is the family's combined living, sleeping, and kitchen area, the only place from which as-salon can be accessed. The living areas are therefore public, whereas normally Arab houses are built so that guests walk first into a hallway or straight into as-salon, the space of hospitality, which, as the only truly public room in a home, is distinct and should be kept separate from intimate family life. The arrangement of the house thus crudely embodies Freud's notion of the uncanny as what exists between being homely (heimlich) and unhomely (unheimlich). While it has been furnished and made livable, the house seems still a temporary home that does not evoke care of or pride in the premises to either Amina or her family. Even the front yard is strikingly barren, although the village in which they live is known to have rich, fertile soil and front yards that are often lush with fruit trees. Only on my return in 2008 were her frail mother's careful efforts to grow trees beginning to result in leaves and a few lemons, tangerines, and pomegranates. The house still felt as if it had never been lived in, although Amina had lived there with her mother, her children, and her sister, and another sister in the next-door flat for almost seven years.

I was constantly reminded of Amina's feeling of uncanniness in her own house. On warm September evenings, she was careful to shut all the windows before we went to sleep, explaining to me that she felt afraid if they were left open. Something might enter. The house felt haunted, an atmosphere brought about by absence: the absence of Amina's husband, of homeliness, and of the assurance of safety. With the aid of her brothers and nephews, Amina had meanwhile constructed a new house nearer to her oldest sister Khuloud's. The ground floor had been finished for a while, but because of Amina's responsibility for her older sister Reema, Reema's daughter, her husband, and their baby girl were living there until they could afford to build a house themselves. Amina moved into the house in July 2009. To Amina, her husband's imprisonment in one sense allowed her more independence from both her consanguineal and affinal families because she was able to live without her husband and apart from her family. This independence was nonetheless fraught with obligations, since Amina had been the person primarily responsible for her mother until Amina moved and left the responsibility to her sister Layla.

The rearrangement of care in and among Amina's female kin as it was linked to her husband's imprisonment was the topic of discussion one night, after a day of picking olives in Amina's fields. Layla, Amina, Khuloud, Khuloud's neighbor, Rawan, and I were sitting in Khuloud's yard talking about the years since the "massacre," which is how the villagers refer to the large-scale demolition of homes, killing of eleven men, and capture of the political activists accused of an assault on the Israeli state. We spoke about how it had affected the family's feeling of closeness. In the dim light of a single fluorescent lamp on the wall of the house, the women slowly gathered around us after I had been talking alone with Khuloud for a while about her son Mahmood, who as noted earlier is a detainee with a life sentence, and her experience of his imprisonment. Amina joined the conversation:

Lotte: Do you wish that it [your husband's imprisonment] never happened?

Amina: Yes. I don't feel secure without my husband, and it's difficult to handle this all alone, and the house; it's a big responsibility, now I am everything for the kids: their father, their mother, and their friend.

Lotte: Tomorrow is the commemoration of the massacre in Dar Nūra. If you think about this family and that event, what are the links between them?

Khuloud: Certainly we remember the massacre, and when they destroyed the house, and the suffering that happened to us, and to the other people. All of this happened in one day, it's difficult.

Lotte: If I was to say anything I would think that your family was among those the hardest hit that day?

Khuloud: Yes, my family was strongly hit that day.

Lotte: What is the difference between the situations of other people and your situation? I mean the situation of the family that has lost the father or the son,[3] or when they are imprisoned, like your son and Amina's husband?

Amina: No one can forget this suffering.

Khuloud: No one can forget this suffering, but I was saying that it was easier for us when we saw that there are people who suffer more than us.

Lotte: What does that mean, Amina?

Amina: I don't want to answer because I will start crying. I can't handle speaking about the massacre.

Lotte: I am sorry.

Khuloud: We cannot forget that now, after they destroyed the house, we are separated all of us, each one lives in a different place. What hurts is not that they destroyed our house but it's because that made us far from each other and that they changed everything. We are not living together anymore. I mean that, at that time when they destroyed our house, my parents and my sister went to live in my sister's house, me and my husband we were in Ramallah under house arrest, we couldn't be in contact with my family, I rarely saw them. What I am trying to say is if we were actually all together at that time, we could be more helpful toward each other. I am sure we all were sad, and we wanted to do something but we could only do it in our hearts. Because of the distance we couldn't actually help, and that was difficult.

Lotte: What about today, do you think you still feel these changes in the family?

Khuloud: Yes, sure, because we are not all together in the same house. I remember when we were all together we were very happy, and it was always noisy because we were sitting together, all of us, but now we are not together.

Lotte: Does that make the family less close?

Khuloud: We are still close to each other and we feel with each other, but the problem is that we are not living close to each other.

Lotte: I was wondering whether a distance in space can mean a distance in emotions?

Khuloud: No, I don't think emotions can be affected.

As Khuloud describes her situation, the family was separated and went from living literally in each other's backyard to being dispersed across towns and cities. Some live in Dar Nūra and others in Ramallah. In practical terms the separation of the family means that they cannot help each other day to day. As Khuloud says, all that is left is the intention and wish to help each other, without the ability to fulfill the wish. And while Amina's forced move from her family home seems to have given her independence from her consanguine and affinal families, the literal dispersal of the family has actually created increased responsibility for her to take care of her mother while also being the sole caretaker of her four children, a responsibility that her family can only partially assist with due to the distance between them. In line with the Palestinian metanarrative of the family standing tall through suffering and destruction, Khuloud contended in a steady yet hesitant voice that emotions could not be affected by distance.

It is worth thinking further about the implications of Layla's remark that evening in Khuloud's yard: "Hard things make people closer, I guess." It seems that both "becoming closer" in terms of literally moving closer and becoming physically separated as a residue of incarceration bring to the fore aspects of kin normativity: *ḥimāya* (protection) in its meaning of care, *ḥakkam* (control), and *mas'uliyya* (responsibility). These three aspects appear

as differentiations of kinship norms, depending on the particularity of relationships in which they appear.

Closing In

Yasmin's brother-in-law would come and go incessantly at her flat, running
errands for her and often calling to check on her. Yasmin's flat, with its fancy,
modern Arabic furniture, was spotless. She wore smart clothes, and served
her guests impeccable food. Without doubt, the reason for Yasmin's privileged material conditions was that she had married into a wealthy family, one
of the most affluent in the entire city. Making sure that she did not lack for
anything, her brother-in-law fulfilled the obligation intrinsic in his role to
care for and protect Yasmin during her detained husband's absence. But
the endless cans of soft drinks and bags of tasty Israeli potato chips could
never compensate for the abiding, resigned loneliness Yasmin felt: "I tried
to buy a car because I did not want to be lonely. Every time I have a visitor,
I want them to stay." When I asked whether the car changed these things
for her, she replied: "No. This feeling is stuck with me, of loneliness. There
is nothing that is nice [fiš iši ḥilu] because the person who makes me happy
is missing. When I go out of the house in the car, people will say that I went
out late, so I do not go out a lot. No, I always organize myself so I have a
destination. I take my children, because I want them to feel like they had a
good experience."

On a later visit, I asked her if she was using the car a lot. She said no,
confirming that she only used it for short trips so that people wouldn't talk
about her. Yasmin attempted to control the gossip of outsiders by ensuring
that her excursions always had a specific destination.

There is another aspect to the protective relationship with Yasmin's
brother-in-law that materialized upon her husband's incarceration. What
should be protected, not least, is the tie between her and her in-laws, including fulfillment of the responsibilities she is obliged to fulfill, whether or
not her husband is present. Control of her movements and activities thus
not only is a matter of what she does during her days inside or away from
her flat but also applies within her in-laws' household.

This resonates with Mervat's account of how her husband's family assumed that she would live up to her obligation as the wife of the oldest son

to undertake their household chores. The feeling of being under constant scrutiny once they start living in the homes of their husbands' families applies to Palestinian women across generations. Interestingly, this is also how the women who are now the mothers-in-law of my primary interlocutors remember their time in their husband's family homes. To be under scrutiny is therefore not a marker that distinguishes detainees' wives from other married Palestinian women. The distinguishing detail with a detained husband's absence is the proximity of the scrutinizing gaze.

Thus, when I visited Maryam I could calculate the minutes before Maryam's mother-in-law would come to stand in the door to the living room. Suddenly, with an authoritative presence, she would walk into the living room without asking to join or sit down. Her entrance into the room, listening, and taking over the conversation is, however, appropriate according to kinship norms in Palestine and shows the multiple meanings it can take as forms of both care and control.

Once, after Maryam's mother-in-law had left the living room and Maryam slowly released the pillow she was squeezing in her lap, she told me how, at the onset of her husband's incarceration, she tried to go about her life, doing her everyday chores as she would have if he had been there. Normally she asked his permission before leaving the house and told him where she was going. In his absence she just went about doing her errands. After a while her mother-in-law reprimanded her, saying that Maryam was running around in the city without a purpose. She made it clear to Maryam that the absence of her husband did not mean that she could do whatever she wanted. Her mother-in-law therefore took on the role of her husband in granting permission for Maryam to go out, and keeping track of her whereabouts.

It is not only mothers-in-law and brothers-in-law of detainees' wives who make lived kinships seem closer to the norm. As Muhawi and Kanaana observe (1989), the relationship between sisters-in-law and wives is characterized by structural antagonism. In her analysis of brother-sister relationships in Lebanon, Joseph argues that the brother-sister relationship should be considered other, and more, than an extension of the honor-shame codex through which parents control and protect their children (1999: 126). Apart from being a structural connection in which the brother is obliged to protect his sister, the brother-sister relationship is foremost a psychodynamic process of gendering (129). Brothers and sisters use each other in their upbringing as models of the other sex, and therefore become each other's significant gendering other, through which boys and girls become men and women, respectively. As a result, the relationship between a woman and her sister-in-law is almost inherently antagonistic, since the husband's object for unfolding sexuality is changed from sister to wife, which then becomes a potential source of jealousy. In addition, not only are brothers obliged to protect their sisters, the sisters are also interested in securing the loyalty of the wife, who, even in endogamous first-cousin marriages, is considered an *ajnabi* (stranger) to the intimate household. A sister-in-law therefore protects her brother's wife by being present during women's conversations about husbands, sex, families, and in-laws, making sure that knowledge of such issues stays in the family.

One example epitomizes how a woman might use these means to ensure her sister-in-law's loyalty. Rawan and I were visiting Fatemeh. We were all talking quietly. The visit lasted longer than the ordinary hospitality visits of the sort that form part of any Palestinian woman's ordinary day (Gjerding 2008). The structure of such visits follows a prescribed sequence, in which initially the guest is served a soft drink or juice, sometimes accompanied by little bowls of crackers, roasted pumpkin seeds, or the more expensive roasted nuts, according to the prosperity of the family. Then a delicately arranged plate of fresh fruit along with a knife is given to each guest. Later, the host offers sweet tea with mint, and after a while the visit should be rounded off with the serving of steaming hot, strong, sugared coffee as a marker that the visit can now end. The ceremonially structured visit ordinarily lasts no more than three-quarters of an hour. Thus, when we had both drunk the soft drinks that Fatemeh's sister had served us and the tea that came a little later, and neither Fatemeh nor we made the recognizable moves to leave, the sister-in-law sat down in the middle of our clearly confidential conversation. We were talking about sex, about Fatemeh's conjugal relationship, and her feelings about both having and not missing sex with her husband, and we were all being delicate in our choice of words.[4] From our voices and expressions Fatemeh's sister-in-law must have understood that we were speaking confidentially. This did not deter her from sitting down and waiting for us to continue the intimate conversation, which I clumsily tried to change into something more innocent so as not to compromise Fatemeh's confidentiality. As with Maryam's mother-in-law, this incident shows how confinement makes a family comply with kin obligations that in other circumstances would have been less pressing. In the following section I outline the senses in which the relationship between a prisoner's wife and her in-laws differs from any other Palestinian woman's relation with her husband's relatives.

Ordinary Obligations

The configuration of living arrangements that follows the detention of a husband implies a subtle but pervasive intensification of the affinal relations surrounding his wife. This accentuation occurs through aspects that are intrinsic to qarabah, in which loyalty and betrayal hinge on the kin-based obligations between a woman and her in-laws. The imperative of protecting and controlling the whereabouts of detainees' wives forms part of the virtual obligation to secure a family's honor, predicated on protecting the modesty of the women of the family (see Abu-Lughod 1986 [2000]). This obligation is transferred from a woman's brother to her husband upon marriage. A husband's detention, however, disperses that responsibility to the detainee's mother and brother, in particular, a task that is easier to perform when the woman in question is living with her in-laws.

The Palestinian understandings of patrilocality and patrilineality imply that the married women's primary everyday relationships become those of their husbands' families. Joseph asserts that a woman remains the responsibility of her agnatic family, despite her marriage (1999: 124). And like Clarke (2007: 383), she emphasizes that the responsibility to protect and control the whereabouts of a woman remains with her brothers (Joesph 1999: 124). In everyday life, however, a married woman's husband's family is decisive in these matters. The in-laws care for her financially and oversee her movements. If her brothers do not agree with their sister's husband, who is primarily responsible for his wife, a family meeting takes place to resolve the dispute. If she is living in their house, however, it is often the women's in-laws to which she is responsible day-to-day. The wife is obliged to her mother-in-law, and must undertake chores in the house, take care of the children of her husband's sisters, and share in the daily running of the household. This is true whether a woman is married to a detainee or to a man who is not imprisoned. But when a husband is imprisoned, he can no longer mediate the relationship between the woman and her in-laws. As Mervat's case demonstrates, her husband showed outstanding loyalty to her, and they moved away from his family home, as she wished. When he was incarcerated, the position of the husband was transferred to his family, and his responsibilities were distributed between his mother, brother, and sister. The lines of affect centered on protection, control, and responsibility are intrinsic to Palestinian notions of kinship, and were also potential sources of tacit, yet ongoing, domestic conflict between Mervat and her in-laws.

Fatemeh's case illustrates the complex and potentially ambiguous relationship between a woman and her brother-in-law, who have to be close but, due to the ambiguity of their closeness, are both *ġarībeen* (close) and *ajnabeen* (strange). Intrinsic to their qarabah is the potential of a sexual relationship that could be consummated upon Fatemeh's husband's death, a likely scenario in the context of the Israeli-Palestinian conflict. The two of them being alone together therefore comes close to compromising Fatemeh's virtue. All it takes is a rumor.

Subtler than a brother-in-law who fulfills the obligation to protect the wife of his brother is the slight mode of control pursued by a sister-in-law. Fatemeh's sister-in-law, for example, wanted to ensure that knowledge of Fatemeh's intimate thoughts did not become known to anyone other than her in-laws, and that she would not leave the house without their knowledge. It was her particular obligation, as the person with access to women's private forums, to ensure that Fatemeh's loyalty was to the sister-in-law's family.[5] The relationship between a woman and her mother-in-law is rarely without complexities.

Due to a woman's dependence on her husband's family for her livelihood, housing, and protection and support for her children, what I call the "whole of obligations" constitutes a space in which a detainee's wife becomes more closely tied to his family (Bergson 1912 [2004]). In this manner, family indeed becomes closer in the face of hardship.

How practices of care and control unfold and make families close can be thought of as constituting the duration of Palestinian notions of kinship— always already there, whether or not a woman's husband has been incarcerated. What occurs when a husband goes to prison is that all the virtual obligations intrinsic to duration are actualized for his wife (Bergson 1912 [2004]: 196). Bergson uses the image of an inverted cone, rising from a base representing contraction, with the entirety of the virtual actualized in the rising and narrowing cone. This image provides an apt picture of this tightening around the detainees' wives.

Whereas this contraction is a way to conceptualize detainees' wives' situations theoretically, it is their lived experience, too: the relationship with their in-laws narrows and closes in on them. In Amina's case, allegedly the opposite happened: her relations with her in-laws were dilated because they live in Amman. Because of the demolition of her family home, her consanguineal family lived farther apart than they would have preferred. In spite of this, Amina shares something with the other women: the relational contraction of her life, in the sense that she was even more entangled in familial gestures of care than she would have been before her husband's incarceration. For detainees' wives, becoming close therefore means a closing in of the relational space around them.

Evidently, this phenomenon does not pertain only to my interlocutors. Any situation in which a family is under pressure would most likely result in a similar contraction of lifeworlds, be it due to illness, poverty, or even male absence due to immigration (see, for example, the work on wives of Moroccan immigrants by Alice Eliott (2015)). This is because the contraction is always already present as part of Palestinian duration. The outline here therefore speaks to Amalia Sa'ar's (2001) analysis of how Palestinian women in Israel must strike a balance between weakness and power in order to gain the protection and help of their families. Although Sa'ar's interlocutors seem to be primarily working women who enjoy social status and certain privileges, her analysis is in tune with my own in this chapter, as exemplified above all by the title of her article: "Lonely in Your Firm Grip." The difference between Sa'ar's interlocutors and mine is the increased firmness of the grip on detainees' wives during their husbands' confinements.

Doubt and Duration of Palestinian Kinship

As al-Ali portrayed in his cartoon, the stronghold of the Palestinian family rests on gendered complicity: men fight and give their lives for Palestine; women support them and reproduce new generations of Palestinians. We may think of this dynamic as an aspect of the Palestinian duration. The absence of an incarcerated husband triggers obligations that are part of this duration, which I have also termed the "whole of obligation." The foregrounding of temporality in both of these terms make them especially apt for understanding the complexities of those left behind after incarceration. Lines of connectivity and affect are reconfigured, as the husband's absence is repeatedly realized in the mundane practices of control, protection, and responsibility that are exercised over the wife in his absence. A similar movement of absence constantly making itself felt unfolds through the practices a detainee's wife engages in to stay related to the detainee.

Perhaps counterintuitively, detention does not appear to dissolve Palestinian families. Rather than being ripped apart, the social relationships surrounding a detainee become closer. Aspects of control, protection, and responsibility are intensified—aspects that delineate how the wives of detainees are cared for in the wake of their husbands' incarcerations.

But whereas these protective mechanisms hold the family together, make its members closer, and allow them to cope with external encroachments, my concern has been to show how this in fact situates the wife as a figure with enlarged responsibilities, and one who experiences an enclosure of her feelings of living in that situation. My concern is the extent to which this enclosure amounts to an instance of aspect blindness in the Palestinian moral discourse on the family as the stronghold that keeps the Palestinian community intact in the face of occupation: this moral imperative means the slow but steady contraction of relationships around a wife. As the ethnography clearly shows, this contraction of care affords the wife of a detainee a subject position that she can inhabit and use to make her lifeworld livable, even without her husband (see Butler 1997 and Gammeltoft 2013). In the case of an absent husband's wife, kinship appears as an unchanging signpost of belonging. My interest in this chapter has been to delineate the rhythm of kinship relations and the thin line between care and control.

Carsten's recent engagement (2011) with notions of substance and relatedness can help us think about the wider political implication of such a narrowing of care around the prisoners' wives. If we think of substance, here, in the sense of consanguine relations, it seems that even in an endogamous society like Palestine, where affinal ties are in fact always already consanguine, there is an element of doubt as to how they can be trusted. I had numerous discussions with my baffled informants about the fact that I lived with my partner but we were not married. Of course, they knew that this has long been the norm in Europe, yet I had difficulties in communicating how I could actually trust this person when we were not married. The leap of faith I made seemed completely unsubstantiated to my interlocutors, across generations.

In his work on Palestinian kinship in refugee camps in Lebanon, Sylvain Perdigon argues that knowing one's spouse is closely linked to Islamic notions of *ar-rahim*, the God-given womb (2011, 2014). He concludes that the way in which Palestinian kinship is lived in Palestinian refugee camps in

Lebanon hinges on Islamic theology. I am hesitant to unequivocally apply this conclusion to contemporary Palestine. Yet Perdigon's elegant analysis of the imbricated matters of trust and consanguinity may enlighten our understanding of the potentially suffocating circumstances of the confined husband's wife. The husband is what ties a woman, his wife, to his family. Through his role as a father of her children, their blood is mixed. While she will always be a stranger to his family in some sense, the blending of substance through their children renders her a legitimate part of the family. In his absence, it becomes clear that this link was in fact always fraught with doubt. The lack of faith that a wife's loyalty will stay with her in-laws in her husband's absence surfaces precisely in the enclosing maneuvers of care undertaken to ensure that very same loyalty. This points to the primacy of consanguine relations, that is, endogamous marriage, as the foundation on which the idea of a collective of Palestinians rests. Twinned to it in importance, however, is doubt in kinship's potential to offer substance to any idea of a collective of Palestinians. This feeling of doubt runs like an undercurrent in every gesture of sisterly care, public speech, and political effort that goes into showing how vital and long-standing an institution the Palestinian family is. The braiding of importance with doubt has only tightened further with every year the occupation continues, as the Palestinians fear, if not extinction, then dilation. Their doubt in the duration of the Palestinian family is the poison they swallow.

CHAPTER 5

―――

Solitude in Marriage

Lonely the day came to you
Lonely
A lonely day came to you from the window
And all you opened [for it] was the silence of
    the closet
(where your wakeful remains lie
on blood frozen on the floor tiles)
                    —Ghada al-Shafi'i

This verse by al-Shafi'i evokes loneliness, silence, and a sense of being frozen—all feelings my interlocutors conveyed to me about the years of living with an absent spouse. But as an outsider to Palestinian culture and society, I hesitate to claim knowledge about married life for detainees' wives.

In her seminal article "Wittgenstein and Anthropology," Das makes a plea for "a hesitancy in the way in which we habitually dwell among our concepts of culture, of everyday life, or of the inner" (1998: 172). This compelling juxtaposition of hesitancy and argument seems crucial, particularly with regard to ethnographic engagements with contexts suffused with myriad forms of violence.

The Israeli-Palestinian conflict is one such context, and within it, arguments are made forcefully, stubbornly, and without the slightest hint of doubt. If nothing else, I hope this book offers my readers at least a moment's hesitancy before they close their minds and thoughts to what it means to live as the family of a Palestinian detainee. To achieve this aim I rely on Das's reading of Cavell on the theme of how to receive or grasp knowledge of the other and how his work invites an analysis of how knowledge, rather than being something to be found, is something that one can (only) aspire to (see Das 2011). Das advances our understanding of this problem by proposing that "the problem of knowledge has two sides, what is it to know but also how can I bear to be known, thus pairing the problem of knowing with that of confessing" (2011: 949). Crucial to this particular chapter is how Das offers us a gendered division of knowledge, and in doing so takes the register of confession, or the "daring to bear the gaze of another on oneself," to have a feminine form (950).

In pairing with the question of how it is possible to know and be known by another human being, this chapter asks what kinds of marriage and what forms of intimacy are possible in the wake of Israel's detention of Palestinian men.

I examine what it means to be part of a conjugal relation in which being together means seeing each other once, twice, or, in the best case, maybe twenty times annually for forty-five minutes through scratched Plexiglas. During such a visit to the prison, conjugal intimacy means exchanging words through a phone in an atmosphere of anxious need for intimacy, sometimes with a whole range of relatives, including mother, wife, children, and sisters, all present and sharing that need. Sometimes, spouses are not allowed to visit, and information about the other passes through a detainee's mother to his wife, or through the couple's children. Other times, knowledge about one another is exchanged through letters whose words are redacted and desensitized, revealing nothing but facts that could be shared with anyone.

Beginning with the means and forums available to my interlocutors to sustain intimacy during the husband's incarceration, I investigate how the conjugal relationship is configured in such a context—a context one could relate to Pinto's (2014) work in India about women on the margins of marriage. Here I would add, though, that in the "captive conjugate"—a term I use to refer to a detained husband and wife—both husbands and wives inhabit, albeit differently, conjugal marginality. I therefore ask what intimacy means and what fills the void left by the detained husbands' physical absence in the habitual and emotional lives of their wives. In doing so I hope to repair a common misreading of Cavell that, as Das argues, concerns the point that "in making the knowledge of others a metaphysical difficulty, philosophers deny how real the practical difficulty is of coming to know another person, and how little we can reveal of ourselves to another's gaze, or bear of it" (2011: 949). Here I flesh out how the knowledge of the other during incarceration is precisely a practical difficulty that inhibits intimacy among Palestinian detainees, their wives, and their families.

In his essay "The Uncanniness of the Ordinary," Cavell evokes marriage as an image of domesticity employed in tragedy: "It stands to reason that if some image of human intimacy, call it marriage, or domestication, is the fictional equivalent of what the philosophers of ordinary language understand as the ordinary, call this image of the everyday as the domestic, then the threat to the ordinary that philosophy names skepticism, should show up in fiction's favorite threats to forms of marriage, namely, in forms of melodrama and tragedy" (1988: 176). To render marriage emblematic of the ordinary invites examination of how the conjugate is configured during incarceration, despite the gloss that it is ordinary in the occupied Palestinian territories, owing to the sheer number of Palestinian families with a male relative incarcerated in Israel.[1] This examination is informed by Cavell's notion of tragedy as imbued with enduring skepticism. The notion of tragedy in relation to Palestinians incarcerated in Israel is nonetheless far from an invocation of pride in the national struggle for statehood and the notion of sumūd in the face of the occupation. When I evoke the notion of tragedy, it is to focus on the meaning of incarceration for the wives of the detainees, rather than the meaning it has for Palestinians as a collective, or for detainees themselves.

Furthermore, I take Cavell's notion of marriage as my point of departure for inquiry into the ordinary through the lens of conjugal intimacy: "Marriage here is being presented as an estate meant not as a distraction from the pain of constructing happiness from a helpless, absent world, but as the scene in which the chance for happiness is shown as the mutual acknowledgment of separateness, in which the prospect is not for the passing of years (until death parts us) but for the willing repetition of days, willingness for the everyday (until our true minds become unreadable to one another)" (1988: 178). Here, one senses Cavell's reliance on Wittgenstein's ideas of forms of life as a premise for intelligibility and community (Viefhues-Bailey 2008: 5). This reliance becomes evident in how Cavell conceives of marriage as an entanglement between an ordinary resting on both the "repetition of days" and acknowledgment of the other. Acknowledgment occurs through reading, and allowing oneself to be known by, the other. According to Cavell's definition, marriage lasts as long as it is possible, or willed, for the partners to be intelligible to each other.

Cavell's definition of marriage could in fact be seen to resonate with notions of mutual respect and obligation intrinsic to Muslim marriage according to the Islamic philosopher al-Ghazali (1058–1111; see Farah 1984). To al-Ghazali, marital obligations regard moderation and good manners in twelve matters including cohabitation, jealousy, intimate relations, and producing children (Farah 1984: 93). These obligations are translated into the practical arrangements that enable marriage to take place in an atmosphere of mutual recognition (Farah 1984: 98). In contrast, Cavell's notion of marriage hinges on the seemingly metaphysical "willingness for the everyday." In this sense, the two definitions seem far apart. Nonetheless, both emphasize what it takes for a marriage to dissolve. To al-Ghazali, a marriage can be dissolved if mutual obligations are not met. To Cavell, marriage ends when the spouses' true minds become unreadable to each other. Since incarceration simultaneously severs the possibility of fulfilling obligations and the possibility of knowing and making each other known through the willing repetition of the everyday, the juxtaposition of al-Ghazali and Cavell invites us to question whether a marriage in which one spouse is incarcerated is, in fact, still a marriage.

Invoking the idea of an analytical continuum, I analyze the absent body on the one hand with reference to the Palestinian notion of sumūd (Sayigh 1993), according to which the absence of a detainee from the lives of his relatives does not alter the bonds between them; if anything his absence is supposed to strengthen the bonds, because of the honor generated by his activities of resistance. One the other hand, I consider Cavell's reading of Wittgenstein, according to which the body is the field of expression of the soul (Cavell 1979: 356). Cavell remarks that I neither *have* nor am *in* my body: my body is simply who I am (397–398). In this sense, the body becomes the only way in which to know the other, albeit imperfectly, by engaging in the willing reading of each other's bodies.

Practicing Captive Conjugality

The ethnography in this section describes how aspects of the habitual are central to an understanding of how a husband is not felt to be lost even though he has in fact disappeared from the everyday life of a detainee's wife. Amina is a good example of this situation. As mentioned earlier, she now lives in a village in the West Bank, together with her four children in a newly built concrete house. Her husband has been sentenced to twenty-seven years for activities against the Israeli state, of which he has served fourteen. Amina talks about her situation in ways that fit her personality as a *niswan bassita*, a "simple woman." Her vocabulary is often understated, and her mode of speaking is different from the predominant mode of narrating suffering among Palestinians as a source of honor and a sign of proper Palestinian-ness. I asked how she did it, living through the first five years without per-mission to visit her husband. She replied, "It was difficult, I used to make him breakfast in the morning before he went to work and lunch when he came back. But after he was imprisoned I got used to the idea that he is not here."[2] I asked her if she missed her husband all the time or only on special occa-sions. Amina answered, "No, always. And especially when I feel bad, or when I have a problem or feel tired . . . when we were sitting together and spoke with each other. And his way of making me feel better when I am exhausted or when there is something making me angry."

Cooking breakfast for a spouse is probably one of the least dramatic aspects of a conjugal life, yet to Amina, it was how her day started when her husband formed a part of her daily life. She still gets up and cooks breakfast, gets her three youngest daughters ready for school, and makes sure her mother has her first cup of sweet tea. The only thing missing is her husband. Her mention of this ordinary moment of life indicates how, to her, it is first and foremost the habitual elements of life that are altered because of her husband's imprisonment. Now that she has temporary permission to visit him twice a month, Amina and her husband can talk over issues during visits, but such exchanges do not replace the habitual togetherness inherent in sharing a meal.

The absence of an ordinary part of a married couple's life is experienced by a detainee's social network, too. Fardoz too told me that she can no longer participate in conversations with other women about relationships and sex because of her husband's imprisonment. When other women discuss these issues, Fardoz has nothing to bring to the conversation, as her sexual life is considered nonexistent in the absence of her husband: "What can I say? If I say something it will be misunderstood." She elaborated to me that, whereas detainees' wives know what it is like "to miss the person who makes me most happy," other women might judge her words to mean that she is not showing sumūd or waiting for her husband to be released. An admission that she misses him, or misses a sexual life, amounts to weakness, which potentially threatens public discourse about support for detainees and the national struggle. Doubt about a woman's support for the revolutionary national movement and her morality promotes suspicion and rumor, so indicative of conflict. What alters Fardoz's mode of being in close friendships is thus the lack of a reference point, the man with whom her feelings of desire can be stored safely. We spoke about what she does when these feelings arise, and she asked, "Should I dream about it or forget it? His sentence is a hundred years. When my dreams fly away I try to do other things, I read, or speak to my children. I try to think of it as a test from God. But at night, the dreams come. What can I do about it?" In the absence of her husband, Fardoz cannot acknowledge her longing for him. Aaron Goodfellow understands the reverberations of a break in a sexual relationship as a "passing of a way of being in the world" (2008: 290). As Amina and Fardoz show, the incarceration of their husbands has dissolved a habitual way of being, and of being together, that is intrinsic to a conjugal relationship in the eyes of both themselves and their relatives and friends.

Contours of a Heroic Absence: The Bed Is Cold at Night

Among the gallery of Palestinian heroic figures, some occupy a distinct space in narratives of revolutionary struggle. One such figure is Yara's husband, whom we heard about in the Introduction. He has been in and out of both Israeli and Palestinian prisons for decades due to his opposition to both the Israeli occupation and the Palestine Liberation Organization's acceptance of the Oslo Accords in 1993. He is now imprisoned in Israel based on accusations that he was centrally engaged in violent acts of resistance against the Israeli state. Yara is a close friend and neighbor of a Palestinian friend of mine who introduced us early during my time in the West Bank. She met her husband when she was thirteen, but it was twelve years before they were married, due to his political activities. Yara knew that politics was the air her husband breathed, and she herself became involved in politics: "I was really in love with him, and I did not care about other things. I think it was enough that my name was related to his name; I did not want to think further than that." Yara's marriage crystallizes a "political marriage," in which both spouses are active politically within the same movement, and it is their political rather than their agnatic status that designates this as a preferred union (Johnson, Abu Nahleh, and Moors 2009; see also Rosenfeld 2004). Yara and her husband lived together for three years before he was arrested, at which time she was pregnant with their third child:

> I lived it moment by moment because it was the first time [he was imprisoned] when we were married. He stayed one hundred days in the [isolation] cells, he was interrogated for three months, and we cannot see him, we know nothing about him. The lawyer was the only one who can see him. That was difficult, I had two kids, I was pregnant, and I was working, I didn't stop going to work. I guess it gives you power when you decide to continue your life. Maybe, if I were to face it now, I will not be able to continue, but at that time, I was full of energy because everyone experienced the same suffering and we were all in pain; all the people were united and we helped each other.

The intensity of Yara's account of the time of her husband's most severe imprisonment shines through in how she alternates between the present and past tense. It happened then, but the feelings of it are with her, now. This resembles Cavell's reflections on the value of returning to his entries in his autobiography, thereby allowing himself "to follow a double time scheme, so that I can accept an invitation in any present from, or to, any past, as memory serves and demands to be served" (2010: 8). We saw this coexistence of past, present, and future temporalities in Chapter 3 as well, and, in Yara's case, it reveals that her husband's imprisonment persistently invites her to be at once in her past and her present. It is an invitation she cannot refuse. Revisiting her past both allows and condemns her to reflect on the weight of her past feelings. This dual temporality is evident in Yara's reflections on her feelings then and now: "I did not feel that he was away. I was sad inside, but I was not thinking about it, because I did not want myself to reach a situation of sadness. When I was younger, I was not that sensitive; now I cannot stand life without him. . . . I did not allow myself to be a weak person, but I am sure that it affected me negatively. Now I feel how sad I am, and these nightmares I have every night about soldiers coming to take my husband, it is recent, I have never felt like this before." Yara's personal life folds into the Palestinian revolutionary movement. Her toggling between the personal and the political, the past and present, elucidates the impossibility of escaping the conflict over temporalities of hope, collective loyalty, and betrayal as she analyzes her personal feelings. As Yara's life demonstrates, affect comprises both how feelings are managed publicly and politically and how feelings are lived. When we finished our conversation, she sat for a while in her chair, as if realizing the significance of her story. I stumbled for appropriate words; all I could come up with was "ṣaʿb, ṣaʿb jiddan. ʿindik šaḵsiyya qawiyya" (It is hard, very hard. You have a strong personality), in an insufficient attempt to acknowledge the force of her story. She looked at me, shrugged and said, "Yes, but the bed is cold at night."

Yara's pride as a Palestinian who has a husband struggling in the collective movement for statehood coexists with the desolation of living with a void left by an absent spouse. Yara casts her present sensitivity in light of her aging; she is nearing fifty. Her sensitivity is entangled with collective fatigue from a struggle that has come to what feels like an indefinite halt. This entanglement is part of why she no longer feels able to endure life without her husband. Her choice of words is significant, since her husband is one of the few detainees who still enjoys public acknowledgment, both locally and nationally. Despite his presence in the public discourse, she feels that she is living without him. Understanding the "without" leads us toward her final utterance: "The bed is cold at night." Resonating with Fardoz's account of floating desire, these words concern her husband's physical absence.

The stories of Yara, Fardoz, and Amina illustrate the reconfiguration of the affective lines of physical intimacy that occur with incarceration. Al-Ghazali stresses that marriage is a container of desire (see Farah 1984), but the physical absence of the husband from his wife's realm, as the accounts here suggest, thwarts the idea of marriage as a container of desire. For instance, al-Ghazali outlines the preferable time and place in an ordinary month for a husband and wife to find a space for conjugal intimacy (Farah 1984: 107). Since incarceration makes intimate relations impossible, the question is whether desire can in fact be contained in the form of marriage that incarceration allows.

Because desire is saturated with morality, it is a sensitive topic to discuss, even in a confidential setting. For my interlocutors, physical desire was something contained within the personal realm and something that could proliferate in public spheres as rumors (that this or that woman was wearing makeup and going to parties in order to attract male attention). Detainees' wives are thus constantly reminded of the absence of their husbands. The form of marriage is still intact, yet in place of its substance is a void, one that is not experienced as a lack but that is woven inextricably into the women's lives. Due to national politics and the value attached to resistance against Israel, this change is not voiced, but is merely assumed to be a worthy national sacrifice that calls for sumūd.

The unacknowledged sexuality of detainees' wives also concerns the therapists who offer these women psychosocial assistance. One psychotherapist pointed out that if she could get the women to speak about how it felt to be physically alone, she would consider it an achievement. As noted earlier, in public Palestinian discourse, the acknowledgment of distress seems to rest on the visual evidence of trauma and violence, and the categorization of victimhood. Consequently, for a detainee's wife, her desolation is not visible, and the vocabulary available to represent her life revolves around pride and derivative suffering. Cavell asserts that the detachment of words from the body engenders doubt in the world. From this point of view, focusing only on visual markers of suffering when attempting to understand the experiences of detainees' wives engenders doubt as to what their distress actually consists of, or whether it actually exists. To acknowledge the experiences of detainees' wives, then, requires that we reconfigure the relation of visuality, words, and corporeality.

The Possibility of Knowing the Other During Incarceration

I now wish to consider the materialization that appears in, and fills, the void of physical nearness, namely, letters and diaries:

> In the name of God, one day I was so upset and angry and I did not know what to do, so I just took a piece of paper and a pen and started to write a letter to my husband; I sat down and began to express my feelings in words. I did not know how to start and what to write, but then I just wrote what I felt and suddenly I found the paper full. Then I read the letter and I was surprised of the words I could write. I do not know how I wrote them, I felt that my heart made the pen move and draw the letters on the paper.
>
> I felt so happy and realized that I was able to write all this. Sometimes I hold my husband's pictures and start to talk to him and tell him about everything. I tell him what makes me happy and what makes me angry, and I look for a long time at his picture, and

after that I start to cry because I know that he does not hear me and
he cannot respond to my calls and to my complaints. I find myself
crying, just looking at his picture, no one around me feels with me.
I feel that I am alone even though I have three kids surrounding
me, but they do not know how I feel. I always feel that there is
something missing. When I visit friends I feel good, but when I
come back I feel sad again because I go by myself and come back
by myself.

This excerpt from Maryam's diary alludes to the possibility of finding a
language through which to let her husband know her feelings. However, she
knows the limits of talking to a photo, and her efforts to make herself known
to her husband leave her in tears. Her husband's absence is tangible in the
sense that she can enter into other relations situationally, yet she enters and
leaves them alone, despite the fact that she is the mother of three children.
Another excerpt from Maryam's diary points toward the ineffability of her
feelings and how they are contained in her body: "God, how do the days pass
when I am alone and sad? I could not find anyone to talk to, so I looked at
the moon and told it about my feelings and how my life is, and I asked the
moon about my husband and how he is doing and what is he doing right
now? Is he sleeping? Is he thinking about me as I think of him now? Is he
looking at you as I look at you right here? I cried until I fell asleep and prayed
to God to help me, to protect me and my kids and my husband as well." This
excerpt concerns the possibility of knowing and making oneself known
when bodily coexistence is severed by incarceration. This brings me to Cavell's
writings on skepticism in light of the relationship of the body and the soul
(see Csordas 1994, 2008; Gammeltoft 2008).

Skepticism and tragedy, Cavell argues, "conclude with the condition of
human separation, with a discovering that I am I; and the fact that the alternative to my acknowledgment of the other is not my ignorance of him but
my avoidance of him, call it my denial of him" (1979: 408). Maryam does not
deny her husband. In the above excerpt, she expresses a wish to acknowledge
her husband. What dawns on her is that she is alone, paradoxically because
she is part of a conjugal relationship—she forms part of a "one," but incarceration has broken the conjugate by separating the spouses. The experience
of being separate when she is in fact one *with* her husband implies that she is
forced not to acknowledge him. She must unwillingly avoid acknowledgment

because she cannot know him. How to claim that she does not know the man who is the father of their three children? Cavell elaborates:

> The idea of the allegory of words is that human expressions, the human figure, to be grasped, must be read. To know another mind is to interpret a physiognomy, and the message of this region of the Investigations is that this is not a matter of "mere knowing." I have to read the physiognomy and see the creature according to my reading, and treat it according to my seeing. The human body is the best picture of the human soul—not, I feel like adding, primarily because it represents the soul but because it expresses it. The body is the field of expression of the soul. The body is of the soul; it is the soul's; a human soul has a body. (1979: 356)

During incarceration, husband and wife become unreadable to each other. Maryam cannot read the expressions of her husband because his "body [as] the field of expression of the soul" is absent. Present instead are the disjointed lines that connect her quotidian obligations to an imaginary conversation. In this conversation, the affect described above emerges as the subject that is Maryam. Maryam's situation breeds skepticism in her. When there is no body to acknowledge, she cannot experience her separateness from her husband, beyond profound doubt. Doubt here is not a residue to the absence of a body. Rather, doubt emerges because it is through and with the body that Maryam and her husband create and sustain a place in language for them to know and be known by each other—thus evoking Das's insight that coming to know and bear the gaze of another is indeed a practical difficulty (2011: 950). Notably, Maryam's failure to acknowledge her imprisoned husband is not due to any inherent discrepancy between her feelings and her ability to express them. Her diaries can be aligned with Cavell's hesitancy toward the "private language argument": "So the fantasy of a private language, underlying the wish to deny the publicness of language, turns out, so far, to be a fantasy, or fear, either of inexpressiveness, in which I am not merely unknown, but in which I am powerless to make myself known; or one in which what I express is beyond my control" (1979: 351). Here Cavell suggests that the basic premise for a lived experience to be known and acknowledged by others is the existence of an adequate standing language—one that allows for a place to know and acknowledge that experience (355). The distinction between knowing and acknowledging is key in a standing language. To know does not necessarily mean to acknowledge, since the latter implies that one is engaging in a process of reading the other and making oneself read. Failure to acknowledge, in this view, does *not* rest on the fact that certain types of lived experience are per se inexpressible, but on the fact that the standing language available to describe them is inadequate. In other words, it is an incomplete standing language that renders lived experiences inexpressible. Whereas language is never complete, the circumstance of incarceration intensifies such inexpressibility.

From this perspective, incarceration configures the possibilities for both Maryam and her husband to acknowledge each other. According to Cavell's analytical premise regarding the body as the field of expression of the soul, the impossibility of acknowledging the other would be due to the absence of a body through which at least some knowledge of the other can be gained.

I would argue, however, that the difficulty of Maryam and her husband acknowledging each other rests less on the fact that the body as the medium of reading the other has disappeared. Rather, the body's disappearance causes a displacement of language so that, in the absence of her husband from everyday talk and interaction, Maryam has only the standing language about national heroes available to her to know and make herself known to her husband. This indicates how the conjugal relationship in this situation, despite the still-extant legal marriage, causes a separation between the spouses, one that is arguably unique to a conjugal relation: it occurs through the carving out of the couple's bodies from the domestic intimacy that they shared. According to Cavell, acknowledging the other's separateness from oneself is a condition of knowing, of being able to acknowledge the other. The above, however, makes apparent how the separateness caused by incarceration makes it impossible to allow oneself to be read by the other, since the way in which husband and wife are supposed to read each other is displaced from habitual practices to dreamy conversations with the moon, or words in a diary. Cavell, describing everyday language, asserts, "I do not picture my everyday knowledge of others as confined but as exposed. It is exposed, I would like to say, not to possibilities but to actualities, to history. There is no possibility of human relationship that has not been enacted" (1979: 433). Imprisonment, however, confines knowledge and mutuality so that they cannot become exposed and enacted, thus fundamentally subverting the possibility of marriage during incarceration.

Knowing and Doubt

Habit is one clue to the making of the link between doubt and the larger issue of skepticism, in the sense of the enactment of everyday practices, including speaking together (see Das et al. 2014). Cavell asks, "Could we say that the practices are both an answer to skepticism because human relationships are enacted through them? And that they produce skepticism because you (over time) do not know the other but he looks like the one you knew?" (1979: 433). The invocation of everyday practice as both a response to and a ground for skepticism mirrors the failed attempt by Maryam to make herself known by talking to her husband's photograph. In order to investigate how skepticism becomes part of the configuration of affect caused by incarceration, I analyze excerpts from the correspondence between another interlocutor, Aisha, and her detained husband. The first excerpt is written by Aisha's husband: "You are a part of me, no; actually you are all of me, not just a part. Maybe I am not being fair when I relate you to me, and to be clearer, I am part of you, not the opposite, and this part can be all, I love you a lot, and you are my love in all languages. The only thing I need after praying to God is to be with you, to be close to you forever." This reads as a conjecture that it is possible for spouses to acknowledge each other even when they do not share an everyday life. Alluding to the ambiguity of this point, however, are Aisha's husband's last words, which express a wish to be close to his wife. The desire to be close in the everyday appears, too, in the following letter from Aisha to her husband:

> I await each visit for you, visiting you without actually visiting you;
> I try to prove my love to you and how much I miss you by letters
> that you can translate in your or in our own way, you do not leave
> any word that can explain your unlimited and your warm love to
> me without telling me it. I await your letters, I read them while we
> drink our noonday coffee together. Oh my love, how much I long
> for you, and how much I miss experiencing with you the small
> details of life be it in bad or good circumstances, I am always sure
> that I have chosen the right choice (you), you are a great thing for

me, I thank God each day for giving me you, the presence of you in my life is what makes me continue and makes me stronger, and more patient. You are here with us, even if you are not here, sharing every moment with us, at home, and in school, we have the most beautiful kids, Meiza and Ahmad, so let us pray for them to have good luck and to be good persons. They are a piece of you, they look like you in everything and in their social behavior too, they love the family, and the house, they are making us, me and you, very proud. How much I love them. They are just two kids but they are special in kind and in behavior.

In an effort parallel to a desire to be close on an everyday basis, Aisha's letter expresses how she feels her husband *is* present, in the way she and their children enact their everyday routines. Aisha also addresses how her husband's written words convey his feelings for her without him speaking them to her, as he would have were he not detained. The correspondence between Aisha and her husband thus contests Cavell's contention of the body as the only means through which one can acknowledge the other. By way of their letters, Aisha and her husband appear to be engaging in a process of reading each other. This becomes possible through their shared language, which is evoked in the letter's first line. Evidently, this possibility does not satisfy Aisha's longing for her husband to be an actual part of her everyday existence. In this sense, the letter reflects the ordinary in its twin meaning as the thing that produces skepticism and as the practice that attempts to counter it.

In the following letter, which Anwar (Aisha's husband) wrote shortly after he was handed his life sentence, we sense the affective configuration of the captive togetherness:

My soul Imm Ahmad,
I just came back from the court. It finished early today at 4 o'clock, I came back to find all the detainees waiting for me, after knowing my sentence from Israeli TV. The court today was full of journalists, they were asking me about my feelings, and whether I regret what I did or not. I answered that I do not regret anything and that I am proud of what I did. I was feeling normal and safe, because I know that God is the only one who can sentence me, and I do not believe in their court. I know God is there, and he will give us our freedom soon.

I didn't care about the sentence of this occupation court. I don't believe in it, I only believe in God's sentence, so I hope you share this feeling with me. The sentence was presented on the TV and on the radio, and I ask God for forgiveness because I asked you to focus on the media. I forgot that God is above all, and he is the only one who can help.

In this letter there is no evocation of connectedness, only comments on the sentence and continuous references to the occupation, the media, the Palestinian cause of the detainees, and God as the only legitimate judge of Anwar's violent acts. How Anwar expresses his reaction to the sentence is reflected in what Aisha wrote to him shortly after he was sentenced:

Your case file has been closed now, we do not believe in this court, nor in the occupation; its existence is not legal, and everything the occupation does is rejected by the Palestinians, and also they [the Israelis] do not even have the right to be in Palestine.

I know how things are going now. I know also how strong you are, and how patient you are. You never give up. Each one of us will support the other, you have given me all the positive parts of my personality, and all that came after I knew you as a lover and as a husband. I know how you will be thinking after this court's sentence, we are two close lovers, despite the occupation and the checkpoints and the suffering.

It's forbidden for me to see you, but my eyes go to you with my kids. I leave you to go to you, and when I am busy away from you I will be thinking about you; your picture is always here with me, it is all over me. I am also a detainee in a difficult prison which is being far from you, and also it is my love to you. There you are standing as a holy tree, we do not care what the sentence will be, nor the theater of the court itself because you are in my heart and my mind always, despite the distance and the walls that separate us. And we will stay together forever, my love.

You will stay with us always despite your distance, we refer to you and we share with you the making of decisions, so do not be surprised if I send you a lot of questions from our children, it is just to make them feel the importance of your role in our life.

Also you are worried about Ahmad, as you told me, you are worried that he does not understand what father means, do not worry, my love, he is on the right track, because he understands what the relationship between children and their father is and he is feeling jealous of the children that have their father at home. He also feels sad when a detainee gets out of the prison and comes back to his children but you are still in there. Does that not show that he realizes what father means?

I argued earlier that Aisha's and Anwar's disavowal of the occupation could be seen as a fight against the skepticism that seems to have seeped into their relationship. Nowhere is this skepticism clearer than in the above letter, which reads like a reassurance that Anwar's detention has not meant anything for their relationship as spouses and as a family. Her final question, "Does that not show that he realizes what father means?" is nonetheless emblematic of Aisha's doubt that her son, who has never lived with his father, will know the meaning of the term. Aisha knows that no amount of cultivating fatherly love can compensate for this lack of an everyday routine. Its disappearance with incarceration reconfigures the lines of affect that circulate in and around the captive conjugate and result in the skeleton of a marriage.

The correspondence between Aisha and her husband resonates with Yara's story. When Yara was younger, she did not feel the absence of, or longing for, her husband. What cannot be overlooked in either of these cases, however, is the doubt. In Yara's account, it is a doubt about whether she can stand the separation any longer. And in Aisha's husband's letter it appears as an unconfirmed feeling that the visits will be severed because of his sentence. The change of tone in both Aisha's letter and her diary mirrors that of her husband, and is devoid of anything but political rhetoric. However, doubt about what the future will bring, in terms of their continuing to be part of each other without being together, is nonetheless present in their correspondence. From writing in a personal register, Aisha and her husband now employ a vernacular of nationalist affect. The change in their writings to each other can be thought of as displacement in language. By employing a nationalistic language that denies the legitimacy of the prison sentence, Aisha and Anwar displace their experience of skepticism in their relationship to a willed expression of skepticism toward the legitimacy of the sentencing body, the Israeli military court.

The void created by the severed conjugate in the cases of Maryam, Yara, and Aisha appears to inspire objectified images of the other. Particularly in the case of Aisha, the detainee and his wife were configured as individuals who can only know each other as the national subjects "the detainee" and "the detainee's wife." The habitual practices belonging to their former life are out of reach for the captive conjugate, who therefore alter their expressions from an intimate language to the standing language. Yara's account showed clearly how the invocation of the other through a vocabulary of national affect does not replace sharing an everyday life. To Yara, having a hero husband in prison does not compensate for her cold bed. In other words, incarceration constrains the possibility for detainees and their wives to engage in the "willing repetition of days, willingness for the everyday (until our true minds become unreadable to one another)." Maryam made this configuration apparent in the way she tried to elicit her husband by imagining that he may be talking to the moon in order to recall the face of his spouse, just like her.

Maryam's case recalls Strathern's idea of what appears in the gap of a severed relation. "Obviation" refers to what appears when a relation is severed. To Strathern, a cut refers to a new configuration of a relation (2004: 81). Within the cut of the severed conjugate, I have argued, appears to be a relation permeated by doubt, to such an extent that we can talk about skepticism. Maryam attempted to replace this skeptical relation of not knowing a husband with the moon in an effort to denounce her feeling of skepticism. The absence of an incarcerated husband therefore both configures a relation as one imbued with doubt and allows for a replacement of the void left by a husband's absence.

Enduring Skepticism

I conclude that incarceration suffuses the captive conjugate with skepticism. In an attempt to characterize skepticism in epistemology, Cavell writes: "At some early point in epistemological investigations, the world normally present to us (the world in whose existence, as it is typically put, we 'believe') is brought into question and vanishes, whereupon all connection with a world is found to hang upon what can be said to be 'present to the senses'; and that turns out, shockingly, not to be the world. It is at this point that the doubter finds himself cast into skepticism, turning the existence of the external world into a problem" (1988: 173). Skepticism—which doubts the connection between the world and what it "is found to hang upon"—illuminates what incarceration does to the relationships around the incarcerated. Skepticism occurs because of the circumscribed possibilities to read another's mind, which may cause spouses to become unreadable to each other. The only reminder of a marriage left for the captive conjugate is the will to take up the repetition of days, and the hope that they one day can read each other's minds.

This analysis speaks on the one hand to the analytical continuum of sumūd, according to which the absence of physical presence does not alter relations, and on the other to Cavell's assumption that the body is the field of expression of the soul—its absence fundamentally alters relations. The language of sumūd may displace the language of intimacy between spouses. This ethnography nonetheless proposes that the premise of sumūd cannot truly replace that which is displaced—namely, the physical presence of the husband and the sharing of an everyday existence. Sumūd, however, does appear as a way of denouncing the skepticism that separation engenders, since it is a language in which skepticism toward the occupation can be expressed. In this sense, my findings support at least to some extent Khalili's (2007) contention that narratives of sumūd offer some solace to Palestinians who cannot contextualize their personal affliction in either heroic or tragic genres of shared narration.

Concerning the body as the soul's field of expression, my analysis complicates Cavell's premise. It shows how conjugality is configured differently in the face of incarceration. It seems that such a configuration includes not only the way in which the spouses become unreadable to each other due to the lack of a habitual everyday routine but also the void of the husband's physical absence and the attendant consequent disappearance of an intimate language. In addition, incarceration seems to actualize captive conjugates, as a conjugality of letter writing that figured in the case of Aisha and Anwar. In this sense, marriage in the face of incarceration is possible, even if it is a volatile entity, over which the threat of skepticism looms large.

This conclusion returns us to the reconfigured triad of visuality, words, and corporeality that are necessary in order for the achievement of acknowledgment in the captive conjugate. Never quite fully there but never quite absent either. In the Palestinian standing language evolving around sumūd, visual markers of hurt is emphasized as a way to know and acknowledge suffering and forms of life.[3] Cavell, in contrast, presumes that knowledge and acknowledgment of the other can only take place if the body as the field of expression of the soul is present. I propose a slight shift of interpretation with regard to Cavell's analytical premise. We saw how a fundamental premise of Cavell's notion of language is how language that becomes detached from the body creates skepticism. Thus, if words stay connected to the body, acknowledgment is possible—even, I argue, when a body is actually missing. This connection is captured aptly by Das in regard to the status of knowledge in anthropology: "As in the case of belief, I cannot locate your pain in the same way as I locate mine. The best I can do is to let it happen to me. Now it seems to me that anthropological knowledge is precisely about letting the knowledge of the other happen to me" (1998: 192). Thus the premise for knowing the other during incarceration is perhaps no less under the threat of skepticism than that of the attempt to let another happen to me as an ethnographer.

The possibility of a captive conjugate can be actualized by each spouse letting the other happen to him or herself in the myriad ways that can happen during incarceration. Secondarily, this may also be a way of acknowledging what is implied by incarceration for the conjugate at a collective level. This acknowledgement seems to be denied in the Palestinian standing language because if all that is endured, not only by the detainee but by the detainee and his wife in relation to each other, were "allowed to happen" to the Palestinian collective, this would engender skepticism about the premise of sumūd itself: It would entail a realization that not everything can be endured.

CHAPTER 6

Enduring the Ordinary

It is a loss, my children lost the word "dad"; to me it is
the loss itself, losing him.

This is how Nadia expressed the loss of her first husband. Here I return to Nadia's situation and use it to analyze loss, endurance, womanhood, and the ordinary. In Chapter 2, I described Nadia's living room décor and we learned that she was the only one among the detainees' wives who was also the widow of a martyr. Expanding on how the loss of her husband affected her relationships, she emphasized how his death had been an invitation for her kin to intrude into her life. The family believed that she should remarry and become the wife of her late husband's brother. At first she did not want to at all, but after a while she agreed. "Now," she said, "I am married, but not in practice. . . . But when people intrude, there is protection." Nadia reveals that her marriage cannot be enacted in the practice of sharing a day-to-day life. Even so, her marriage functions as a shield against intruders, which at least gives her a sense of privacy. Perhaps it even allows her the *safe place* that was evoked by the psychotherapists discussed in Chapter 1 as a therapeutic aim of their interventions. Nadia sees the void left by both her deceased and incarcerated husbands, however, as much more than simply a place: "It's on the inside; there's an empty space, a hole in me."

Nadia's evocation of loss as emptiness refers to the death of her husband. However, paying attention to how she says, "*my children* lost the word 'dad,'" we might consider this loss as something other than bereavement. Nadia's deceased husband is the father of her three oldest children. The father of her last child is her deceased husband's brother, whom Nadia married after her first husband's death. Considering the strong connotations of loss and incarceration respectively, it is worth noting how in the above statement Nadia does not distinguish between the loss experienced by the children of her deceased husband and the experience of her last child, whose father has been detained. In Nadia's wording, all of the children have lost their father. The remaining parent is herself, their mother, regardless of who their father is, and was.

Nadia's words invite us to examine the meaning of motherhood in relation to detainees' wives' sense of womanhood, and in relation to the national discourse that surrounds the prisoners and their intimate ties. By analyzing the feelings of womanhood that incarceration creates for detainees' wives, I examine the configuration of affect during incarceration from the vantage point of the detainees' wives *as women*.

Through an investigation of the meaning of being a mother during a husband's incarceration in light of notions about "the Palestinian Mother," this chapter returns to the therapeutic trope of the safe place introduced in Chapter 1. I ponder whether the establishment of a safe place is in fact a possibility for the women who are the focus of this book: can and do they create an affective place that feels just safe enough to allow them to endure persistently and permanently? My aim is not to validate a therapeutic understanding of the women's lives, but rather to ask why such an understanding may not encompass these lives. In posing this question, I interrogate motherhood as a Palestinian defeat of skepticism in the face of incarceration.

The inquiry opens with a description of the mother as a Palestinian symbol, followed by an outline of how I understand the gap between motherhood as a symbol and my interlocutors' lives as women and mothers. I then analyze how particular aspects of womanhood are simultaneously elicited, obscured, and replaced during husbands' incarcerations. Finally, the chapter discusses the potential of the ordinary—as a site of recovery, of loss, or of the emptiness that Nadia voices.

Women, Mothers, and National Becoming

To understand the meaning of motherhood during incarceration we must return to the way in which some forms of affliction are voiced in occupied Palestine while other forms of distress are inarticulable. Motherhood is configured vis-à-vis a Palestinian moral discourse that revolves around suffering and heroism. Intrinsic to this discourse, to the gendered organization of Palestinian society, not the least with regard to violence, is that its center of gravity is younger men who are perceived to be the heroes of the resistance against Israel. They are the martyrs who have sacrificed their lives, while the detainees have put theirs on hold, all in the name of a Palestinian nation-state (see Nashif 2008; Khalili 2007; Massad 1995; Peteet 1991).

Women figure, too, in discourses about Palestinian national becoming. In contrast to the men who fight, women are evoked as the soil in which "manhood, respect and dignity" grow (Massad 1995: 474). In current national discourse, mothers, daughters, and sisters appear as supportive, yet secondary, figures in the Palestinian narrative (Massad 1995: 473). Through an analysis of the constitutional documents of the Palestine Liberation Organization and political communiqués from the first Intifada, Joseph Massad shows how women are represented as mothers destined to deliver the new warriors and mourn their loved ones and lost sons. This gendered organization of resistance was crystallized in al-Ali's cartoon depicting the family as the embodiment of both the plight and the endurance of Palestinians. Important work in anthropology has documented how Palestinian women, like Leila Khaled and other political heroines of the first Intifada, have participated directly and indirectly in activities of resistance in the public domain (Peteet 2005; Jean-Klein 2003; Sayigh 2008). Meanwhile, the general exhaustion of Palestinian society after the failed Oslo Accords and the second Intifada has meant that the gains around new forms of gendered, social organization under the first Intifada have evaporated (Johnson, Abu Nahleh, and Moors 2009). The gendered organization of resistance activities today can be conceptualized in line with Das's reflections on the intersection of gender and war: "Sex and death, reproduction and war, become part of the same configuration of ideas and institutions through which the nation-state sets up defences to stave off the uncertainty emanating from dangerous aliens and from the ravages of time" (2008: 285). In occupied Palestine one defense to "stave off the uncertainty emanating from dangerous aliens and from the ravages of time" has been to crystallize womanhood into figures that mobilize their work for the care of the nation. As described in Chapter 2 these figures take the form of images of the Palestinian mothers; not only as idiosyncratic mothers but also in the sense of an underlying semantics in which "mother" refers to woman as the motherland, or in the words of the Arabist Nathalie Khankan, "woman as Palestine" (2009: 122). Massad suggests that a reconfiguration of Palestinianness has taken place: to be Palestinian formerly implied to be born in the territorial motherland, whereas being Palestinian at present is thought to be inherited through the agnatic line (1995: 472). The meaning of the mother in the national discourse is thus simultaneously continuous and constant and also somewhat altered.

Emblematic of the contemporary discourse of Palestinian suffering are the mothers of heroic detainees like the woman addressed in the song, as well as the mothers and widows of martyrs, who mourn yet also keep the household and family together in the wake of destitution. Concurring with Allen (2009), I described this discourse in Chapter 1 as a politics of immediation. It permeates the Palestinian media and everyday conversation, and is braided into the policy ambitions of psychosocial interventions aimed at those labeled secondary victims. A significant question, however, is what the national emphasis on heroic men, on the violent, so-called traumatic events they encounter, and on the twin of lamenting, nurturing mothers means for how detainees' wives experience themselves as (Palestinian) women, and how others perceive them, and how the two intersect. To further our understanding, I quote Wittgenstein as rendered in Das's work *Life and Words*:

> The formation of the subject as a gendered subject is then molded through complex transactions between the violence as the originary moment and the violence as it seeps into the ongoing relationships and becomes a kind of atmosphere that cannot be expelled to an "outside." I want to evoke at this point Wittgenstein's sense of there being no outside and the image of turning back that he offers, as thinking of a humble way of using words: "The ideal, as we think of it, is unshakeable. You can never get outside it; you must always turn back. There is no outside; outside you cannot breathe." This image of turning back evokes not so much the idea of a return, as a turning back to inhabit the same space now marked as a space of destruction, in which you must live again. Hence, the sense of the everyday in Wittgenstein as the sense of something recovered. How you make such a space of your own not through an ascent into transcendence but through a descent into the ordinary. (Das 2007: 62)

In Palestine, Wittgenstein's formulation of the permeability between the inner and the outer speaks to how the language of Palestinian national becoming is braided into the intimate sphere of individual detainees' wives. The lack of an alternative context in which women's suffering can be voiced and heard invites us to consider the pertinence of the Palestinian discourse on heroic suffering for the lived experiences of a detainee's wife. With reference to Bergson's concepts of the virtual and the actual (Deleuze 1988), the national discourse here can be said to figure as the realm of the virtual through which is actualized particular differentiations of the subjective duration of the detainees' wives. To consider the actualizations of detainees' wives' lives against the background of national discourse is to interrogate the flickering interstice between national representation and lived experience. The premise that there is no clear delineation between an inside and an outside when it comes to subjectivity offers a vantage point for understanding the imbrication of incarceration and gendered subjectivity.

Furthermore, the Das quotation considers the idea of living through violence as a descent into the ordinary, a descent that holds the potential, though not the promise, of recovery (1997, 2007). Recovery features here as a potential that may unfold through the different manifestations of womanhood that occur in the acts of care for the everyday (Das 2014).

Gender is intrinsic to the conceptualization of the relationship between "event" and the ordinary in the occupied territory, and this can further our knowledge of how some women's lives and everyday existence may not belong either to the national Palestinian narrative (Massad 1995) or the globally circulating discourses about the occupants of the occupied territory as a trauma-ridden population (Fassin 2008; Lindholm-Shulz 2003).

Women in the Shadow of Violent Events

While I hope I have brought to life how the women here are other than therapeutic subjects, I want to return to precisely the kind of gendered subjectivity that is evoked in the encounter between the wives of detainees and the psychosocial services they were offered by the Prisoners' Support Center. Among these women is thirty-one-year-old Yasmin, the affluent woman living in Bāb aš-šams with her six children. As noted earlier, Yasmin's husband was sentenced to one hundred years in an Israeli prison for both his political affiliations and his participation in activities of resistance against Israel. Yasmin's husband was in fact released as part of a prisoners' exchange in 2012, but she still has not seen him and there is scant hope that she will, given the lack of mobility between the West Bank and Gaza. During a conversation with Yasmin, we spoke about her experience with a group therapeutic project with other detainees' wives and how it compared with regular social gatherings of female friends and relatives. I asked her what her situation of being married to someone who had been sentenced to prison for one hundred years meant for her in ordinary social interaction. Yasmin said that it made her feel excluded. She was quiet for a while and then added, "from my own experience." She is married and therefore in theory may participate in regular women's talk and gossip in which husbands are evidently a topic of conversation. Yasmin elaborated that she felt she could not contribute anything to such interactions. If she revealed to other women how it felt to be in her situation, she was sure to be the focus of gossip among her near and distant peers for a long time. Her feelings of loss are at odds with the affect permeating Palestinian moral discourse, in which women such as Yasmin are evoked as the proud and honorable wives of heroic resistance fighters. The fact that rather than being proud, Yasmin sometimes feels empty and lonely is crucial. The ideal of the proud detainee's wife permeates self and social relations, rather than residing comfortably outside them, but it does not encompass the entire spectrum of feelings for these wives. Thus supporting Saint Cassia's argument on that situations with unsettled affect pose a challenge to anthropological understanding (2005:153), since we are disciplined to think that ritual, and I would add local vernacular, covers and indeed offers solace to all forms of feeling. The feelings that suffuse Yasmin's story, and the ones to follow, testify that this is far from always the case.

"In the group [with the other detainees' wives]," Yasmin continued, "I can speak about everything that didn't happen." Yasmin's everyday life is marked by lack: lack of the small and big events that are perceived to constitute the habitual life of a husband and wife. As noted in Chapter 5, however, precisely such habitual repetition is absent from her conjugal relationship. Instead, Yasmin can only participate in regular social forums with her in-laws, sisters, and friends by talking about her children. Thus, her participation is made possible because she is a mother. What she cannot share are those aspects of her life that concern her husband, because it would not only compromise her own image but also inspire doubt about her support for the national struggle.

Yasmin points to a gap between the pride that is supposed to fill the void left by her absent husband and her actual feelings. According to a therapeutic assumption about the healing potential of groups, Yasmin supposedly feels better among women in situations similar to her own, where the absence that saturates their lives binds them together (Bion 1961 [1996]). After all, Yasmin and her peers were included in the group project by the Prisoners' Support Center precisely because they are married to detainees. The violent events of resistance undertaken by their husbands appear to situate and unify the women as detainees' wives married to honorable men.

During my participation in the group therapy in Dar Nūra for detainees' wives, I realized that the intended creation of social bonds on the basis of shared experience captures only part of the affective discourses in and around such therapeutic groups. In the group in Dar Nūra, the women did not talk about "everything that did not happen," but about what structured and filled their everyday routine. To this extent, the void in their togetherness resembles al-Shafi'i's trembling absence. The lines of this contour of absence, though, show in how the content of the therapeutic sessions concerned the women's children, problems with their upbringing, chinks in their relationships with their in-laws, and sometimes financial issues such as how to find the time for a job when one must be responsible for one's children. This was confirmed in the women's diaries, the pages of which were full of worries about children and about what other people thought of them as wives and as mothers. Described at length were also frustrations about how to deal with gossip and "intruders": people trying to help by transgressing boundaries that felt personal to them. These boundaries tightened around the women during their husbands' incarcerations, as family members tried to influence their choices. Husbands were mentioned only in the instance of recent visits to Israeli prisons. These passages expressed intense emotions of frustration, joy, and anger. But shortly after the affective reverberations of a visit had settled in the self and the collective, any mentions of husbands evaporated from the pages once more. Even though the status of their (detained) husbands was the whole rationale for their gathering as a therapeutic group, it appeared that only elements that were practically present in the women's everyday lives; namely, children, family, and social networks, could be shared in the therapeutic forum. The variable intensity of conjugal emotions thus made itself clear in the women's therapeutic forums, their neighborly interaction, and perhaps most intriguingly their writings, too, which addressed no one but themselves and, if they wanted to, me.

Notwithstanding the fact that talk about a detainee consumes a lot of social conversation, what is absent from such talk, including among his family and close friends, is the fact that, apart from being a detainee, he is also a husband. As noted earlier, in such interactions, the question asked is, "kīf al-asīr" (How is the detainee?). I have yet to encounter a situation where women, even if all of them are the wives of detainees, ask "kīf jozik" (How is your husband?).

How great care is taken on part of interlocutors not to mention potential rifts in conjugal life in the wake of imprisonment was made palpable during a visit to an aunt of Amina and Layla. The aunt was nice but a bit weird, Layla hinted. How their aunt welcomed me warmly and started narrating her plight straightaway reminded me of other women I have met during my time in the occupied territory. She served us tea and sweets while telling me vivaciously about how her nephews had been involved in heroic activities during the second Intifada. She started recounting the details, but Amina interrupted, "Stop it, she knows already, she knows Palestine." Despite Amina's plea, and the conspicuous sighs of boredom from Amina's girls, the aunt set the scene for her narrative in 2001, during the first part of the second Intifada. Israeli soldiers came to her house and hurt her when they searched for Amina's husband and the other men in the group involved in violent activities. She asked me, "Do you know about the Israeli soldiers; do you know what they did to me?" Amina's aunt recounted in detail the activities of violence undertaken by Amina's husband and its reverberations for him and for herself as a distant relative of the detainee. Missing from her story were the consequences for Amina and her girls, who were an audience as much as I was that day. Stories are told of honorable relations, yet the wounds and wounding aspects of these relations on the captive conjugate are left out of the accounts.

The discursive absence of married life and spouses in talk about detainees and their relatives is, as conveyed earlier, partially explained by an unwillingness to undermine the Palestinian family as a stronghold against Israel. The family and personal relationships contain feelings so as not to threaten the idea of the Palestinian collective as standing tall in the face of the occupation. The affect of mourning, in contrast, is not perceived as a threat to the cohesion of the Palestinian collective, as Khankan (2009) asserts in her analysis of the female voice in post-Oslo Palestinian poetry. Female poets, who often adopt masculine forms of writing while leaving experimental form to male writers, are included in the Palestinian cultural canon through writing as *ritha* (elegy) (112). A mother or a widow mourning a šahīd is not considered a threat to relational texture, despite her potential to affect social relations. Mourning, however, is not possible for the wives of the detainees. Cavell describes how "Freud regards mourning as the condition, that is to say, of allowing its independence from me, its objectivity" (Cavell 1988: 172). For the detainees' wives, it is impossible to separate themselves from the void left by their incarcerated husbands. Their incarcerated husbands' absence is woven into their lives by a process that is, in its essence, uncanny. Part of what is uncanny is the wives' status as sexually mature women who are simultaneously living alone, a situation that is naturally permeated with emotional longing, the withholding of physical desire, and, not least, doubt—doubt about the other and doubt about the worth of the supposedly heroic action. Together these aspects configure how a wife's relationship to a detainee could be addressed and expressed as separate from its conjugal aspect.

Counterintuitively, this configuration resonates with how detainees' wives are supposedly recognized and thus acknowledged as the *wives* of detainees by being classified as "secondary victims" by the organizations that attempt to ameliorate the social and emotional burdens for detainees' families. Organizations like the Prisoners' Support Center categorize the detainees' wives as therapeutic subjects due to both their relationship to a detainee and, even more importantly, the women's connection to a violent and allegedly traumatic event. The latter is defined through the woman's relationship to a detainee with a violent event behind him. Since the spouses of detainees are acknowledged socially and become subjects of psychosocial intervention because of their indirect relationship to a violent event, the wife's conjugal relationship to her husband is eclipsed the instant she is acknowledged, ironically, as a "detainee's wife." What remains prominent is the violent event and, as the direct victim of it, the woman's husband. The paradox is that a woman's wifehood is both the criterion for acknowledgment and the basis for the erasure of her *conjugal relationship*, which becomes merely a relationship to a detainee. The multiplicity of relationships in which the wife of a detainee is engaged in are blinded by the shadow of the violent event.

Cleaning Bathrooms, Containing Feelings

It was the third day of Eid al-Fitr, and life was slowly returning to normal after the end of the holy month of Ramadan. It was Friday, and, like any other Friday, the three sisters, Amina, Reema, and Layla, were baking bread for the week in the backyard of Reema's house, one of the oldest houses in the village. Reema was the oldest of the three sisters, in her early forties, married with four girls and two boys. That particular Friday, she, Amina, and their younger, unmarried sister Layla were waiting for Aisha to come by for lunch. Aisha's husband orchestrated the political event that led to his life sentence and Amina's husband's twenty-seven years in a high-security prison in Israel. It was a still-warm October day, and Aisha's husband's sentence of life plus eighty years had been handed down by the Israeli military court a week earlier. Layla was sitting on the wall between the courtyard and the garden, peeling cucumbers for the salad with me. Amina was watching the last loaves in the wood-fired oven when Reema came out of the house, slightly annoyed because lunch had already been ready for a long time. Reema asked rhetorically, "Where is Aisha? When is she coming, she was supposed to be here by now. Lunch is ready, it is almost three o'clock, yalla Imm Ahmad."[1] Reema's sister Amina answered her vaguely:

> *Amina:* I called her one hour ago, she said twenty minutes; she will be here soon.
> *Layla:* I called her; she said she had to clean the bathroom because of *al-Eid* and all the visitors.
> *Reema:* She is always cleaning her bathroom; that was also her excuse last week, she is nervous, very nervous.
> *Layla:* Yeah, she has been very nervous lately, always doing something, cleaning, visiting, driving the kids around, always busy.
> *Amina:* Nervous? Well, what can she do, what do you want her to do, lifetime plus eighty years . . . what is she supposed to do?

Aisha had changed in the wake of her husband's sentence. She was nervous and restless, and avoided eye contact. Aisha did eventually come to lunch, but when I went to her house with her after the meal, Aisha herself said to me that, after seven years of imprisonment, the fact that her husband had received his final sentence had caused feelings she had never experienced before, feelings that did not go away, no matter what she did to keep herself busy, be it cleaning or even praying. According to her self-perception as a devout Muslim, it unsettled her that her prayer seemed to have no effect. She kept herself busy, performing her job with sincerity and persistence, working every available hour that was not spent nurturing and studying with her two children, taking care of her family and her husband's family, or visiting and receiving visits from villagers who wanted to ask her a favor or pay their respects. In one of our first conversations, she said adamantly, with regard to the then undecided length of her husband's absence, that she had not lost him, she only missed him, because "missing is romantic." Yet what she felt during the weeks after the final sentence was, she said, like being lost.

In her attempts at first to contain her feelings of being lost within the romantic connotations of longing, Aisha eclipses her identity as a wife with an absent husband through her everyday activities and by keeping herself busy. To some extent, she writes down what is detached from her subjectivity in her diaries and in the letters she writes to her husband. Through these expressive media, she partially actualizes herself as a wife. Even in the letters, though, Aisha does not tell her husband about how her sense of self unraveled when she was informed of the sentence—she says only that Palestine will be victorious some day (Buch Segal 2014a). Her affective expressions are thus meticulously kept within the language of national struggle, which legitimizes any kind of personal loss or suffering. The sorrow for the loss of a particular way of being (together) that a wife of a detainee may experience must be left out of her story and her way of inhabiting a social world in order for her to fit the character of a woman who bears the brunt of her husband's detention and the military occupation. At the same time, she is an example for other women by her comportment. This form of implicit censorship of particular feelings could be seen as an act of burying something that could potentially threaten social life in Palestine.

Another example of the entanglement between subjective feelings and the example one wishes to set can be seen in how Amina expresses herself to her husband through photos of herself she sends or asks her children to take to him in prison. Usually, as a seasonal farmer and a weaver with little money, Amina dresses very simply, never acting in a way that could be considered vain or that would imply she wants to attract a new man. In contrast, the photos she sends her husband show a woman with her hair done simply but elegantly by the hairdresser. In these photos, Amina is not wearing the hijab, since her husband is allowed to see her unveiled, and she is dressed in smart women's wear that connotes discreet sensuality. However, in the part of Amina's everyday activity that is not about herself as a wife in an expressive relationship with her husband—by far the majority of her life—there is no trace of this woman. A further example of this contrast can be seen in a stanza from the poem "My Messengers to the Desert" by al-Shafi'i.

Like this
from a day that departs in the tolling [sound] of gold
to a day that swims in clouds
they walk
inheriting [their] longing
storing it in clay jugs [made to hold drinking water].[2]

Khankan describes al-Shafi'i's poetry as a contemplation of the nexus of
lack and want (2009: 129)—for instance, as applied to the national homeless-
ness of the Palestinians (133). Longing in the poem is contained in the
everyday objects of clay jugs, perhaps suggesting that the only materialization
such a longing can assume is that of ordinary objects. While the subject
matter of the poem is not personal longing but rather the collective Palestinian longing for statehood and freedom, two aspects of the poem are
relevant for this analysis: first, the transfiguration of longing into everyday
objects and, second, the image of containing longing.

Longing that is configured into everyday objects is somewhat crudely
illustrated by Amina's work as a weaver in a small local factory, which sustains her family. In this factory, she produces pillows that bear the image of
Che Guevara, the global icon of a heroic figure who not surprisingly also
symbolizes Palestinian resistance to the occupation. This was made clear
to me on a quiet autumn afternoon, when I had been picking olives with
Amina, her kids, and two of her sisters on her land near her village. When we
were done, her nephew, who came to pick us up in a ramshackle car, asked
me, tongue in cheek, "Do you know Che?" clearly hoping for a discussion
about the legitimacy of the Palestinian freedom fighters in light of the revolutionary icon Che Guevera. Having participated in this kind of discussion
numerous times before, I said, "Yes." When Ibrahim asked me what I thought
of him, I shrugged my shoulders. Not happy with my lack of spirited counter-
argument, he went on to tell me why Che was a hero in occupied Palestine.
Ibrahim need not have, since Che Guevera is in fact so iconic that his photo
figures on tapestries, woven pillows, and the letters and pieces of handicraft produced by the Palestinian prisoners in Israeli detention, now on display
in the living rooms of their relatives across the occupied territory.

I wish to dwell on how the letters to husbands containing photos and
woven pillows featuring Che are no less ordinary objects than the clay jugs
storing longing in al-Shafi'i's poem. For Amina and Aisha, such objects dem-
onstrate the entwinement of the ordinary and the extraordinary in their

everyday lives, and their husbands' physical disappearance from the every-day. The personal longing of Amina and Aisha is inseparable from the in-herited, collective longing for freedom. Moulding their everyday practices no less than other structuring principles, incarceration marks their entire lives, their close relationships, and their domestic sphere. The pillows showing Che Guevara are thus emblematic of the revolutionary struggle in two ways, and their production is a dual act of national solidarity and breadwinning. In fact I would argue that Amina's motivation for weaving such a pillow is less a desire to make a heroic contribution to the fight for national liberation than it is the task of nurturing and sustaining a home and a life for her family.

The poem's containment of longing in clay jugs may be likened to the objects in which the loneliness and emptiness of Aisha, Amina, and other women with them are contained, namely, their diaries, photos, and letters. Containment of such feelings is necessary, as has been described elsewhere, notably in Lila Abu-Lughod's sensitive work on emotions among the Awlad-Ali in Egypt and more broadly on gender in the Middle East (1986 [2000], 2013). If these feelings were actualized in public rather than in private, they would severely compromise the example set by detainees' wives, who are sup-posed to feel only honor and pride (Nashif 2008). Loneliness and emptiness are thus best kept at a distance; they must not be spoken, because they have no place in the standing language. Containing these feelings is woven into Aisha's constant cleaning of the bathroom, Amina's weaving, and Yasmin's restless attempt to come up with errands she can run in her big Land Cruiser. The ongoing effort to contain such feelings may do the job on a subjective level but, as shown in Amina, Reema, and Layla's discussion of Aisha's restless cleaning, these efforts produce other fissures. The question is whether the obligations and the women's mundane, containing acts of cleaning, weaving, and driving fill the abyss in their everyday lives, or expand further the emo-tional void they are attempting to close.

Antigone and Awkward Witnessing

To cast the above ethnography in an alternative light, I wish to bring up a figure who has long informed social analysis of women who balance hero-ism and its consequences: Antigone (Das 2007; Butler 2000; Willner 1982). In an act intended to secure the heroic burial of her brother, she defeats her uncle Creon and, as a consequence, is walled up in a tomb, where she commits suicide. By insisting on burying her brother, Antigone chooses obligation to kin over the state, at the cost of her own life. To Judith Butler, Antigone's choice is a conflict between the law of the state and the law of the family (2000: 6).

Antigone's choice also informs Das's (2007) examination of how the violence of the partition between India and Pakistan in 1947 is folded into kin relations through women's silence about the violence of the state as they attempt to stitch together sundered families. Das's analysis of Antigone is salient here because, referencing Lacan, she frames Antigone as a female witness who finds her voice in the zone between two deaths (2007: 61). To Das, voice "is a spectacular, defiant creation of the subject through the act of speech" (61) Voice is something other than speech in the sense that speech, as we have seen, does not always allow for subjective experience to be expressed. To Das, the voice of Antigone emerges in the moment of transgression; "transgression" here refers to the instant in which the crime of the law is realized by the killing of Antigone's brother, to which Antigone is a witness (61). In what sense, may we ask, is Antigone as a female witness of transgression relevant to an analysis of womanhood in Palestine? Though the link to Palestinian widows of martyrs is all too easy to make, I flag it nonetheless because it shows precisely what kind of witness women who have (only) lost their men to imprisonment can never become. Like Antigone, martyrs' widows indeed live through the transgression caused by their husbands' deaths in the name of the Palestinian state-to-be. In contrast, the wives of detainees find themselves balancing on the sword edge of a transgression that has not yet fully occurred. That which has not happened, of course, is death. An exemplary witness is the one standing beside the death of a near one, whereas detainees' wives do not witness death, only possible death. This makes it impossible even for Aisha to stand out as an exemplary witness. All women like her can hope for is to become awkward witnesses.

There is a further resemblance between the Greek tragedies and the ways in which Palestinian women are supposed to inhabit the world after detention in the sense that my interlocutors are primarily understood by what they are not. The difference between the Greek tragedies and my interlocutors' situations is that the linearity of the tragedy and the way in which death offers a solution to the tension, albeit a tragic one, does not offer a framework for comprehension for Palestinian wives. Cavell asserts that Shakespeare's tragedies are distinct in that they are imbued with what he terms a "skeptical structure" (1987: 19). According to Cavell, the skepticism in Shakespear-ean tragedies refers to the withdrawal of the world as one knows it (1987: 19). Cavell analyzes the tragic story of Othello and Desdemona as being about a man whose tragedy is not a lack of knowledge of the other but a lack of trust in the certainty of this knowledge. How can he be sure of what he knows—how can he be sure of Desdemona's virginity upon their marriage (Cavell 1979: 490)? Othello demands visual proof of his wife's intactness in the sense of her fidelity, a proof Desdemona fails to deliver due to the interven-tions of Othello's aide Iago (Cavell 1979: 495). The only thing that can prove Othello's doubts incorrect is Desdemona's death. Othello kills her, and she is metaphorically intact as only the inhuman can be (1979: 481). By killing his wife, Othello attempts to protect his knowledge of her from skepticism, allowing death to bring about a degree of certainty that human life never possesses. Othello's final act of suicide underlines the tragic juxtaposition of death and clarity.

In what sense can Shakeaspearean tragedy be of relevance in the context of the West Bank? The emphasis on keeping out of sight particular aspects of womanhood in Palestine could be conceptualized as a national requirement to turn certain types of emotion to stone—an allegory that was often used by my interlocutors, albeit in a different sense, namely, that their strength was *zay al-jabal*—like the mountain. No matter what occurred, they would endure. Sa'ar (2006) argues that local expressions of women as *qawiyyi* (strong) are used as a mode of praise that deploys the women's strength to affirm shared values of, in the Palestinian case, national revolution. The trag-edy of such praise lies in the dynamic of simultaneously praising a woman's strength, thereby turning her into an example, and denying her other feel-ings: loneliness, despair, or even a wish to divorce. What is denied is pre-cisely what can be endured, because it does not count as tragic: in this case, male absence from a marriage caused by detention that continues and does not end with the violent, spectacular death offered by martyrdom. The tragedy of the detainees' wives is in this sense their ambiguous heroism.

Antigone, by being heroic in the face of her brother's burial, breaks the law of the state. For the wives of detainees, it seems to be the other way around. They reproduce the nation and live up to its requirements by dis-playing heroic strength while hiding their longing behind a public face of heroic womanhood. In ethnographic terms, the cracks nevertheless appear in the carefully constructed masks of the women like Aisha, who out of fear of rumors must prove again and again that they guard the intactness of the voided marriages.

Children—Underscoring and Weakening Woman as Palestine

To say that the women's everyday gestures of care revolve around their children is a grave understatement. The majority of the women's waking hours is devoted to raising children, worrying about them, and nurturing them. If the women work, it is because having an absent husband has compelled them to do so, save for Aisha, who with her MA in gender and development and her political orientation thrives in a job that involves great responsibility and long hours. In this quotidian life, as the wife of a famous and heroic detainee, her marital relation is oddly absent. As the anecdote above showed, Aisha's close friends and kin all know about her situation, but her nervousness is not spoken about as something related to her husband's life sentence. Rather, she is criticized by the others (except Amina, who is in a similar situation) for being too busy, thus compromising her role as a mother, and for being too nervous. Whereas this criticism can and often does befall any professional woman in the occupied territory as well as anywhere in the world, the fact that Aisha is married to a detainee means that she is less able to defend her chosen priorities. No different from those of Amina or any of the other housewives, Aisha's responsibilities as a mother absorb a majority of her time, and elicit concern and inquiries from kin and social relations.

Being a "detainee's wife" is a criterion for being acknowledged in Palestinian women's social and intimate relations, as well as by psychosocial organizations. This event-centered criterion does more than obscure the marital relationship that made the wives visible in the first place: the aspect of subjectivity implied by wifehood is *replaced* by an image of motherhood. And in the everyday life of detainees' wives, their subjectivity as mothers eclipses other social relations that constitute their identities.

The configuration of gendered subjectivity unfolds in the complex structure of an everyday where everything appears normal, yet its compositional structure is arranged around the shadow cast by their husbands' absences. As we learned earlier, a day, a week, indeed an entire life are all structured according to the practices detainees' wives must engage in to sustain their marital relationships. Intermittently organizing the passage of each day, however, is care for their children. All of my interlocutors' children go to school, so the day starts with getting them out of bed, making them breakfast, and walking or driving them to school. During school hours, the women cook lunch for the children, attend to the household chores of cleaning and mending clothes, and perhaps visit family or friends. Around three in the afternoon the children come back and eat, and their mothers help them with their homework. Together they relax, watch television, or receive guests in the evening before going to bed. In this regard, life with children in the families of detainees is hardly any different than life for other families in the occupied territory, or families globally, either.

But the children in detainees' families figure quite differently in the national discourse, and in relation to their mothers as national subjects. Nadia's firstborn son, for instance, carries the name of his father, Baha'. People in the community are generally familiar with the story of Nadia's martyred husband. Learning the name of this younger Baha', they therefore know that he is the son of a šahīd. This casts not only Baha' but also Nadia in an honorable light, even though Baha' was named before his father's death: people do not know that Baha' was born before his father was killed, and even if they did, his name could allude to how Nadia had a hunch about her husband's coming martyrdom. In this sense, Nadia is actualized as an honorable and suitably proud widow because her son is an extended relation of herself.

The first time I participated in the therapeutic group in Dar Nūra, I went home with Amina afterward. On the way, we had to pick up her children, who were in the children's club downstairs in al-balladiyeh (the town hall). The children's club was run by Reema, Amina's sister. After she had taken me on a tour of the premises, Reema asked Rawan and me to sit down in front of the television and watch a video. The video showed Meiza, Aisha's eleven-year-old daughter, on stage agitatedly half-singing, half-shouting a song to the glory of the detainees. Around her were children who enacted being imprisoned in an Israeli prison. When the song neared its end, the children broke their chains, symbolizing the freedom of Palestine. The video was from the Palestinian Prisoners' Day, held annually on April 17 all over the occupied territory. In Dar Nūra, which at that time had just over one hundred of its four thousand citizens detained in Israel, the day is celebrated at the school, where the children perform songs, dramas, and recitals for a crowd of their parents, detainees' families, and official representatives of the community. Reema, Amina, and Meiza observed me intently, eager to hear my reaction to the show. The instance made it clear that although the women and men of the occupied territory must wrestle with both the absence of detainees and the longing for freedom, this complicated emotion is inherited no less by their children.

The value attached to martyrs and prisoners in Palestinian society thus forms not only part of the conjugal relationship but an equally important part of the relationship between parents and children. In Mervat's home, the entanglement of parents, children, and the national discourse played out on different occasions. On one of the first occasions I visited her home, her six children, two of her sisters, and a cousin were present in her living room, where I expected us to talk about how her life had evolved after her husband had been incarcerated six years earlier. Yet a stranger's visit was clearly an event for the entire family. I tried to keep the conversation to what I took to be a polite and nonconfidential tone, but Mervat urged me to pose my questions. When I asked my first question and Mervat started to answer it, she was interrupted by her oldest son, Ibrahim. He was fifteen years old at the time and preparing for *at-Tawjīhi*, the final exam in secondary school for Palestinian pupils. I asked Mervat to give her account of the events of her husband's capture, how she felt while he was a fugitive, and what it was like finally to know that her spouse had been detained. Ibrahim kept asking me if I did not want to hear about his father's story, why he was haunted and how the Israelis had missed him due to his slyness and choice of hiding place. Realizing that the visit was becoming a lesson in co-narration and the power to tell the right story, I listened to Ibrahim's account while inviting the other children to participate. On later occasions, when I had become less of a guest and more of a regular in Mervat's house, she would not bother to change from her tracksuit into a jilbab, nor was she wearing a hijab when I entered the house. In the hope of hearing Mervat's version of the story next to but separated from Ibrahim's account, I arranged to be with Mervat in the mornings when the children were all in school. When Ibrahim came back from school and found us chatting in the kitchen he commented that his mother was not decently dressed and asked her if she was wearing mascara. He warned her not to go out like that.

A woman's reputation thus extends beyond herself, and not least to her children. How Ibrahim enacted his obligations as the oldest son by making his father the center of gravity in the family's story and by taking over his father's obligations led me to ponder whether we can consider Ibrahim as configured into the role of his father upon taking on the detainee's obligation toward his wife, obscuring the fact that he is a son. I speculated that Ibrahim's efforts to constantly invoke the significance of his father are related to the fact that, upon turning fifteen, sons are no longer permitted to visit their fathers in an Israeli prison. If they are, it may be imperative, not least emotionally, for Ibrahim to insist on his father's presence in the family and to underline his own relationship to him. This is because, when he still had a permit to visit his father, it was a way of staying within the marital relationship of his father and mother due to his role as their mediator and messenger. Once his permission to visit his father comes to an end, he becomes extraneous to the marital relationship, just as his father is external to the domestic sphere of his family.

The crucial role of children in the very tangible acts of stitching together a sundered family leads me to argue that incarceration makes children pivotal in the marital relationship. As Joseph writes about Lebanese children, the quotidian lives of these children are permeated by their relationships to their mothers because it is mothers who engage with them practically, temporally, and affectively (1999: 176). Fathers are no less important, but traditionally in Levantine countries the mother expresses parental care, while the father represents authority (176). In the case of enduring imprisonment, however, the relationship between children, their mother, and their father is reconfigured. Whereas the mother is still the one close to the children, the father's distance is accentuated. Because the conjugal relationship is cut, which is emphasized through a lack of permission to visit a husband, the child or the children step in as a mediating relation between mother and father. It is the children who frequently shuttle photos, presents, and letters between their mother and father. This is naturally a great responsibility, but entwined with it is the capacity to be in control of the flow of information to and from the captive conjugate.

Children's position as mediators cannot be underestimated. Illustrating their crucial role in keeping families intact, detainees' wives often extend their approved visitors' permits to each other's children. In one case, Mervat had long-standing permission for her and her children to visit her husband once every fortnight. As Mervat said with a contemptuous shrug of the shoulder, "the Israelis do not recognize the children in the photos of the mother's ID," thereby reinforcing the common idea among Palestinians that to the Israelis any Palestinian is but a crystallization of the Palestinian other. Thus families can swap children so that every now and again, Amina's children visit their father instead of Mervat's children visiting theirs. Since the visits take place in a collective visitors' room, there are in practice no limitations as to whom visitors can address among the detainees.

In the case of children visiting their fathers as mediators between their parents, we may even consider their role as a substitution for both husband and wife in the instant they pass over letters, gifts, and photos in either direction. The children step into the conjugal relationship precisely where it is cut. Thus Ibrahim served dually as a replication of his father in the domestic sphere and as a substitution for both mother and father in the public sphere of the prison visits.

This pivotal role of detainees' children illustrates in the most concrete fashion my earlier suggestion that motherhood substitutes for wifehood: the children literally step in where the father or the mother cannot go in the marital relationship.

The ways that motherhood overshadows other aspects of womanhood surface in the entanglement of the national discourse, in attempts at containing disturbing emotions, and in the children's physical trips to prisons. Whereas the body of each the mother and father was formerly the medium through which the two of them could read and know each other, the children's bodies have taken their places, allowing a marital reading to occur only derivatively. In order to fully understand these gaps between motherhood, wifehood, and womanhood, I devote the next section to a discussion of how these gaps are configured and what kind of ordinary life is made possible for the detainees' wives through a return to the theme of gender, the ordinary, and skepticism.

'Ādi: Absence, Skepticism, and the Ordinary

Recall that a frequent response in everyday conversations to questions like "kīfik" (How are you?), "šu aḵbārik" (What's your news?), and "kīf aḥsāsik" (How do you feel?) is "'ādi" (nothing unusual or spectacular, plain ordinary). "'Ādi" was also a response to my question concerning if and how life had changed after a husband had gone into prison. Although everything appeared normal for the wives of long-term detainees, the way in which lives were stitched together was not the same as before their husbands' detentions. How could they answer "'ādi" to a life that has become uncanny at its seams?

A response to this question demands a detour. This concerns how the event-centered criterion for being acknowledged as a detainee's wife in its

actualization actually eclipses the aspects of subjectivity that grant fulfillment of the event-centered criterion in the first place, namely a detainee's
wife's relationship to a violent event through her detained husband. The
wife-husband relationship is not only eclipsed; as noted, it is replaced by
an image of motherhood. We have seen how both lived motherhood and
motherhood as a national emblem fill the void in the everyday, enveloping
its temporal structure and children, in national discourse and practice.
This emblematic idea of motherhood determines what is and is not considered ordinary and acceptable for detainees' wives. The question I have tried
to answer here is why do all the various and different connections that, together, constitute womanhood seem to become eclipsed by motherhood in
daily life?

One answer is that everyday life for women married to detainees is composed of the tasks of caring, nurturing, and ensuring a livelihood for their
families, mainly their children. Left without a man, as the women noted,
they have to be both mothers and fathers in their families. Because they fill
both roles, the gendered connotation of "events," related to male domains of
subjectivity, and everyday life, related to female domains of subjectivity, is
complicated yet further. Making life ordinary for the wives of detainees rests
on the eclipse of all other aspects of their subjectivities by motherhood. For
detainees' wives, the only way in which one can answer "'ādi" in response to
"kīfik" is by substituting motherhood for conjugal womanhood.

This argument makes relevant a return to the politicized and national-
ized image of the suffering, nurturing mother who sustains everyday life in
the absence of a son (Jean-Klein 2003). If wives emphasize those aspects of
womanhood that are connoted by motherhood, life remains recognizable
even in the absence of a husband. A mother still has to keep the family together by making sure that the everyday is normal in its structure: getting
children ready to school, cooking for them, studying with them, earning
money, and caring for them. When the husband is absent, these tasks still
function routinely. Accordingly, even though a violent event happened,
the mother is what makes life safe amid the chaos. The symbol of "the Palestinian mother" therefore literally secures Palestine as a homeland while
her sons engage (or train to engage) in resistance to the occupation. Re-
ducing womanhood to motherhood also sustains the Palestinian struggle
for a nation-state insofar as nurture and support ensure that violence does
not fragment the Palestinian collective. In a sense, the women are frozen
as the epitome of stability, whereas detainees in prison are free to transform

themselves: in fact it is expected of them,[3] this being the end of a liminal phase (Nashif 2008). In short, conceiving womanhood as motherhood during male incarceration is a collective attempt to defeat skepticism.

In regard to the concept of skepticism, there is, today, doubt in occupied Palestine about the worth and value of the national struggle. Skepticism makes it impossible to know and to fully acknowledge the loss of a life as a holy sacrifice, or a thirty-two-year prison sentence as a necessary price to pay. As conveyed in the previous chapter, skepticism figures most clearly with regard to the conjugal relationship. Replacing the conjugal with the maternal is therefore an attempt to keep skepticism at bay.

The image of the Palestinian mother achieves more than the preservation of an intact Palestine for the collectivity of Palestinians. Making an everyday life that is actually ordinary through motherhood is just as much a means of creating a "safe place" for detainees' wives themselves, precisely by immersing them in everything that is still "normal," even in the absence of the husband. Were the women themselves, their social relations, and the organizations attempting to address their problems to focus on the relationship between husband and wife, it would mean that nothing could feel intact, because of the obvious ways that incarceration alters the captive conjugate.

In contrast, were we to focus solely on the absence of a husband from the marital connotations of a woman's subjectivity, nothing is "'adi" or normal in his absence. Thus if womanhood were eclipsed by wifehood, the image of the Palestinian collective as practicing sumūd and the corresponding activities of resistance would be shattered. To keep the notion of a nation-state intact, it is necessary to replace conjugal womanhood with motherhood. Whereas motherhood may be said to be part and parcel of the conjugal relationship due to its objective of reproducing warriors (Massad 1995), the slight but important inflection in the background of the marital relationship is significant for understanding what is altered in the lives of women who live with incarcerated husbands. That alteration is what causes skepticism in the Palestinian collective.

Recovering a Safe Place?

Within this book's overarching analysis of the intimate, gendered relations that are the backbone of sociality in Palestine, this chapter has called attention to how the wives of detainees are central yet invisible in the Palestinian portrait of its key figures. That this oversight reaches beyond Palestine is clear in the analysis of international, institutional images of who needs amelioration, why, and how.

My analysis has centered on the emotional labor in and of the everyday in the occupied territory, initially to understand *how* a settling into the ordinary takes place among the Palestinian wives of detainees. The main conclusion, however, poses a different question. This analysis contemplates thinking in terms of descent when a violent event is nonlinear and lacks finality. In reality, for the wives of detainees, the violent event did not stop when the gun went off. Due to its constant presence in the wife's life through her husband's absence, the violent event becomes continuous rather than finite, thereby blurring into the everyday. What kind of descent into the ordinary does this then allow for?

The first chapter of this book opened with a Spanish therapist and teacher, pondering how to make Amina feel better. In response to the therapist Muna's frustration that Amina did not improve, the Spanish teacher said, "We have to help Amina create a safe place." What should have become clear throughout this book is that, for a detainee's wife, there is no "safe place," in the sense of a return to the ordinary that existed before Amina's husband disappeared, which happened more than fourteen years ago. Cavell discusses return in this manner: "The return of what we accept as the world will then present itself as a return of the familiar, which is to say, exactly under the concept of what Freud names as the uncanny. That the familiar is a product of a sense of the unfamiliar and of the sense of a return means that what returns after skepticism is never just the same" (1988: 166).

This book has revealed that the ordinary, as sited in the domestic sphere, has become uncanny for the detainee's wife for the duration of her husband's incarceration. The familiar has been made unfamiliar, and the ordinary un-canny. When this happens, how should we think about the ordinary as a site of recovery? To the wives of detainees, there is no return to the everyday, in the sense of a return to a (recovered) realm of the ordinary. The uncanny is always a facet of the ordinary, but here there are circumstances—military occupation, violence, and confinement—that constrict the ordinary and make it increasingly difficult to distance oneself from a sense of omnipres-ent uncanniness.

My analysis, however, anticipates an adjacent conclusion: that a safe place can potentially be created. Such a safe place can be experienced when Amina and the other women set aside the aspect of their identities that made them therapeutic subjects in the first place: the relationship to their heroic husbands. Replacing conjugal womanhood with motherhood is a way to sustain and nurture not only their children but also the Palestinian collective as it engages in violent events of resistance and struggle for a state, yet without allowing this violence to dissolve the collective in the process. Through this substitution, the violent event, as well as the importance, the necessity, and the legitimacy of engaging in resistance, remains in focus. Yet the eclipse that casts detainees' wives solely in the light of motherhood is important for the women themselves. It allows them to stay themselves and live ordinarily in the face of an altered ordinary.

To where, then, is the womanhood connoted by marriage displaced? It is actualized in a photo of a sensual wife, in contrast to the woman as an everyday mother. Or it is woven into pillows featuring Che Guevara, waiting in the living room to celebrate the day of the detained husband's return. Or the womanhood connoted by marriage is projected, like Aisha's letters, invisibly from everyday life into the heart of the Israeli prison.

This conclusion invites us to challenge an event-based notion of suffering as the only viable way to understand violence—its creation, its shape, and its aftermath. As the analysis in this chapter shows, the event-based criterion for suffering misses what may look the same but is in fact altered for these women—namely, ordinary life. The transformation resides in the ineffable, in the affective registers of empty eyes and busy hands, in everything that is invisible when the only criterion used to acknowledge suffering is that of the traumatic event.

Conclusion

When I was finishing this book, war was raging in Gaza. Again. On July 7, 2014, Israel launched Operation Protective Edge, a military incursion that left Gaza a scene of devastation hitherto unmatched in the history of the conflict. Defending the operation publicly, Israel blamed the kidnapping and murder of three Israeli teenagers whose slayers Israel announced were affiliated with Hamas. As it turned out, and as Israel knew all along, Hamas had nothing to do with the killing of the teenagers. Never in the history of the Palestinian-Israeli conflict had so many images of dead, mutilated bodies gone viral. If ever in doubt, the summer of 2014 delivered the proof of Allen's argument that Palestinian moral sentiment is steeped in a discourse of immediacy (2009). Palestinians themselves have insisted for many years that the world should know, that the outside world needs to see, to feel, and to hear what an Israeli incursion actually means for those being invaded.

That summer, the world knew. I have known ever since my first engagement with Palestine in 2004 what this intimacy with war means. Yet I have wondered for just as long if it is only through catastrophic scenes of misery that we recognize what is right in front of us. The answer is twofold. The first is provided by Tobias Kelly in his book *This Side of Silence* (2011), in which he reminds us that lack of acknowledgment is less about the impossible expression of someone in pain than about the failure to listen to precisely what is being said. The second response to such a question is, I hope, this book. Throughout, I have explored the forms of life that never make the headlines of neither international nor Palestinian news, because they lack the eventfulness of violence and stand, in the language of Povinelli (2011), as testimonies to how lives are reshuffled between abandonment and belonging, the effect of this reshuffling nowhere to be seen.

That the pull of spectacular events is a social force extending beyond academic texts and social media hit home for me during fieldwork in the West Bank in March 2008, when Israel launched, by its standards, a small invasion into Gaza. The incursion killed approximately one hundred Palestinians over a spring weekend. In Ramallah and East Jerusalem shops closed in a gesture of public mourning. People remained in front of their televisions, exchanging e-mails and pictures of spectacular fatalities and the latest death tolls. Political parties arranged demonstrations at Sa'at Manara (Manara Square) in Ramallah, which sparked public outrage and suspicion that the parties were not in total solidarity with those suffering in Gaza but acted only to enhance public opinion of themselves. I joined Rawan at a demonstration one night in Ramallah, populated by a small crowd of Ramallah literati, Palestinian intelligentsia, foreign activists, researchers, and aid workers. Palestinian Legislative Council member Mustafa Barghouti spoke to the crowd, which was largely peaceful. The only attempt to undermine the demonstration occurred when the crowd reached Yasir Arafat's mausoleum at al Muqata, the headquarters of the president of the Palestinian Authority. Here, Fatah politicians scolded Hamas for its irresponsible acts, which they said had forced Israel to employ collective punishment in Gaza—the same argument that Israel made while Gaza was burning in the summer of 2014. The following day, I spent the morning in the Prisoners' Support Center, where staff gathered at the windows to see whether the demonstrators in al-Manara would actually show up. I asked if the center would also close or whether anyone from the staff would go; most people shrugged, they all had work to do. Meanwhile Rawan and I spoke on the phone more than once to discuss what we were doing in the afternoon. The plan had been to go to Dar Nūra, where Weeam had invited us for lunch at her house. She had promised to cook us chicken, a dish for which she was famous among the other woman in Dar Nūra. However, since the demonstration was on in al-Manara and Rawan and I felt helpless and saddened by what was going on Gaza, we were torn between going to the demonstration to show solidarity with the people in Gaza and going to visit Weeam, who was going through a rough patch, but of course not anywhere near the acute crisis for the people in Gaza. Knowing that Weeam had wanted to invite us to lunch for a long time, that she had most certainly put her heart into it, and that all the other women in the village knew we were going to her house, I insisted that we visit Weeam. I do not mean to say that Rawan did not feel as obliged as I did to Weeam. Rather, her profound doubt and guilt compelled her to want to publicly acknowledge yet another incident in which Gaza had borne the brunt of the occupation: the territorial dilation of the Palestinians caused her pain, as did the impossibility of aid from West Bank

Palestinians. When we left Weeam's house later that night, Rawan said that, though she had felt hesitant beforehand, it felt right not to let Weeam down.

The episode reminds us that the acknowledgment of suffering privileges spectacular violence and outrageous events, not the kind of lives that Weeam and my other interlocutors can display. I, too, have felt some guilt— particularly in the summer of 2014—that I am writing about these women who are doing well enough, while the people of Gaza are only now catching their breath after a summer of fear and loss.

Again and again, I return to the simple fact that the prisoners' wives about whom this book is written compel me to scrutinize aspects of human life that challenge the systems of thought we have available to understand them—systems such as mourning, religion, or ideology. João Biehl, facing a similar concern regarding his continuous return to his main protagonist, the woman Catarina living in the institution VITA, contends that "ethnographic subjects allow us to return to the places where thought is born" (2014: 99). To me, the prisoners' wives in Palestine are so structurally, emotionally, and relationally compelling that I do not think that anthropological knowledge about them is exhausted. If anthropological knowledge ever is.

Trembling Absence

In resonance with the merging of self and void in the al-Shafi'i poem that opened this book, the Palestinian families of detainees are defined by the reverberations of an absence. I have investigated the trembling of a void, or an absence, that superficially seems to leave nothing but a welcome badge of honor and pride among those whose lives are, in fact, greatly affected by the absence of their imprisoned husbands. The duration of incarceration is worked into social realms and relations around the detainees' wives. This conception of incarceration as an enduring, nonlinear temporality rests on how, in the context of the Israeli-Palestinian conflict, a prison sentence could always be shortened due to negotiations between the conflicting parties about the "detainee issue"—and it could also be lengthened by Israeli appeals to the hackneyed trope of "security concerns." Due to the inherent nonlinearity of Israeli detention, the trembling of the absence left by a detained husband remains powerful but easy to miss in the indiscernible ways it is felt in those realms and relations around a detainee's wife. It only partially meets the criteria for recognition in the standing language. Meeting only one of these proxies of suffering—the wives are related to heroic husbands who are perceived as the victims of violence—the lives of these women appear ordinary. The violence has left no marks.

The premise for much of the anthropology of adversity is the violent event and its aftermath, or consequence. Here, the violent events include both my interlocutors' husbands' violent activities of resistance against Israel and their attendant incarceration where violence during capture, detention, and imprisonment may occur. Yet the distance or proximity of these events in the lives of the men's wives is not a settled matter, nor are the effects on their wives' ordinary lives. I have pondered what the ordinary means under such circumstances of absence caused by incarceration. This is why I intentionally didn't offer an a priori definition of the ordinary. Rather, my analysis has emphasized the spheres that make up *their* particular ordinary, namely the lives lived in the braiding of Palestinian and psychological understandings of suffering, the domestic sphere, lived temporality, kin relations, the conjugal relation, and selfhood-as-motherhood.

The absence of detainees' wives in the standing language is nonetheless due to more than the failure of the criteria to include the women's suffering in the register of acknowledgment. I have shown how such an acknowledgment would potentially threaten a Palestinian moral discourse on suffering and resistance in which the Palestinian family figures politically as a stronghold against the Israeli occupation. The experiences endured by detainees' wives are therefore contained not only by the women individually but equally so by their close relations. Relations among Palestinians are all that is left to protect and continue the struggle, without a territorialized nation-state. Under these circumstances it becomes crucial to keep the Palestinian family intact. Acknowledging the profound alterations that incarceration entails for the conjugal relationship would be tantamount to an admission that the struggle for statehood has had a most profound, enduring, and disruptive effect on the Palestinian family, and thus on the collective. It would be an admission that the effects of Israeli security procedures had indeed infiltrated even the family and the domestic stronghold. And if community were as frayed as the dispersed occupied territories themselves, what, then, remains as the basis of a legitimate claim to Palestinian statehood?

Detainees' wives seem to be included among the deserving victims, but are in fact excluded because their suffering is not encompassed by the notions through which proper affliction is known by the standing language.

This is the context of life married to a detainee enduring a sentence in an Israeli prison.

In parallel with an examination of the configuration of affect, I have tried to understand the experience and effects of absence. How is absence endured, actualized, and made to disappear into the weave of the ordinary of the detainees' wives? My attempt to comprehend the effects of an absence that leaves no visible or expressible mark in the lives of those left behind has occurred in conversation with Das's and Cavell's writings on subtle alterations in intimate relations and the ways in which a relation or emotion is expressed, or contained, in the making of the ordinary. My intention has been to show how the outer and inner are constituted by each other in the sense of a Möbius strip. This translates into a concern with how private experience is actualized along the lines of affect and understandings of what the inner might be and how it should be managed. Precisely how emotions concerning imprisonment of a husband are managed forms a mode of expression that establishes intelligibility, and thus community. Emphasizing these coping strategies has allowed me to juxtapose an investigation of experience with an analysis of how aspects of experience are elicited or eclipsed in both public Palestinian narrative and inner self-understanding.

A Note on Suffering

Intense conversations about the place of suffering in anthropology force us to think about how and why we describe our interlocutors in terms of their affliction as much as in terms of their ethnic, relational, or ontological worlds. Yet my ongoing research on detention and kinship in the Middle East at the height of the discourse about the region as the "axis of evil" complicated the issue of how to think analytically about the intimate dynamics around imprisonment in occupied Palestine. The two most obvious frameworks available to me were the framework of Muslim women suffering at the hands of patriarchy, conflict, and, Islam, or, second, what has often been understood as its opposite, Saba Mahmoud's conceptualization of agency in the Middle East as a human capacity unleashed from liberal undercurrents (2004). As Abu-Lughod asserts (2002, 2013), academics are as responsible for the othering discourses of Muslim women as are politicians and the media. I concur with Abu-Lughod that oppression is often politically rather than religiously engendered, and overwhelmingly so. Moreover, I am also hesitant to use an analytic that celebrates agency "in spite of," so I chose not to make Islam the vehicle of my analysis. Akin to the findings in the work of Samuli Schielke (2010), religion and religious practice are braided undramatically into the everyday lives of many among my female interlocutors, and I have followed their cues not to make it stand out.

In line with Joel Robbins's (2012) call to locate anthropological analysis solidly in terms of culture, a graduate colleague once urged me to deliberately avoid suffering in my texts and write about birthday parties or other social events that were not about the occupation, suffering, or violence as such. While I attempted to reorient my focus onto the rich complexity of social life in the occupied territory, the ethnographic reality was, and continues to be, suffused by specific markers of the conflict—including, in fact, children's birthday parties. For example, Luma's daughter's fifteenth birthday was also an opportunity for Luma to show she copes heroically, despite her husband's untimely death. As Goodfellow (2015) argues in regard to the making of kinship among gay fathers in the United States, the challenge for anthropology is to conceptualize suffering in the instances where suffering and its instantiations, rather than taking on the character of an external force, are at the heart of our interlocutors' everyday lives.

In such instances—life in Palestine among them—there is no exterior realm of local culture that is *not* marked by suffering. Wittgenstein's challenge of the idea of a realm of the interior as a private space becomes relevant. Although I do not assume that there is an interior realm untouched by social life, this book's point of departure has been the personal feelings of being in the position of an absented wife, how it feels to be in such a position, and how such feelings go beyond collective representations of heroic affect and collective endurance. Toward the end of her book *In My Mother's House,* Sharika Thiranagama observes that "those who imagined themselves as one at a moment of violence nonetheless remain differentiated after the riots" (2011: 240). Thiranagama here addresses the Tamil-Sinhalese riots in Colombo in 1983. Though the context of the Palestinian-Israeli conflict is a different scene entirely, Thiranagama's words speak to the tension that instigated this entire project—namely, the relationship between collective language (and the claims made within such a language about an individual's affliction) and the residual feelings of that particular individual. Because public speech centers on women's call to show sumūd, I have focused my inquiry on the labor of endurance. It is an immense, ongoing effort for individuals and families to do the quotidian work of actually enduring.

Here I echo Han in her monograph *Life in Debt: Times of Care and Violence in Neoliberal Chile* (2012) and her response to reviews of the book (2013). Han (2013) describes her work as an anthropologist in a context where poverty and violence, structural and otherwise, are braided into quotidian life. It seems, argues Han, that anthropologists working in such contexts either choose to write about "the good" that emerges despite hardship and affliction or to document human beings' capacity to suffer, though they are aware of the risk that ethnographic description of hardship can become quasi-pornographic voyeurism (Kelly 2013). It seems that the question requires a different formulation, hinted at both in Das's (2013) comments to Han, and Han's (2013) response; namely, what becomes of social relations at the limits of society, where the risk of falling out is acute, if it hasn't already happened?

To me, Palestinian society has slowly but persistently moved toward the limits of the evocative call to endure, to stand tall and show sumūd in the face of military occupation. If this is a voyeuristic portrayal of a human being's capacity to feel pain, it is because of its opposite—the tragic caricature of Palestinians as feeling no pain at all. To me, there is also a moral impulse in this description: descriptions of agency and steadfastness in spite of occupation constitute at best a broken mirror of how Palestinians see the situation, and themselves within it. As such an impulse, this book is my attempt to sketch the contours of the limit of endurance, when endurance has come to belong to the register of the everyday.

Ordinary Doubt

What does it mean to say that uncanniness is something that constitutes rather than perturbs the ordinary? I have documented how the sense of time and place is saturated with uncanny affect for detainees' wives. I have also been shown how affinal and consanguineal relationships close in on women during their husbands' absences. A husband's absence also implies that what is left of the captive conjugate is an empty shell whose meaning in the life of the detainee's wife is further eclipsed by her role as both the national symbol of the Palestinian mother and the tangible mother of the detainee's children. For my interlocutors, this configuration of affect engenders a feeling of doubt in the world, and in the relations within which their selves are created. And the idea of doubt here calls for a discussion of skepticism. For Cavell, skepticism is intrinsic to what he terms a masculine way of knowing (1987: 16).

A masculine understanding of knowledge resonates with the modern attraction of absolute certainty, objectivity, and neutrality. Skepticism is the struggle for this understanding, in tandem with the knowledge that it is unobtainable (16). Das's premises of how it is possible to know and be known by another human being are profoundly relevant for my attempt to depict what kinds of intimacy are possible in the event of Israel's detention of Palestinian men (2010: 12).

When we consider how detainees' wives can "know" the other of their captive partner, it is important to understand that doubt simply becomes part of being the wife of a detainee. Naturally, such doubt about the world and fundamental relations vary according to axes of class, and the status of the particular violent acts of resistance undertaken by the husband. But whatever the case, and however heroic the acts of resistance are perceived, nothing compensates for a cold bed, the image invoked by Yara. A fundamental doubt about the husband, the world, and the future becomes part of living as the free party of a captive conjugate.

This sense of the nonlinear duration of incarceration renders the captive conjugate, and its affect, uncanny. The link between uncanniness and skepticism, or doubt, is created by the unsettled temporality of a prison sentence, and the ways this ambiguity works on the ordinary, both spatially and temporally. This is precisely why Shakespearean tragedy is an apt image of the incarcerated couple: rather than a tragic ending emblematic of the Greek tragedies that evolve around conflict and paradoxes inherent to family and kin relations, Shakespearean tragedies are imbued with a skeptical structure. According to Cavell, the tensions invoked in the tragedy are not resolved through a tragic ending, but rather linger in the form of penetrating skepticism. The enduring skepticism is an accompaniment to the uncanniness. The elicited image of the proud Palestinian family contains in its shadow the skepticism and uncanniness inherent in the captive conjugate. Thus, the Palestinian family is both an unwavering stronghold and a site threatened by skepticism.

Acknowledging Uneventful Lives

The frequently overlooked or unseen aspects of the daily existence of Palestinian detainees' wives carry a message for psychosocial organizations working with secondary victims both in the occupied territory and globally where similar conditions apply. Therapists and staff on the ground should be encouraged to step back and not assume anything, but instead listen and learn what actually constitutes the everyday existence of those whose conditions they are attempting to alleviate. With regard to anthropological theory specifically, I hope this book will be read as an engagement with Das's (1998) discussion about the potential of certain forms of violence to enunciate the limits to forms of life and thus to humanity. The violence Das (1997) refers to is the brutal, sexualized, and humiliating violence inflicted on Muslim women during the partition of India.

The findings of my research have, however, made me wonder whether violence that is less brutal or less in violation of fundamental moral codes can similarly threaten the forms of life known to be human. My research compels me to answer in the affirmative. I have documented how the subtle but enduring forms of suffering I have investigated—those implicit to being the wife of a Palestinian detainee—might lead us to deconstruct our notions of violence and question just how "normal" violence can become. I have no answer to this question, but I suggest that the simple posing of the question, the fact that it could arise at all, delimits what forms of existence can be contained within a Palestinian national narrative. I suggest that the answer rests on this simple but unchanging fact: enduring suffering in Palestine has become as ordinary as the occupation itself. It is 'adi.

We are left to wonder what the healing potential of the ordinary is when the ordinary itself is engulfed by daily tribulations and the emotional labor required to endure. During my ethnographic engagement with Palestine I have often wondered about the power of analysis. I could easily have written this book as a testimony to the overwhelming sense of agency universally present in occupied Palestine in spite of the occupation. I have not chosen to do so throughout because I have found something more pressing underlying such expressions of vitality: it is the opposite of hope, which is doubt in the future. How these two horizons—hope and doubt—combine every day to define the ordinary lives of the women whose lives have been at the center of my inquiry. Hope and doubt are what allow and oblige them to go on, yet these emotions also make endurance utterly exhausting.

No Place for Grief could easily be read as saying there ought to be a place to grieve for the women about whom this book is written. A place in which a voice would find its way in the void of the language available to mourn, recollect, and even make note of the multiple forms of loss caused by the Israeli occupation of Palestine. I have, however, tried to convey precisely how, if such a place existed, a voice would speak of a sadness that could not possibly be mourned. Therefore the grief suffusing this book finds its voice only in the mode of doubt—and only if we dare to listen.

NOTES

Introduction

Epigraph: From the poem "Maps of Absence" by Ghada al-Shafi'i, in al-Shafi'i's collection *al-mashhad yukhabbi' sahilan* [The scene hides neighing] (al-Shafi'i 1999:69), translated by Nathalie Khankan (2009) and transcribed for the purpose of this book by Christina Copty.

1. A most famous passage to convey the elusiveness of this argument is found in §206, where Wittgenstein writes, "Shared human behaviours is the system of reference by means of which we interpret unknown language."

2. The history of the military occupation of Palestine and the Palestinians by Israel runs through the book as an undercurrent yet it is not the explicit object of investigation. My point of reference for this history however is the work of Ilan Pappé (2004, 2006) and Rashid Khalidi (2006) and for the metaanalysis of the representation of Palestinians in history and beyond, Edward Said (1977).

3. Occupied Territory is the term used by the UN Office for the Coordination of Palestinian Affairs for the Palestinian territory occupied by Israel www.ocha.org.

4. See the conclusion for elaboration.

Chapter 1

1. Details about the Prisoners' Support Center are provided later on in this chapter. Both its name and its location are fictional in order to protect the confidentiality of the organization and its employees. Since I do not consider this book to be an institutional ethnography, the information I provide about the center mainly takes the form of ethnographic examples that offer insight into the notions of suffering that the organization reveals.

2. In patrilateral parallel first cousin marriage, which is practiced in Palestine and elsewhere in smaller communities across the Levant, the man and the woman are the children of siblings. Preferable a young woman is married to her father's brother's son (*ibn ammi*). Thus, their extended families are already closely related to one another (Joseph 1999: 176). In practical terms this also mean that in a village, even if families

are not consanguinely related but only through affinity, a marriage that would be considered exogamous actually folds back into the same agnatic line (Eickelman 2002 [1981]: chapter 7; Bourdieu 1977 [1995]: 35).

3. William Connolly defines resonance as "relations of dependence between separate factors, morph[ing] into energized complexities of mutual imbrication and inter-involvement, in which heretofore unconnected or loosely associated elements fold, bend, blend, emulsify, and dissolve into each other, forging a qualitative assemblage resistant to classical models of explanation" (2005: 870).

4. Convergence is, according to Deleuze, the point at which lines "intersect again, where the directions cross and where the tendencies that differ in kind link together again to give rise to the thing as we know it" (1988: 28).

Chapter 2

1. In this context, my assumption is that structural violence in the occupied territory rests on two interrelated pillars: the Israeli-Palestinian conflict and the dysfunction of the Palestinian government (Giacaman et al. 2009).

2. An Israeli prison known to be the highest security prison in the Negev Desert.

3. An Israeli prison located near Lake Tiberia in the north of Israel.

4. See http://www.btselem.org/statistics/detainees_and_prisoners.

5. This is exemplified by the rumors of exchange regarding the Israeli war prisoner Ghalit Shalid. At the time of negotiations between Israel and the Palestinians in the autumn of 2009, rumors circulated in the Palestinian and regional media that his exchange might release up to one thousand Palestinian detainees in Israeli prisons. For a crystallization of such rumors see, for instance, the article "Hamas: Prisoner Swap Talk Ongoing," Palestinian news website Maan News (http://www.maannews.net/eng /ViewDetails.aspx?ID=240773.)

6. None of my interlocutors are refugees, which is why I do not give any detail to the issue of Palestine refugees in this book.

7. In Palestine the use of teknonymy is wide spread. Imm Hazem thus means mother of Hazem.

8. See Afana et al. 2010.

9. This notion of inexpressibility has proliferated in anthropology inspired by literary studies. The proponents of this view are mainly Elaine Scarry (1987) and Cathy Caruth (1996).

10. I have discussed with Mark Vacher whether the parable of Abraham about to sacrifice his son Isaac is a valuable perspective on Imm Hazem's narrative. I am hesitant about such an evocation because the sacrifice is in this instance not only religious. As both Jayyusi (2007) and Asad discuss, the idea of martyrdom in Islam as such is not a sacrifice; but in the Palestinian context the (religious) martyr is represented as a national sacrifice in the struggle for a Palestinian state (Asad 2007: 49).

11. This verse was written by former detainee and singer Ayman Ramadan in 2005. My assistant Mayy listened to the song and wrote down the lyrics, which were translated by Christina Copty. As is documented by Esmail Nashif, the time of imprisonment for the detained often includes the production of handicraft, poetry, and ornaments that are sent to his family (2008). The Abu Jihad Museum for the Prisoners Movements Affairs in Abu Dis holds a rich collection of such artifacts and writings.

12. This analysis might have included attention to the current concern in psychological anthropology with Paul Ricoeur's hauntologie and hauntings more generally (see for instance Gammeltoft's 2014 book *Haunting Images*). I have chosen not to because of the certainty involved in how the death and absences that I describe occurred: they can be traced clearly to the violence of the occupation and the struggle against it.

13. There was an exchange of detainees right after our conversation due to the Annapolis conference in 2007 when the United States hosted talks where the Palestinian bid for statehood was reconsidered. As expected though, there were no foreseeable solutions or agreements on the table. Nadia's husband was not part of the exchange.

14. In his analysis of how Islam forms part of Palestinian nationalism, Nels Johnson shows how the term *thawrah* (revolution) is used to convey the redemptive implications of the process of the Palestinian revolution. Participation in at-thawrah holds a promise of redemption in itself: redemption is not something that occurs once the revolution has occurred (1982: 83).

15. This is discussed in Chapter 4.

16. The history of Dar Nūra' is distinctive, and research into the village's geographic and demographic trajectory has been undertaken by archaeologists. It is, however, a history that, if disclosed, will reveal the identity of the village and thereby my interlocutors. The information I have provided above is important in order to understand the closely braided relationality of the village. I have restricted myself from further expansion on this subject out of concern for the anonymity of my interlocutors.

17. In the Levant, such extended families, or more precisely clans, are referred to as *hamula* (see Johnson 1982: 63). I do not employ the term elsewhere in the book since it was never used by my interlocutors. Speaking about family and relatedness with them, the term used was *al-ʿāʾila* (family).

18. I employ Pierre Bourdieu's notion of "preferred marriage" to convey the idea that, although patrilateral parallel cousin marriage may be considered the ideal form of marriage, this does not mean that such marriages are always possible or preferable (1977 [1995]: 35). As described in Chapter 4, this form of marriage prevails largely in villages across the West Bank, but it is upheld in urban areas too.

Chapter 3

1. See Amahl Bishara's film *Degrees of Incarceration* for a visualization of the themes of this chapter.

2. Jilbab is the Arab term for a piece of clothing that for women in contemporary Palestine takes the form of an ankle-length loosely fitted coat. Hijab is the headscarf used to cover a woman's hair and thus secure and signal her modesty.

3. Around 1.3 percent of the detainees are women, therefore I write about the detainees as masculine. And as Nashif (2008: 18) and Massad (1995) point out, the Palestinian national project overall is characterized as masculine while the spaces for women are delineated within the overall frame of resisting the Israeli occupation. Here a line could be drawn to the Palestinian patriarchal kinship norm where men and women occupy different but independent roles.

4. The interlocutor in question was a client at the Prisoners' Support Center, who was aware of the alleged torture of her son. The center has an opportunity to involve the Israeli organization Public Committee Against Torture Israel in a lawsuit against the Israeli state.

5. Deleuze defines this as "the contemporaneity of the past with the present it was" (1994: 81).

6. Anticipation is defined by Frida Hastrup as the capacity to project a future trajectory of life (2009: 212).

Chapter 4

1. My own reaction was to cringe, rather than be amused. My colleagues Mark Vacher and Henrik Rønsbo have readily shared their interpretation of the drawing with me.

2. Alex Argenti-Pillen's study on how women contain violence in Sri Lanka can be seen to resonate with the questions I ask here (Argenti-Pillen 2003).

3. The comparison was made because Khuloud's neighbor was present, and she had lost a husband to a lightning strike, which she was very eager to talk about that evening.

4. The themes of sexuality, affect, and imprisonment are investigated further in Chapter 5.

5. This also influenced my ability to tape conversations. Frequently, my interlocutors were reluctant to tape conversations for fear that the sound files would fall into Israeli hands. But the in-laws were also an unspoken deterrent. Twice, women I was speaking with would not agree to be tape until their mothers-in-law had also agreed to it, in my presence.

Chapter 5

Epigraph: From "Lonely the Day Came to You," by Ghada al-Shafi'i, in al-Shafi'i's collection *al-mashhad yukhabbi' sahilan* [The scene hides neighing] (al-Shafi'i 1999: 33), translated by Nathalie Khankhan in Khankhan (2009). For the purpose of this book Christina Copty translated the poem from Arabic to phonetic Arabic: "Waḥīdan atāk an-nahār / aḥīdan / atāk an-nahār al-waḥīd min an-nāfiḏa / w-lam naftaḥ lahu ḡaira ṣamt al-ḵazāna / fīha baqayāka sāhira / 'ala damm yatajammidu fawqa al-balāṭ."

1. According to the Israeli human rights organization B'Tselem, there are currently 5,298 Palestinian prisoners in Israeli jails (http://www.btselem.org/statistics/detainees _and_prisoners). Since 1967 a total of 700,000 Palestinians have been detained in Israeli prisons.

2. All excerpts from interviews and diaries are translated from Arabic (Palestinian dialect) to English by my Palestinian assistants Mayy Abu Meizar and Rawan Odeh.

3. While arguing for the primacy of vision in communication of suffering among Palestinians, I am aware of the argument concerning the primacy of "the Arab ear" over the eye, as Kanaanah argues (2005 [1990]).

Chapter 6

1. Aisha also goes by the name of Imm Ahmad since she is Ahmad's mother.

2. From "My Messengers to the Desert," by Ghada al-Shafi'i', in "Eternal Guests of Fire" in al-Shafi'i's collection *al-mashhad yukhabbi' sahilan* [The scene hides neighing] (al-Shafi'i 1999: 89), translated by Khankan and transcribed from Arabic to phonetic Arabic by Christina Copty (Khankan 2009: 135): ''w-hākaḏā . . . / min yaum ḏāhib fī ranīn al-ḏahab / ila yaumin 'a'imin fī as-saḥb / yasīrūna / w-humm yatawāraṯūna al-ḥanīn / w-yukazinūnahu fī il-jarār il-mu'adat li-ma'i iš-šurb."

3. I owe this point to my colleague Dr. Frida Hastrup.

REFERENCES

Abenante, Paola. (2012). Inner and Outer Ways: Sufism and Subjectivity in Egypt and Beyond. *Ethnos* 78 (4): 490–514.

Abu Hein, Fadel, Samir Qouta, Abdel-Assis, Thabet, and Eyad El Sarraj. (1993). Trauma and Mental Health of Children in Gaza. *British Journal of Psychiatry* 306(6885): 1130–1131.

Abu-Lughod, Lila. (2013). *Do Muslim Women Need Saving?* Cambridge, MA: Harvard University Press.

———. (2002). Do Muslim Women Really Need Saving? Anthropological Reflections on Cultural Relativism and Its Others. *American Anthropologist* 104(3): 783–790.

———. (1993 [2008]). *Writing Women's Worlds: Bedouin Stories.* Berkeley: University of California Press.

———. (1986 [2000]). *Veiled Sentiments: Honor and Poetry in a Bedouin Society.* Berkeley: University of California Press.

Abu-Lughod, Lila, and Ahmad H. Sa'adi. (2007). *Nakba: Palestine, 1948, and the Claims of Memory.* New York: Columbia University Press.

Afana, Abdel Hamid, Duncan Pedersen, Lawrence Kirmayer, and Henrik Ronsbo. (2010). "Endurance Is to Be Shown at the First Blow": Social Representations and Reactions to Traumatic Experiences in the Gaza Strip. *Traumatology* 16(2): 43–54.

Allan, Diana. (2013). *Refugees of the Revolution: Experiences of the Palestinian Exile.* Stanford, CA: Stanford University Press.

Allen, Lori. (2013). *The Rise and Fall of Human Rights: Cynicism and Politics in Occupied Palestine.* Stanford, CA: Stanford University Press.

———. (2012). The Scales of Occupation: "Operation Cast Lead" and the Targeting of the Gaza Strip. *Critique of Anthropology* 32(3): 261–284,

———. (2009). Martyr Bodies in the Media: Human Rights, Aesthetics, and the Politics of Immediation in the Palestinian Intifada. *American Ethnologist* 36(1): 161–180.

———. (2008). Getting by the Occupation: How Violence Became Normal During the Second Palestinian Intifada. *Cultural Anthropology* 23(3): 453–487.

———. (2006). The Polyvalent Politics of Martyr Commemorations in the Palestinian Intifada. *History and Memory* 18(2): 107–138.

APA (American Psychiatric Association). (2000). *Diagnostic and Statistical Manual of Mental Disorders-IV-TR*. Washington, DC: American Psychiatric Association.

Argenti-Pillen, Alex. (2003). *Masking Terror: How Women Contain Violence in Southern Sri Lanka*. Philadelphia: University of Pennsylvania Press.

———. (2000). The Discourse on Trauma in Non-Western Cultural Contexts. Pp. 87–102 in *International Handbook of Human Response to Trauma*, ed. A. Y Shalev, R. Yehuda, and A. C. McFarlane. New York: Kluwer Academic/Plenum.

Asad, Talal. (2007). *On Suicide Bombing*. New York: Columbia University Press.

Austin, John L. (1962 [2000]). *How to Do Things with Words*. Oxford: Oxford University Press.

Baker, Abeer, and Anat Matar. (2011). *Threat: Palestinian Political Prisoners in Israel*. London: Pluto Press.

Basoglu, M., M. Livanou, E. Salciouglu, and D. Kalender. (2003). A Brief Behavioural Treatment of Chronic Post-traumatic Stress Disorder in Earthquake Survivors: Results from an Open Clinical Trial. *Psychological Medicine* 33(4):647–654.

Bear, Laua. (2007). Ruins and Ghosts: The Domestic Uncanny and the Materialization of Anglo-Indian Genealogies in Kharagpur. In *Ghosts of Memory: Essays on Remembrance and Relatedness*, ed. Janet Carsten. Oxford: Wiley-Blackwell.

Bergson, Henri (1912 [2004]). *Matter and Memory*. Mineola, NY: Dover.

———. (1910). *Time and Free Will*. London: Macmillan.

Biehl, João. (2014). Ethnography in the Way of Theory. Pp 94–118 in *The Ground Between: Anthropologists Engaging Philosophy*, ed. Veena Das, Michael Jackson, Arthur Kleinman, and Bhrigu Singh. Durham, NC: Duke University Press.

———. (2005 [2013]). *Vita: Life in a Zone of Social Abandonment*. Berkeley: University of California Press.

Biehl, João and Amy Moran-Tomas. (2009). Symptom: Subjectivities, Social Ills, Technologies. *Annual Review of Anthropology* 38:267–288.

Bille, Mikkel, Frida Hastrup, and Tim Flohr Sørensen. (2010). *An Anthropology of Absence: Materialisations and Transcendence of Loss*. New York: Springer Press.

Bion, Wilfred. (1961 [1996]). *Experiences in Groups and Other Papers*. London: Routledge.

Bisson, Jonathan. (2008). Cognitive Therapy Improves Post-traumatic Stress Disorder Associated with Civil Conflict in Northern Ireland. *Evidence Based Mental Health* 11(1): 25.

Bourdieu, Pierre. (2001). *Masculine Domination*. Cambridge: Polity Press.

Brison, Karen, and Stephen Levitt. (1995). Coping with Bereavement: Long Term Perspectives on Grief and Mourning. *Ethos* 23(4): 84–90.

B'Tselem. (2010). *Kept in the Dark: Treatment of Palestinian Detainees in the Petah Tikva Interrogation Facility*.

———. (2015). *Detainees and Prisoners: Statistics on Palestinians in the Custody of the Israeli Security Forces*. Retrieved from http://www.btselem.org/English/Statistics/Detainees_and_Captives.asp.

Bubandt, Nils Ole. (2008). Ghosts with Trauma: Global Imaginaries and the Politics of Post-Conflict Memory. Pp. 75–301 in *Conflict, Violence and Displacement in Indonesia*, ed. Eva-Lotta Hedman. Ithaca, NY: Cornell Southeast Asia Program Publications.

———. (2005). Vernacular Security: The Politics of Feeling Safe in Global, National and Local Worlds. *Security Dialogue* 36(3): 275–296.

Buch, Lotte. (2010). Derivative Presence: Lives and Loss in Limbo in the West Bank. In *An Anthropology of Absence: Materializations and Transcendence of Loss*, ed. Mikkel Bille, Frida Hastrup, and Tim Flohr Sørensen. New York: Springer Press.

Buch Segal, Lotte. (2015). Mourning, Grief, and the Loss of Politics in Palestine: The Unvoiced Effects of Military Occupation in the West Bank. In *An Anthropology of Living and Dying in the Contemporary World*, ed. Veena Das and Clara Han. Berkeley: University of California Press.

———. (2014a). Disembodied Conjugality. Pp. 55–68 in *Wording the World: Veena Das and the Scenes of Inheritance*, ed. Roma Chatterji. New York. Fordham University Press.

———. (2014b). Why Is Muna Crying? Acknowledgment and Criteria for Evaluating Suffering in the Occupied Palestinian Territories. Pp. 179–197 in *Histories of Victimhood*, ed. S. Jensen and H. Rønsbo. Philadelphia: University of Pennsylvania Press.

———. (2013). Enduring Presents: Living a Prison Sentence as the Wife of a Detainee in Israel. Pp. 122–140 in *Times of Security. Ethnographies of Fear, Protest and the Future*, ed. Martin Holbraad and Morten Axel Pedersen. London: Routledge.

Burmeister, Jorge and Manuela Maciel (eds). (2007). *Psychodrama: Advances in Theory and Practice*. London: Routledge.

Butler, Judith. (2004). *Precarious Life: The Powers of Mourning and Violence*. New York: Verso.

———. (2000). *Antigone's Claim: Kinship Between Life and Death*. New York: Columbia University Press.

———. (1997). *Excitable Speech: A Politics of the Performative*. New York: Routledge.

Carsten, Janet (ed.). (2013). Blood Will Out: Essays on Liquid Transfers and Flows (edited). Special Issue, *Journal of the Royal Anthropological Institute*. 19.

———. (2011). Substance and Relationality: Blood in Contexts. *Annual Review of Anthropology* 40: 19–35.

———(ed.). (2007). *Ghosts of Memory: Essays on Remembrance and Relatedness*. Oxford: Wiley-Blackwell.

———(ed.). (2000). *Cultures of Relatedness: New Approaches to the Study of Kinship*. Cambridge: Cambridge University Press.

Caruth, Cathy. (1996). *Unclaimed Experience: Trauma, Narrative, and History*. Baltimore: Johns Hopkins University Press.

Caton, Steven C. (2014). Henri Bergson in Highland Yemen. Pp. 234–253 in *The Ground Between: Anthropologists Engaging Philosophy*, ed. Veena Das, Michael Jackson, Arthur Kleinman, and Bhrigu Singh. Durham, NC: Duke University Press.

Cavell, Stanley. (2010). *Little Did I Know: Excerpts from Memory*. Stanford, CA: Stanford University Press.

——. (1988). *In Quest of the Ordinary*. Chicago: University of Chicago Press.

——. (1987). *Disowning Knowledge in Six Plays of Shakespeare*. Cambridge: Cambridge University Press.

——. (1979). *The Claim of Reason: Wittgenstein, Skepticism, Morality, and Tragedy*. Oxford: Oxford University Press.

——. (1976). *Must We Mean What We Say?* Cambridge: Cambridge University Press.

Clarke, Morgan. (2007). Closeness in the Age of Mechanical Reproduction: Debating Kinship and Biomedicine in Lebanon and the Middle East. *Anthropological Quarterly* 80(2): 379–402.

Collins, John. (2004). *Occupied by Memory: The Intifada Generation and the Palestinian State of Emergency*. New York: New York University Press.

Connolly, William E. (2005). The Evangelical-Capitalist Resonance Machine. *Political Theory* 33(6): 869–886.

Crapanzano, Vincent. (2014). Must We Be Bad Epistemologists? Illusions of Transparency, the Opaque Other, and Interpretive Foibles. Pp. 254–278 in *The Ground Between: Anthropologists Engaging Philosophy*, ed. Veena Das, Michael Jackson, Arthur Kleinman, and Bhrigu Singh. Durham, NC: Duke University Press.

——. (2011). *The Harkis: The Wound That Never Healed*. Chicago. University of Chicago Press.

Csordas, Thomas. (2008). Intersubjectivity and Intercorporeality. *Subjectivity* 22: 110–121.

——. (1994). Introduction: The Body as Representation and Being-in-the-World. Pp. 1–24 in *Embodiment and Experience: The Existential Ground of Culture and Self*, ed. Thomas Csordas. Cambridge: Cambridge University Press.

Das, Veena. (2015). *Affliction*. New York: Fordham University Press.

——. (2014). Action, Expression, and Everyday Life: Recounting Household Events. Pp. 279–306 in *The Ground Between: Anthropologists Engaging Philosophy*, ed. Veena Das, Michael Jackson, Arthur Kleinman, and Bhrigu Singh. Durham, NC: Duke University Press.

——. (2013). Neighbors and Acts of Silent Kindness. *HAU: Journal of Ethnographic Theory* 3(1): 217–20.

——. (2011). Time Is a Trickster and Other Fleeting Thoughts on Cavell, His Life, His Work. *MLN* 126(5): 943–953.

——. (2010). Engaging the Life of the Other: Love and Everyday Life. Pp. 376–400 in *Ordinary Ethics: Anthropology, Language, and Action*, ed. Michael Lambek. New York: Fordham University Press.

——. (2008). Violence, Gender, and Subjectivity. In Annual Reviews of Anthropology 37: 283–299.

——. (2007). *Life and Words. Violence and the Descent into the Ordinary*. Berkeley: University of California Press.

————. (1998). Wittgenstein and Anthropology. *Annual Review of Anthropology* 27:171–195.

————. (1997). *Critical Events: An Anthropological Perspective on Contemporary India.* Delhi: Oxford India Paperbacks.

————. (1977). *Structure and Cognition: Aspects of Hindu Caste and Ritual.* Delhi: Oxford University Press.

Das, Veena and Renu Addlakha. (2001). Disability and Domestic Citizenship: Voice, Gender, and the Making of the Subject. *Public Culture* 13(3): 511–531.

Das, Veena, Jon M. Ellen, and Lori Leonard. (2008). On the Modalities of the Domestic. *Home Cultures* 5(3): 349–372.

Das, Veena, Michael Jackson, Arthur Kleinman, and Bhrigupati Singh. (2014). Experiments Between Anthropology and Philosophy: Affinities and Antagonisms. Pp. 1–26 in *The Ground Between: Anthropologists Engaging Philosophy*, ed. Veena Das, Michael Jackson, Arthur Kleinman, and Bhrigupati Singh. Durham, NC: Duke University Press.

Das, Veena, Arthur Kleinman, Mamphela Ramphele, and Pamela Reynolds. (2001). *Remaking a World.* Berkeley: University of California Press.

————. (2000). *Violence and Subjectivity.* Berkeley: University of California Press.

Day, Sophie. (2007). *On the Game: Women and Sex Work* (Anthropology, Culture and Society). London: Pluto Press.

Day, Sophie, Akis Papataxiarchis, and Michael Stewart. (1998). *Lilies of the Field: Marginal People Who Live for the Moment.* Boulder: Westview Press.

Deleuze, Gilles. (1994). *Difference and Repetition.* London: Continuum Books.

————. (1988). *Bergsonism.* New York: Zone Books.

Eickelman, Dale F. (1998). *The Middle East and Central Asia: An Anthropological Approach.* 3rd ed. Upper Saddle River, NJ: Prentice-Hall.

Elliott, Alice. (2015). Paused Subjects: Waiting for Migration in North Africa. *Time & Society* 1–15.

Emerson, Ralph Waldo. (1844). *Essays: Second Series.* Boston: J. Munroe and Co.

Farah, Madelain. (1984). *Marriage and Sexuality in Islam. A Translation of al-Ghazali's Book on the Etiquette of Marriage from the Ihya'.* Salt Lake City: University of Utah Press.

Fassin, Didier. (2014). The Parallel Lives of Philosophy and Anthropology. Pp. 50–70 in *The Ground Between: Anthropologists Engaging Philosophy*, ed. Veena Das, Michael Jackson, Arthur Kleinman, and Bhrigupati Singh. Durham, NC: Duke University Press.

————. (2008). The Humanitarian Politics of Testimony Subjectification Through Trauma in the Israeli–Palestinian Conflict. *Cultural Anthropology* 23(3): 531–558.

Fassin, Didier and Richard Rechtman. (2009). *The Empire of Trauma: An Inquiry into the Condition of Victimhood.* Princeton, NJ: Princeton University Press.

Feldman, Ilana. (2015). Looking for Humanitarian Purpose: Endurance and the Value of Lives in a Palestinian Refugee Camp. *Public Culture* 27(3): 427–448.

Fischer, Michael J. (2007). To Live with What Would Otherwise Be Unendurable: Returns to Subjectivities. Pp. 423–446 in *Subjectivities: Ethnographic Investigations*, ed. João Biehl, Byron Good, and Arthur Kleinman. Berkeley: University of California Press.

Francis, Sahar and Kathleen Gibson. (2011). Isolation and Solitary Confinement of Palestinian Prisoners in Israeli Facilities. In *Threat: Palestinian Political Prisoners in Israel*, ed. Abeer Baker and Anat Matar. London. Pluto Press.

Freud, Sigmund. (1928 [1969]). *Beyond the Pleasure Principle: The Pioneer Study of the Death Instinct in Man*. Trans. James Strachey. New York: Bantam Books.

———. (1919 [2003]). *The Uncanny*. New York: Penguin Classics.

———. (1917 [1957]). *Mourning and Melancholia*. Penguin Freud Library. 11. London: Penguin Books.

Gammeltoft, Tine. (2014). *Haunting Images: A Cultural Account of Selective Reproduction in Vietnam*. Berkeley: University of California Press, 2014.

———. (2008). Childhood Disability and Parental Moral Responsibility in Northern Vietnam Towards Ethnographies of Intercorporeality. *Journal of the Royal Anthropological Institute* 14(4): 825–842.

Gersons, Berthold P. R. and Miranda Olff. (2005). Editorial: Coping with the Aftermath of Trauma. *British Medical Journal* 330: 1038–1039.

Giacaman, Rita, Awad Mataria, Angela Stefanini, Nirmala Naidoo, Paul Kowal, and Somna Chatterji. (2009). The Quality of Life of Palestinians Living in Chronic Conflict: Assessment and Determinants. *European Journal of Health Economics* 10: 93–101.

Giacaman, Rita, Yoke Rabaia, Viet Nguyen-Gillham, R. Batniji, Raija-Lena Punamäki, and D. Summerfield. (2011). Mental Health, Social Distress and Political Oppression: The Case of the Occupied Palestinian Territory. *Global Public Health* 6(5): 547–559.

Gjerding, Sarah. (2008). Demolishing Homes—Remaking Identities: Social Rupture and Nationalism Among Palestinian Women in East Jerusalem. Master's thesis. Department of Anthropology and Ethnography, University of Aarhus, Moesgaard.

Goodfellow, Aaron. (2015). *Gay Fathers, Their Children, and the Making of Kinship*. New York: Fordham University Press.

———. (2008). Pharmaceutical Intimacy: Sex, Death, and Methamphetamine. *Home Cultures* 5(3): 271–300.

Goodfellow, Aaron and Sameena Mulla. (2008). Compelling Intimacies: Domesticity, Sexuality, and Agency. *Home Cultures* 5(3): 257–269.

Granquist, Hilma. (1926). *Marriage Conditions in a Palestinian Village*. Helsingfors: Societas Scientiarum Fennica.

Gren, Nina. (2009). *Each Day Another Disaster: Politics and Everyday Life in a Palestinian Refugee Camp in the West Bank*. Gothenburg: School of Global Studies.

Hammami, Rema. (2004). On the Importance of Thugs: The Moral Economy of a Checkpoint. *Middle East Report* 231(Summer): 26–34.

Han, Clara. (2013). Suffering and Pictures of Anthropological Inquiry: A Response to Comments on Life in Debt. *HAU: Journal of Ethnographic Theory* 3(1): 231–240.

———. (2012). *Life in Debt: Times of Care and Violence in Neoliberal Chile*. Berkeley: University of California Press.

Han, Clara and Veena Das. (2015). *Living and Dying in the Contemporary World: A Compendium*. Berkeley: University of California Press.

Hanafi, Sari and Linda Tabar. (2005). *Donors, International Organizations, Local NGOs: The Emergence of the Palestinian Globalized Elite*. London: Pluto Press.

Hastrup, Frida. (2009). Weathering the World: Recovery in the Wake of the Tsunami in a Tamil Fishing Village. Ph.D. dissertation, Faculty of Humanities, University of Copenhagen.

Hastrup, Kirsten. (1995). *A Passage to Anthropology: Between Experience and Theory*. London: Routledge.

Heidegger, Martin. (1962). *Being and Time*. New York: Harper & Row.

Hein, Fadel. Abu Samir Qouta, Abel Aziz M. Thabet, and Eyad El Sarraj. (1993). Trauma and Mental Health of Children in Gaza [letter]. *British Medical Journal* 6885: 1130–1131.

Helweg-Larsen, K. and M. Kastrup. (2007). Consequences of Collective Violence with Particular Focus on the Gender Perspectives. *Danish Medical Bulletin* 54: 155–156.

Henare, Amiria, Martin Holbraad, and Sari Wastell. (2006). *Thinking Through Things: Theorising Artefacts Ethnographically*. London: Routledge.

Herman, Judith. (1992). *Trauma and Recovery*. New York: Basic Books.

Hodges, Matt. (2008). Rethinking Time's Arrow: Bergson, Deleuze and the Anthropology of Time. *Anthropological Theory* 8(4): 399–429.

Holbraad, Martin, and Morten Axel Pedersen. (2012). Revolutionary Securitization. An Ethnographic Extension of Securitization Theory. *International Theory* 4(2): 165–197.

Isotalo, Riina. (2007). *Palestinian Return: Reflections on Unifying Discourses, Dispersing Practices and Residual Narratives*. Berlin: Springer Heidelberg.

Jackson, Michael. (2014). *Harmattan: A Philosophical Fiction*. New York. Columbia University Press.

———. (2002). The Politics of Storytelling: Violence, Transgression, and Intersubjectivity. Museum Tusculanum Press, University of Copenhagen: Copenhagen.

Jayyusi, Lena. (2007). Iterability, Cumulativity, and Presence: The Relational Figures of Palestinian Memory. Pp. 102–134 in *Nakba: Palestine, 1948, and the Claims of Memory*, ed. Lila Abu-Lughod and A. H. Sa'adi. New York: Columbia University Press.

Jean-Klein, Iris. (2003). Into Committees, out of the House? Familiar Forms in the Organization of Palestinian Committee Activism During the First Intifada. *American Ethnologist* 30(4): 556–577.

Jensen, Steffen and Henrik Rønsbo, eds. (2014). *Histories of Victimhood*. Philadelphia: University of Pennsylvania Press.

Johnson, Nels. (1982). *Islam and the Politics of Meaning in Palestinian Nationalism.* London: Kegan Paul International.

Johnson, Penny, Lamis Abu Nahleh, and Annelise Moors. (2009). Weddings and War: Marriage Arrangements and Celebrations in Two Palestinian Intifadas. *Journal of Middle East Women's Studies* 5(3): 11–35.

Joseph, Suad. (1999). *Intimate Selving in Arab Families: Gender, Self, and Identity.* Syracuse, NY: Syracuse University Press.

Kanaaneh, Mosleh, Heather Bursheh, Stig Magnus Hursén, and David McDonald. (2012). *Palestinian Music and Song: Expression and Resistance Since 1900.* Indiana: Indiana University Press.

Kanaana, Sharif. (1990 [2005]). *Struggling for Survival: Essays in Palestinian Folklore and Folklife.* Al- Bireh: Society of Ina'ash El-Usra.

Kelly, Tobias. (2013). A Life Less Miserable? *HAU: Journal of Ethnographic Theory* 3(1): 213–216.

———. (2011). *This Side of Silence: Human Rights, Torture, and the Recognition of Cruelty.* Philadelphia: University of Pennsylvania Press.

———. (2010). In a Treacherous State: The Fear of Collaboration Among West Bank Palestinians. Pp. 169–187 in *Traitors: Suspicion, Intimacy and the Ethics of State-building,* ed. Tobias Kelly and Sharika Thiranagama. Philadelphia: University of Pennsylvania Press.

———. (2009). The UN Committee Against Torture: Human Rights Monitoring and the Legal Recognition of Torture. *Human Rights Quarterly* 31(3): 777–800.

———. (2008). The Attractions of Accountancy: Living an Ordinary Life During the Second Palestinian Intifada. *Ethnography* 9(3): 351–376.

———. (2006a). *Law, Violence and Sovereignty Among West Bank Palestinians.* Cambridge: Cambridge University Press.

———. (2006b). Documented Lives: Fear and the Uncertainties of Law During the Second Palestinian Intifada. *Journal of the Royal Anthropological Institute* 11(1): 89–107.

Kelly, Tobias and Sharika Thiranagama. (2010). *Traitors: Suspicion, Intimacy and the Ethics of Statebuilding.* Philadelphia. University of Pennsylvania Press.

Khalidi, Rashid. (2006). T*he Iron Cage: The Story of the Palestinian Struggle for State-hood.* Boston: Beacon Press.

Khalili, Laleh. (2007). *Heroes and Martyrs of Palestine: The Politics of National Com-memoration.* Cambridge: Cambridge University Press.

Khamis, Vivian. (2008). Post-Traumatic Stress and Psychiatric Disorders in Palestin-ian Adolescents Following *Intifada*-Related Injuries. *Social Science* 67(8): 1199–1207.

Khan, Naveeda. (2012). *Muslim Becoming: Aspiration and Skepticism in Pakistan.* Dur-ham, NC: Duke University Press.

Khankan, Nathalie. (2009). Breathing Sun-Drenched Horizons: The Possibility of Poetry in Post-Oslo Palestine. Ph.d. dissertation, University of California, Berkeley.

Kublitz, Anja. (2013).Seizing Catastrophes. The Temporality of Nakba among Palestinians in Denmark. Pp. 103–122 in *Times of Security. Ethnographies of Fear, Protest and the Future,* ed. Martin Holbraad and Morten Axel Pedersen. London: Routledge.

Lévi-Strauss, Claude. (1955). The Structural Study of Myth. Pp. 81–106 in *Myth: A Symposium*, ed. Thomas A. Sebeok. Bloomington: Indiana University Press.

Leys, Ruth. (2007). *From Guilt to Shame: Auschwitz and After.* Princeton, NJ: Princeton University Press.

———. (2000). *Trauma: A Genealogy.* Chicago: University of Chicago Press.

Lindholm Schulz, Helena. (2003). *The Palestinian Diaspora.* New York: Routledge.

Lucht, Hans. (2008). Darkness Before Daybreak. Existential Reciprocity in the Lives and Livelihoods of Migrant West African Fishermen. Ph.D. dissertation, Department of Anthropology, University of Copenhagen.

Madianos, Michel G, Adnan Lufti Sarhan, and Evmorfia Koukia. 2012. Major Depression Across West Bank: A Cross-sectional General Population Study. *International Journal of Social Psychiatry* 58(3): 315–322.

Mahmoud, Saba. (2004). *Politics of Piety. The Islamic Revival and the Feminist Subject.* Princeton: Princeton University Press.

Massad, Joseph. (1995). Conceiving the Masculine: Gender and Palestinian Nationalism. *Middle East Journal* 49(3): 67–83.

Mattingly, Cheryl. (2014). *Moral Laboratories. Family Peril and the Struggle for a Good Life.* Berkeley: University of California Press.

———. (1998). *Healing Dramas and Clinical Plots: The Narrative Structure of Experience.* Cambridge:. Cambridge University Press.

Mattingly, Cheryl, Nancy Lutkehaus, and Jason Throop. (2008). Bruner's Search for Meaning: A Conversation Between Psychology and Anthropology. *Ethos* 36(1): 1–28.

Mauss, Marcel. (1954 [2008]). *The Gift: The Form and Reason for Exchange in Archaic Societies.* London: Routledge.

McDonald, David. (2013). *My Voice Is My Weapon: Music, Nationalism, and the Poetics of Palestinian Resistance.* Durham, NC: Duke University Press.

Meari, Sumud. (2014). A Palestinian Philosophy of Confrontation in Colonial Prisons. *South Atlantic Quarterly* 113(3): 547–578.

Meo, Sani P. (2008). The Palestinian Mother. *This Week in Palestine* 119 (March): 98.

Merry, Sally Engle and Susan Biebler Coutin. (2014). Technologies of Truth in the Anthropology of Conflict. *American Ethnologist* 41(1): 1–16.

Mittermaier, Amira. (2014). Bread, Freedom, Social Justice: The Egyptian Uprising and a Sufi Khidma. *Cultural Anthropology* 29(1): 54–79.

———. (2011). *Dreams that Matter: Egyptian Landscapes of the Imagination.* Berkeley. University of California Press.

Moreno, Jacob. (1946). *Psychodrama Volume 1.* New York; Beacon House.

Muhawi, Ibrahim and Sharif Kanaana (1989). *Speak Bird, Speak Again: Palestinian Arab Folktales.* Berkeley: University of California Press.

Nashif, Esmail. (2008). *Palestinian Political Captives: Identity and Community*. New York: Routledge.

Ochs, Elinor and Lisa Capps. (1996). Narrating the Self. *Annual Review of Anthropology* 25: 19–43.

Ochs, Juliana. (2011). *Security and Suspicion: An Ethnography of Everyday Life in Israel*. Philadelphia: University of Pennsylvania Press.

Orsi, Robert A. (2005). *Between Heaven and Earth: Religions People Make and the Scholars Who Study Them*. Princeton, NJ: Princeton University Press.

Palestinian Center for Human Rights (PCHR). (2014). Report on Crimes of Torture in Palestinian Prisons and Detention Centres. Accessed on November 2nd 2015, http://www.pchrgaza.org/portal/en/index.php?option=com_content&view =article&id=11282:report-on-crimes-of-torture-in-palestinian-prisons-and -detention-centers&catid=47:special-reports&Itemid=191

Pappé, Ilan. (2006). *The Ethnic Cleansing of Palestine*. Oxford: Oneworld.

———. (2004). *A History of Modern Palestine: One Land, Two Peoples*. Cambridge: Cambridge University Press.

Papilloud, Christian. (2004). Three Conditions of Human Relations: Marcel Mauss and Georg Simmel. *Philosophy and Social Criticism* 30(4): 431–444.

Peacock, James L. and Dorothy Holland. (1993). The Narrated Self: Life Stories in Process. *Ethos* 21(4): 367–383.

Pedersen, Morten and Martin Holbraad. (2013). Introduction: Times of Security. Pp. 1–27 in *Times of Security: Ethnographies of Fear, Protest, and the Future*, ed. Morten Axel Pedersen and Martin Holbraad. London: Routledge Studies in Anthropology.

———. (2009). Planet M: The Intense Abstraction of Marilyn Strathern. *Anthropological Theory* 9(4): 371–394.

Peltonen, Kirsi, Samir Qouta, Eyad El Sarraj, and Raija-Lena Punamäki-Gita. (2010). Military Trauma and Social Development: The Moderating and Mediating Roles of Peer and Sibling Relations in Mental Health. *International Journal of Behavioral Development* 34: 554–563.

Perdigon, Sylvain. (2014). Ethnography in the Time of Martyrs: History and Pain in Current Anthropological Practice. Pp. 21–37 in *Wording the World: Veena Das and Scenes of Inheritance*, ed. Roma Chatterji. New York. Fordham University Press.

———. (2011). The One Still Surviving and Viable Institution. Pp. 165–179 in *Palestinian Refugees: Identity, Space and Place in the Levant*, ed. Sari Hanafi and Are Knudsen. London: Routledge.

Peteet, J. M. (2005). *Landscape of Hope and Despair: Palestinian Refugee Camps*. Philadelphia: University of Pennsylvania Press.

———. (1991). *Gender in Crisis: Women and the Palestinian Resistance Movement*. New York: Columbia University Press,

Pinto, Sarah. (2014). *Daughters of Parvati: Women and Madness in Contemporary India*. Philadelphia: University of Pennsylvania Press.

Political Cartoon Gallery. (2008). *Shooting the Witness: The Cartoons of Naji Al-Ali*. London: Political Cartoon Gallery.

Povinelli, Elizabeth A. (2012). After the Last Man: Images and Ethics of Becoming Otherwise. *E-flux* 35(5).

——. (2011). *Economies of Abandonment: Social Belonging and Endurance in Late Liberalism*. Durham, NC: Duke University Press.

Public Committee Against Torture in Israel (PCATI). (2011). Periodic Report. Doctoring the Evidence. Abandoning the Victim. On the Inclusion of Medical Professionals in the

——. (2009). *And We Were Tortured*. Exhibition Catalogue. Jerusalem: PCATI.

Punamäki, Raija-Leena. (1998). The Role of Dreams in Protecting Psychological Well-being in Traumatic Conditions. *International Journal of Behavioral Development* 3: 559–588.

Punamäki, Raija L., Samir Qouta, and Eyad El Sarraj. (1997). Models of Traumatic Experiences and Children's Psychological Adjustment: The Roles of Perceived Parenting and the Children's Own Resources and Activity. *Child Development* 4:718–728.

Punamäki, Raija-Leena, Samir Qouta, Joop de Jong, Ivan Komproe, and Mustafa el Masri. (2005). The Role of Peritraumatic Dissociation and Gender in the Association Between Trauma and Mental Health in a Palestinian Community Sample. *American Journal of Psychiatry* 162: 545–551.

Pupavac, Vanessa (2001). Therapeutic Governance: Psycho-Social Intervention and Trauma Risk Management. *Disasters* 25(4): 358–372.

Ramphele, Mamphela. (1997). Political Widowhoood in South Africa: The Embodiment of Ambiguity. Pp. 99–118 in *Social Suffering*, ed. Arthur Kleinman, Veena Das, and Margareth Lock. Berkeley: University of California Press.

Reed, Adam. (2003). Papua New Guinea's "Last Place": Experiences of Constraint in a Postcolonial Prison. Oxford: Berghahn Books.

Robbins, Joel. (2012). Beyond the Suffering Subject: Toward and Anthropology of the Good. *JRAI* 19 (3): 447–462.

Rosenfeld, Maya. (2004). *Confronting the Occupation: Work, Education, and Political Activism of Palestinian Families in a Refugee Camp*. Stanford, CA: Stanford University Press.

Ross, Fiona. (2001). Speech and Silence: Women's Testimony in the First Five Weeks of Public Hearings of the South African Truth and Reconciliation Commission. In *Remaking a World: Violence, Social Suffering, and Recovery*, ed. Veena Das, Arthur Kleinman, Margareth Lock, Mamphela Ramphele, and Pamela Reynolds. Berkeley: University of California Press.

Roy, Sara. (2007). *Failing Peace: Gaza and the Palestinian-Israeli Conflict*. London: Pluto Press.

Rubenberg, Cheryl. A. (2003). *The Palestinians: In Search of a Just Peace*. Boulder: Lynne Rienner.

Sa'ar, Amalia. (2006). Feminine Strength: Reflections on Power and Gender in Israeli-Palestinian Culture. *Anthropological Quarterly* 79(3): 397–431.

———. (2001). Lonely in Your Firm Grip: Women in Israeli-Palestinian Families. *Journal of the Royal Anthropological Institute* 7(4): 723–739.

Sabbagh, Suha (ed.) (1998). *Palestinian Women of Gaza and the West Bank*. Bloomington: Indiana University Press.

Said, Edward. (1977). *Orientalism*. London. Penguin.

Saint Cassia, Paul. (2005). *Bodies of Evidence: Burial, Memory and the Recovery of Missing Persons in Cyprus*. Oxford: Berghahn Books.

Salo, Jari, Raija-Lena Punamäki, and Samir Qouta. (2005). The Role of Adult Attachment in the Association Between Experiences and Post-Traumatic Growth Among Former Political Prisoners. *Anxiety, Stress and Coping: An International Journal* 18: 361–378.

Sayigh, Rosemary. (2008). *The Palestinians: From Peasants to Revolutionaries*. London: Zed Books.

———. (1993). Palestinian Women and Politics in Lebanon. Pp. 175–194 in *Arab Women: Old Boundaries, New Frontiers*, ed. Judith Tucher. Bloomington: Indiana University Press.

Scarry, Elaine. (1987). *The Body in Pain: The Making and Unmaking of the World*. Oxford: Oxford University Press.

Schielke, Samuli. (2010). Second Thoughts About the Anthropology of Islam, or How to Make Sense of Grand Schemes in Everyday Life. *ZMO Working Papers* 2: 1–16.

Schryock, Andrew. (2004). The New Jordanian Hospitality: House, Host, and Guest in the Culture of Public Display. *Comparative Studies in Society and History* 46(1): 35–62.

Shafi'i, Ghada al-. (1999). *Al-mashhad yukhabbi' sahilan* [The scene hides neighing]. Beirut: al-Mu'assasa al-'arabiyya li al-dirasat wa al-nashr and House of Poetry.

Solomon, Zahava, and R. Dekel. (2007). Secondary Traumatization Among Wives of War Veterans with PTSD. Pp.137–160 in *Combat Stress Injury: Theory, Research, and Management,* ed. C. Figley and W. P. Nash. New York: Routledge Psychosocial Stress Book Series.

Solomon, Zahava, Mark Waysman, Gaby Levy, Batia Fried, Mario Mikulinger, Rami Benbenishty, Victor Florian and Avi Bleich. (2004). From Front Line to Home Front: A Study of Secondary Traumatization. *Family Process* 31(3): 289–302.

Stevenson, Lisa. (2014). *Life Beside Itself: Imagining Care in the Canadian Arctic*. Berkeley: University of California Press.

Sørensen, Birgitte Refslund. (2012). Gendering Violent Conflicts. Pp. 448–456 in *Elgar Handbook of Civil War and Fragile States*. ed. Graham Brown and Arnim Langer. Cheltenham, UK: Edward Elgar.

Strathern, Marilyn. (2004). *Partial Connections*. London: Rowman Altamira Press.

———. (ed). (2000). *Audit Cultures: Anthropological Studies in Accountability, Ethics and the Academy*. EASA series in Social Anthropology. London: Routledge.

———. (1987). An Awkward Relationship: The Case of Feminism and Anthropology. *Reconstructing the Academy*. Special issue of *Signs* 12(2): 276–292.

Summerfield, Derek. (1999). A Critique of Seven Assumptions Behind Psychological Trauma Programmes in War-Affected Areas. *Social Science and Medicine* 48: 1449–1462.

Swedenburg, Ted. (1990). The Palestinian Peasant as National Signifier. *Anthropological. Quarterly* 63(1): 18–30.

Talebi, Shahla. (2011). *Ghosts of Revolution: Rekindled Memories of Imprisonment in Iran*. Stanford: Stanford University Press.

Tamari, Salim and Reema Hammami. (2001). The Second Uprising: End or New Beginning? *Journal of Palestine Studies* 30(2): 5–25.

Taraki, Lisa. (2006). *Living Palestine: Family Survival, Resistance and Mobility Under Occupation*. Syracuse, NY: Syracuse University Press.

Thabet, Abdelaziz, Omar El-Buhaisi and Panos Vostanis. (2014). Trauma, PTSD, Anxiety, and coping strategies among Palestinians adolescents exposed to War on Gaza. *Arab Journal of Psychiatry* 25(1):71–82.

Thabet, Abdelaziz, Abu Tawahina, Eyad El Sarraj, David Henely, Henrick Pelleick and Panos Vostanis. (2011). Post-traumatic stress disorder and attention-deficit hyperactivity disorder in Palestinian children affected by the war on Gaza. *International Psychiatry* 8(4): 90–91.

Thiranagama, Sharika. (2011). *In My Mother's House: Civil War in Sri Lanka*. Foreword by Gananath Obeysekere. Philadelphia: University of Pennsylvania Press.

United Nations Development Program (UNDP). (2011). Development for Freedom. Accessed 2 November 2015. http://www.ps.undp.org/content/dam/papp/docs/Publications/UNDP-papp-research-devforfreedom.pdf.

———. (2007). Poverty in the Occupied Palestinian Territory 2007. *Development Times* (Jerusalem) 1 July.

UNVFVT (United Nations Voluntary Fund for Victims of Torture). (2007). *United Nations Voluntary Fund for Victims of Torture Guidelines of the Fund for the Use of Organizations*. Retrieved from http://www.ohchr.org/Documents/Issues/UNVFT guidelines2008EN.pdf.

Van der Kolk and Spinalozza Blaustein. (2005). Posttraumatic Stress Disorder Treatment Outcome Research: The Study of Unrepresentative Samples. *Journal of Traumatic Stress* 18(5): 425–436.

Van Velsen, J. (1967). The Extended-Case Method and Situational Analysis. Pp.129–149 in *The Craft of Social Anthropology*, ed. A. L. Epstein. London: Tavistock.

Viefhues-Bailey, Luedger. (2008). Bearing the Beyond: Women and the Limits of Language in Stanley Cavell. Pp 1–10 in *gender-forum* 20: special issue: gender and language.

Vinh-Kim Nguyen, (2005). Antiretroviral Globalism, Biopolitics, and Therapeutic Citizenship. Pp. 124–144 in *Global assemblages: technology, politics, and ethics as anthropological problems*, edited by Aihwa Ong and Stephen J. Collier. Malden, MA: Blackwell.

Wagner, Roy. (1991). The Fractal Person. Pp. in *Big Men and Great Men: Personifications of Power in Melanesia*, ed. Marilyn Strathern and Maurice Godelier. Cambridge: Cambridge University Press.

———. (1986). *Asiwinarong: Ethos, Image, and Social Power Among the Usen Barok of New Ireland*. Princeton, NJ: Princeton University Press.

Willner, Dorothy. (1982). The Oedipus Complex, Antigone, and Electra: The Woman as Hero and Victim. *American Anthropologist* 84:58–78.

Wittgenstein, Ludwig. (1953 [2009]). *Philosophical Investigations*. Oxford: Wiley-Blackwell.

Young, Allan. (1995). *The Harmony of Illusions: Inventing Post-traumatic Stress Disorder*. Princeton, NJ: Princeton University Press.

Zerach, G. (2015). War Captivity: Effects on Spouses and Marital Relationships. In MFRI International Research Symposium on Military and Veteran Families.

INDEX

ACKNOWLEDGMENTS

Writing this book has given me a profound sense of gratitude toward the people who have in different ways left their mark on my work. I wish to acknowledge each one, none more so than the women whose lives I have tried to describe in order to share their experience with my readers. All their names here are made up, as are the names of their villages, towns, or cities. I know, however, that they realize that this book is about them, their lives, and their relations. It is my hope that they accept my deep thanks for the time and trust they gave when letting me listen to their words, stay in their houses, and take part in their lives.

The time I spent in Palestine learning about these women's lives was suffused by the engagement, curiosity and gestures of kindness by many people. Acknowledging individuals in Palestine by name may jeopardize trust and confidentiality, so if I have omitted a name here, it is out of such a concern. During my engagement with Palestine, both while living there and today, a number of individuals and organizations have welcomed me and contributed time, questions and constructive comments to my study. Among those I want to mention are the people at the Gaza Community Mental Health Program, who were not directly involved in my study but helped shape my questions about the gendering of the conflict, not least Marwa Abu Dayah and Abdel Hamid Afana. In the West Bank the organization I term the Prisoners' Support Center kindly offered me a place from where to start my inquiry, and I could not have entered this field without their generous interest and support. They allowed me to be a part of and scrutinize aspects of their tireless and valuable work. Particularly I thank the group of young female therapists whose encouraging welcome inspired me to probe deeper with my study. Numerous individuals and agencies have engaged willingly in discussion about how to understand the effects of long-term conflict upon Palestinian men and women. At Birzeit University I had the pleasure of getting to know the work of Professors Rita Giacaman, Esmail Nashif, and Penny

Johnson. Our conversations about researching imprisonment were extremely inspiring and valuable. Other organizations, in the West Bank as well as in Jerusalem, helped me gain insight into the tapestry of conditions, services, and ways of recognition of the prisoners, the martyrs and their families. Among those who played a major role are welcoming individuals at the Palestine Counseling Center, Addammeer, Women's Centre for Legal Aid and Counseling, YMCA in Beit Sahour, Mandela Institute for Human Rights and Political Prisoners, GTC counselling Centre, Bethlehem Mental Hospital, Abu Jihad Museum for the Prisoners Movement Affairs, Red Cross Family Visits Office in Jerusalem, PASSIA, PCATI, and Btselem. In Geneva, the offices of the UNVFVT, UNRWA, and the CFD were very forthcoming in setting up interviews with the relevant employees for my project and allowing me to participate in seminars.

During my fieldwork I was lucky to meet and be taken in by some special people to whom I extend my gratitude. Rose Copty generously opened her home and shared her life with me. Coming home to a cup of Nescafé on her balcony in Sheikh Jarrah was a true sanctuary and at the same time taught me about how the occupation is lived differently in Jerusalem and the occupied territories respectively and how, even so, there is no escaping the occupation. Laila Atshan, whose sensitive insights and black humor has colored my memory of the West Bank, contributed sharp-witted analysis of resistance and the human psyche that forced me to think twice about my observations. I thank Hanan Abu Ghosh for her friendship and for showing me how to share concerns and work together. I am also grateful for the trust she had in me to the extent that she introduced me to "Yara." Conversations with Majed Nasser and Luna Handal offered a much-needed space for metareflection during fieldwork. Invaluable is the word for the tireless work of my three assistants Rawan Odeh, Mayy Abu Meizzar, and Maysoon Bseiso, whose thoughts on my study have helped shape my inquiry. Always ready with critical comments and productive questions to yet another researcher in the West Bank was Sharif Kanaana, whose sharing of his vast knowledge I appreciate warmly. My conversations with Dana Hercbergs and Louis Frankenthaler about conducting fieldwork in the moral minefield of the Israeli-Palestinian conflict have helped me understand aspects of the conflict that I would not have known otherwise. I am indebted to Nathalie Khankan, whose tutoring as an academic in the occupied territory and a distinct kind of sisterhood has guided me through the process and whose expertise on Palestinian literature is a source of insight and a reminder that ethnography

is only one way to learn about people and places. For thinking with me yet
again about the cover design and constantly showing me the force of art I
thank both her and Kristine Siegel, a powerful reminder that friends are those
who know you best.

At Penn, Tobias Kelly has been a wonderful reader, and I am grateful for
his belief in this project from the very beginning and at times where I myself
doubted it. His comments and sobering critique have made my thoughts so
much clearer. Peter Agree has been a truly supportive editor and his advice
on how to get my book in shape, including the introduction to Pamela
Haag, made all the difference. Pamela's reading of the manuscript left me in
awe. Thanks to Noreen O'Connor for running the process smoothly and to
Rachel Taube for an initial proofreading.

Academic milieus around the globe have shaped how I think about
my work. In Copenhagen I sincerely thank Birgitte Refslund Sørensen for
her superior knowledge of conducting fieldwork in conflict areas, which
made fieldwork approachable and ensured this study of a firm ethnographic
grounding. I remain indebted to my long-time mentor Henrik Rønsbo who
has supported me intellectually and collegially. I consider myself privileged
to continue our collaboration.

I am humbled by the immense engagement that Veena Das has had not
only with this book but also in conversations and projects reaching far beyond it. Her influence, evidenced in her remarkable intellectual generosity,
friendship, hospitality, and interest, is perceptible throughout the book.

I am grateful to my inspiring colleagues at the Institute of Anthropology. I wish to mention here those special individuals who helped me, in
different ways, find my way in academic life as well as were always ready to
shake my intellectual footing. For friendship and conversations that never
end: Anja Kublitz, Helene Risør, Bjarke Oxlund. For reading and comment-
ing I owe special thanks to Frida Hastrup. Kasper Tang Vangkilde, Nina
Gren, Nerina Weiss, Susanne Bregnbæk, Matthew Carey, Vibeke Steffen,
Mark Vacher, Henrik Vigh and Morten Hulvej Rod. Andreas Bandak and
Lars Højer forced me to think clearly about my analysis and I am truly happy
to be part of their intellectual community. The initiative of Martin Holbraad
and Morten Axel Pedersen of thinking about security through ethnography
and their sharp and constructive editorial comments have allowed me to
make temporality a central trope in this book, and their critical comments
have no doubt helped me clarify my thinking. Over the past couple of years
I have been fortunate to work more closely with Tine Gammeltoft and Vibeke

Steffen, whose concerns with interiority in anthropology, and in particular our conversations about psychology in anthropology, have inspired me to follow emerging ideas and pursue other avenues of analysis. Over the years I have had the pleasure to share an interest at the boundaries of anthropology and psychology with Nanna Johannesen.

At Dignity–Danish Institute Against Torture, talks and writing projects with Andrew Jefferson and Steffen are a collaborative treat. Søs Nissen and Jens Modvig have inspired and continue to inspire me at the threshold of the limits of anthropological knowledge and intervention in an applied setting. For assisting with transliteration of Arabic I have been fortunate to have the aid of Christina Copty. At different stages of writing this book I have had the luxury to spend time at the Anthropology Department at Johns Hopkins University. That time pushed my thinking about this project and I am still humbled by the department's willingness to engage so wholeheartedly with my work. My conversations there with, in particular, Naveeda Khan, Clara Han, Aaron Goodfellow, Andrew Brandel, and Sylvain Perdigon were most productive.

The research projects that laid the groundwork for this book were supported by the Carlsberg Foundation and Council for Development Research (FFU) of the Danish Ministry of Foreign Affairs. I extend my thanks to these generous foundations for acknowledging the importance of and supporting my work.

I am often asked "How did this become your field of research?" The answer is not straightforward, but I do know that my parents Lisbeth and Helge Buch have showed me the way to acknowledge and act upon any form of injustice I encountered. This mode of attention, I think, underpins my concern with unheralded affliction. I thank them and my brother Steen for their boundless support, curiosity, and belief in their daughter and sister, however distant the discipline may be for them. Later, the numerous times I have called on them to take care of David, in Denmark and Palestine, and later Elias, in order to have some hours to write, have been such a luxury. My parents-in-law Jytte and Geoff Segal help bring our everyday life closer to a balance of work and family. Together with Otilija and Emma, these individuals are my family and they show me the power of kinship every day. Also deserving special mention for their support, love, and patience with an absentminded friend still working on "that book": Susanne Kalstrup, Ida Hyllested, Nathalie Soelmark, Kristina Bendtzen Rashid, Sofie Kirk Kristiansen, and Karoline Foss.

Overall, I am indebted to Sune Buch Segal for sharing the process, thoughts, and the entire project with such enthusiasm, for visiting me in the West Bank, and for tireless critical reading. Mostly, though, I am grateful to him for being with me and for being such a wonderful father to David and Elias, who bring me back home whenever the themes of my research undo my world. I love you.

*   *   *

An earlier version of portions of Chapter 1 was published as "Why Is Muna Crying? Event, Relation, and Immediacy as Criteria for Acknowledging Suffering in Palestine," in *Histories of Victimhood* edited by Henrik Rønsbo and Steffen Jensen (Philadelphia: University of Pennsylvania Press, 2014). An earlier version of Chapter 2 was published as "Derivative Presence: Loss and Lives in Limbo in the West Bank," in *The Presence of Absence,* edited by Frida Hastrup, Tim Flohr Sørensen, and Mikkel Bille (New York: Springer Science+Business Media, 2010), with kind permission from Springer Science+Business Media © 2010. An earlier version of a portion of Chapter 3 was published as "Enduring Presents: Living a Prison Sentence as the Wife of a Detainee in Israel," in *Times of Security: Ethnographies of Fear, Protest and the Future,* edited by Morten Axel Pedersen and Martin Holbraad (New York: Routledge, 2013). Parts of Chapter 5 appeared in earlier form as "Disembodied Conjugality," in *Wording the World: Veena Das and the Scenes of Inheritance,* edited by Roma Chatterji (New York: Fordham University Press, 2015). An earlier version of Chapter 6 was published as "The Burden of the Example: National Sentiments, Female Heroism and Womanhood in the face of Detention in the Occupied Palestinian Territories," *Journal of the Royal Anthropological Institute,* special issue edited by Lars Højer and Andreas Bandak, 21 (2015): 30–46. doi: 10.1111/1467-9655.12164. I wish to thank the journals and publishers for permitting me to use the material.